HU ANGLAIS *Civilisation*

DANS LA SÉRIE TRANSVERSALE DIRIGÉE PAR MICHEL VIEL,
PROFESSEUR À L'UNIVERSITÉ PARIS-SORBONNE (PARIS IV)

CIVILISATION IRLANDAISE

Paul Brennan
Professeur à l'Université de Paris III-Sorbonne Nouvelle

Valérie Peyronel
Maître de conférences à l'Université de Paris XII-Créteil

HACHETTE
Supérieur

ÉDITION ACTUALISÉE

Paul BRENNAN, ancien professeur à l'université de Caen, est depuis 1998 professeur d'études irlandaises à l'Université de la Sorbonne Nouvelle où il dirige le DEA d'Études irlandaises. Il participe à la direction de *L'Irlande politique et sociale*, Publications de la Sorbonne Nouvelle, et de la revue *Études irlandaises* (Universités de Caen, Lille III et Rennes II). Spécialiste de la politique irlandaise, il a publié de nombreux articles sur ce sujet. Il est aussi l'auteur de *The Northern Ireland Conflict*, Paris: Longman, 1995, et de *L'Irlande du Nord*, Paris: La Documentation Française, 1999, et, en collaboration avec Richard Deutsch, *L'Irlande du Nord: Chronologie, 1968-1991*, Paris: Publications de la Sorbonne Nouvelle, 1993. Il contribue régulièrement à la publication annuelle de la Documentation Française: Alfred Grosser (dir.) *Les Pays d'Europe occidentale*. Il a dirigé *La Sécularisation en Irlande*, Presses universitaires de Caen, 1998, et, avec Thierry Dubost, *G. B. Shaw un dramaturge engagé*, Presses universitaires de Caen, 1998.

Après une expérience de dix ans dans le domaine de la négociation internationale puis dans celui du marketing international au sein d'une entreprise anglo-néerlandaise, Valérie PEYRONEL, maître de conférences au département LEA de l'Université de Paris XII-Créteil, s'est spécialisée dans l'étude des relations intercommunautaires en Irlande du Nord et des relations économiques dans les îles britanniques. Elle est l'auteur de plusieurs articles sur ces sujets et d'une thèse sur l'intégration scolaire en Irlande du Nord.

Les auteurs tiennent à remercier Brid Brennan, Bernard d'Hellencourt et Mike O'Neil, ainsi que le service culturel de l'Ambassade d'Irlande à Paris ; l'IDA ; Sunniva O'Flynn et Emer Twomey, Irish Film Archive (The Film Institute of Ireland, Dublin) ainsi que Estelle Epinoux pour leur aide.

Couverture: Alain Vambacas / Tirzah RAVILIOUS, The Magnet. Shops at Bundoran, 1950 (détail). Private collection. © DACS. The Bridgeman Art Library.

Cartographie Hachette Classiques.

Réalisation et fabrication: MOSAÏQUE.

ISBN 2 01 1449316

AVANT-PROPOS

Pour la première fois dans l'histoire de l'édition scolaire et universitaire française, une grande maison publie un manuel entièrement consacré à l'Irlande. On ne peut que la féliciter de cette heureuse et, sans doute, nécessaire initiative. L'Irlande n'est pas absente de certains manuels, mais il s'agit d'ouvrages sur la Grande-Bretagne, et l'esprit peu averti peut penser que ce vieux pays, l'Irlande, appartient toujours au Royaume-Uni alors que voilà plus de trois-quarts de siècle que ce n'est plus le cas, du moins pour la plus grande partie de l'île. Comment cette appartenance a été vécue (mal), par de nombreux Irlandais, voilà le premier thème du livre. Pourtant Londres gouverne toujours l'Irlande du Nord. Pour cette raison les auteurs ne se sont pas limités à la République d'Irlande. Ils prêtent même une attention soutenue aux énormes difficultés auxquelles les habitants du Nord doivent faire face pour parvenir à une véritable paix. Tel est en fait le deuxième thème de ce livre. Mais l'Irlande, Nord et Sud, fait maintenant partie de l'Union européenne. Elle doit s'efforcer, sur les plans aussi bien politique qu'économique et social, de s'adapter au processus de modernisation que cette situation impose. Voilà le troisième grand thème de cet ouvrage.

Les auteurs proposent donc à leurs collègues une autre terre pour enseigner l'anglais, et aux étudiants un autre terrain pour apprendre une langue qui n'est pas seulement celle de Shakespeare, mais celle de Joyce et de ses compatriotes. En même temps, ils les invitent à mieux connaître un pays voisin et ami. Pour que cette connaissance soit aussi large que possible ils ont choisi une approche qui se veut politique, sociologique et économique, le tout dans une perspective historique.

• Le texte est distribué sur quatorze chapitres dont le dernier est consacré à l'histoire récente, voire à l'histoire immédiate.

• Chaque chapitre est suivi de documents d'origine, de nature et de période différentes, ce qui devrait permettre une exploitation riche et imaginative en cours ou en travaux dirigés.

• Au corps du livre s'ajoute un glossaire qui a l'ambition d'être une petite encyclopédie *(Ireland: A to Z)*, à laquelle on renvoie systématiquement l'étudiant à la première occurrence dans chaque chapitre. Cette approche devrait lui permettre de faire également un travail autonome.

• La filmographie ci-après complétera agréablement, nous l'espérons, la connaissance du contexte irlandais.

Pour certains, l'Irlande n'est qu'une petite île située derrière une autre, et pas n'importe laquelle! Mais beaucoup de Français se sont toujours intéressés à la réalité cachée par l'ombre de la présence britannique en Irlande. Cette réalité constitue en quelque sorte un héritage commun: des liens unissent Irlandais et Bretons; des moines irlandais ont assisté à la naissance de la France; la France a été terre d'asile pour des catholiques irlandais; des soldats français ont aidé les Irlandais qui tentaient d'établir leur première république, peu après la naissance de la leur. Par la suite, et jusqu'à nos jours, la France a offert un foyer aux révolutionnaires et aux artistes et écrivains irlandais. Ce manuel se situe donc, à son niveau, dans le cadre d'un système de relations franco-irlandaises profondément enraciné dans l'histoire.

LES AUTEURS

FILMOGRAPHY

Selection of films on Ireland

b/w = black and white	F = feature/drama	***l.p.*** = leading players	vc = video copy held by IFA for
col = colour	G = in Gaelic	***n.*** = novel	reference purposes only
D = documentary	IFA = Irish Film Archive	***s.*** = story	***w.*** = written by
dir. = director	(Dublin: Irish Film Institute)	***s.s.*** = short story	***w.d.*** = written and directed by

1934: **MAN OF ARAN - GB** 76 min. b/w D vc / ***dir.*** Robert Flaherty, ***w.*** R. and F. Flaherty / ***l. p.*** Colman "Tiger" King, M. Dirrane.

1936: **THE DAWN - Ire.** b/w F vc / ***dir.*** Tom Cooper / ***l. p.*** T. Cooper, B. O'Sullivan, J. Gleeson.
GUESTS OF THE NATION - Ire. 50 min. silent b/w F vc / ***dir.*** Denis Johnston, ***w.*** D. Johnston, F. O'Connor, M. Manning / ***ss.*** F. O'Connor / ***l. p.*** B. Fitzgerald, C. Cusack, S. Richards.

1947: **ODD MAN OUT - GB** 115 min. b/w F vc / ***dir.*** Carol Reed, ***w.*** F. L. Green, R. C. Sheriff, ***n.*** F.L. Green / ***l. p.*** J. Mason, R. Newton, F.J. McCormick.

1948: **OUR COUNTRY - Ire.** 8 min. b/w D vc / ***w.d.*** Liam O'Leary / ***l. p.*** S. MacBride, N. Hartnett, N. Browne.

1952: **THE QUIET MAN - USA** 129 min. col F vc / ***dir.*** John Ford, ***w.*** F. Nugent, ***s.*** M. Walsh / ***l. p.*** J. Wayne, M. O'Hara, B.Fitzgerald.

1959: **MISE EIRE/I AM IRELAND - Ire.** 90 min. b/w D G vc / ***dir.*** George Morrison, ***w.*** G. Morrison, S. Mac Reamoinn.
SHAKE HANDS WITH THE DEVIL - GB 110 min. b/w F vc / ***dir.*** Michael Anderson, ***w.*** I. Goff, B. Roberts, ***n.*** R. Connor / ***l. p.*** J. Cagney, D. Wynter, G. Johns.

1968: **ROCKY ROAD TO DUBLIN - Ire.** 75 min. b/w D film in IFA / ***w.d.*** Peter Lennon / ***l. p.*** S. O'Faolain, C. Cruise O'Brien, J. Huston.

1970: **RYAN'S DAUGHTER - GB** 206 min. col F vc / ***dir.*** David Lean / ***w.*** R. Bolt / ***l. p.*** S. Miles, R. Mitchum, C. Jones.

1982: **ANGEL** (USA title: **DANNY BOY**) - **Ire./GB** 92 min. col F vc / ***w.d.*** Neil Jordan / ***l. p.*** S. Rea, H. Heffernan, V. Quilligan.
THE BALLROOM OF ROMANCE - Ire. 52 min. col F vc / ***dir.*** Pat O'Connor, ***w.***, ***s.s.*** W. Trevor / ***l. p.*** B. Fricker, J. Kavanagh, C. Cusack.

1984: **ANNE DEVLIN - Ire.** 124 min. col F vc / ***w.d.*** Pat Murphy / ***l. p.*** B. Brennan, B. Hogan, D. McAleer.
CAL - GB 102 min. col F vc / ***dir.*** Pat O'Connor, ***w.***, ***n.*** B. Mac Laverty / ***l. p.*** H. Mirren, J. Lynch, R. McAnally.
PIGS - Ire. 79 min. col F vc / ***dir.*** Cathal Black, ***w.*** J. Brennan / ***l. p.*** J. Brennan (*also narrator*), G. Shane, M. O'Donoghue.

1987: **THE DEAD - GB/USA/W. Germ.** 83 min. b/w F vc / ***dir.*** John Huston, ***w.*** T. Huston, ***s.s.*** J. Joyce / ***l. p.*** A. Huston, D. McCann, D. O'Herlihy.

1989: **MY LEFT FOOT - GB** col F vc / ***w. d.*** Jim Sheridan, ***w.*** S. Connaughton / ***l. p.*** D. Day Lewis, R. McAnally.

1990: **DECEMBER BRIDE - GB** 7,908ft col F vc / ***dir.*** Thaddeu O'Sullivan, ***w.*** D. Rudkin, ***n.*** S. Hanna Bell / ***l. p.*** D. McCann, S. Reeves.

1992: **THE CRYING GAME - GB** 10,043ft col F vc / ***w.d.*** Neil Jordan / ***l. p.*** S. Rea, M. Richardson, Forest Whitaker.
INTO THE WEST - Ire. 9,184ft col F vc / ***dir.*** Mike Newell, ***w.*** J. Sheridan, ***s.*** M. Pearce / ***l. p.*** G. Byrne, E. Barkin, C. Fitzgerald, R. Conroy.

1993: **IN THE NAME OF THE FATHER - GB** col F / ***w.d.*** Jim Sheridan, ***w.*** T. George / ***l. p.*** D. Day Lewis, E. Thompson, P. Postlethwaite.
THE SNAPPER - GB 8,003ft col F / ***dir.*** Stephen Frears, ***w.***, ***n.*** R. Doyle / ***l. p.*** C. Meaney, T. Kellegher, R. McCabe.

1994: **THE BISHOP'S STORY - Ire.** col F vc / ***w.d.*** Bob Quinn / ***l.p.*** D. McCann.
HIGH BOOT BENNY - Ire. col F vc / ***w.d.*** Joe Comerford / ***l.p.*** M. O'Shea.
AILSA - Ire./Fra/All, 78 mn, col F / ***dir.*** Paddy Breathnach, ***w.*** C. Morris, ***n.*** Ailsa, J. O'Connor / ***l. p.*** B. Coyle, A. Irvine, D. Kelly.
THE BISHOP'S STORY, Ire., 83 mn, col/b/w/sepia, F / ***dir.*** Bob Quinn, ***w.*** B. Quinn, n. Suil le Breith by P. Standun, l.p. D. McCann, M. Fegan, R. McBride.

1995: **CIRCLES OF FRIENDS, Ire./ US,** 102 mn, technicolor, F, ***dir.*** Pat O'Connor, ***w.*** A. Davies, ***n.*** *Circle of Friends* by M. Binchy / ***l. p.*** C. O'Donnell, M. Driver, G. O'Rawe.
GUILTRIP, Ire./Fr/Ital/ Sp, 87/88 mn, col, F / ***dir.*** Gerard Stembridge, ***w. d.*** G. Stembridge / ***l. p.*** A.Connolly, J. Russell, P. Hanly.
KOREA, Ire./Fr/ Germ/ Neth, 75 mn, col, F / ***dir.*** Cathal Black, ***w.*** J. Byrne, ***s.s.*** *Korea* by J.McGahern / ***l. p.*** D. Donnelly, A. Scott, F. Molony, V. Anderson.
NOTHING PERSONAL, Ire/UK, 85 mn, metrocolour, F / ***dir.*** Thaddeus O'Sullivan, ***w.*** D.Mornin, ***n.*** *All Our Fault* by D. Mornin / ***l. p.*** J. Frain, I. Hart, J. Lynch.

1996: **MICHAEL COLLINS, Ire./US,** 132 mn, col, F / ***dir.*** Neil Jordan / ***w.d.*** N. Jordan / ***l. p*** L. Neeson, J. Roberts, A. Quinn.
SNAKES AND LADDERS, Ire./Germ /US, 90 mn, col, F / ***dir.*** Trish McAdam, ***w.d.*** T. McAdam / G. Moxley / ***l. p.*** P. Boyd, G. Moxley, S. Hughes.
SOME MOTHER'S SON, Ire., 112 mn, col, F / ***dir.*** Terry George, ***w.*** T. George / J. Sheridan / ***l. p.*** H. Mirren, F. Flannagan, A. Gillen.
THE VAN, Ire., 100 mn, col, F / ***dir.*** Stephen Frears, ***n.*** *The Van* by R. Doyle, ***l. p.*** C. Meaney, D. O'Kelly, G. Ryan.

1997: **BOGWOMAN, Ire.,** 84 mn, col, F / ***dir.*** Tom Collins, ***w.d.*** T. Collins / ***l. p.*** R. Dowling, P. Mullen, S. McGinley.
I WENT DOWN, Ire./Sp/UK, 107 mn, col, F / ***dir.*** Paddy Breathnach, ***w.*** C. McPherson / ***l. p.*** B. Gleeson, P. MacDonald, P. Caffrey.
THE BOXER, Ire./US, 113 mn, col, F / ***dir.*** Jim Sheridan, ***w.*** J. Sheridan, T. George / ***l. p.*** D. D. Lewis, E. Watson, K. Scott.
THE BUTCHER BOY, Ire./US, 109 mn, technicolor, F / ***dir.*** Neil Jordan, ***w. d.*** N. Jordan, ***n.*** P. McCabe / ***l. p.*** E. Owens, S. McGinley, P. Gower.
THE LAST BUS HOME, Ire., 93 mn, col, F / ***dir.*** Johnny Gogan ***w. d.*** J. Gogan / ***l. p.*** A. Ryan, B. F. O'Byrne, J. Cronin.

1998: **DIVORCING JACK, Ire./UK,** 110, col, F / ***dir.*** David Caffrey, ***w.*** C.Bateman / ***l. p.*** J. Isaacs, L. Fraser, R. Griffiths,.
THE GENERAL, Ire., 120 min, b/w, F / ***dir.*** John Boorman, ***w.d.*** J. Boorman, ***n.*** *The General* by P. Williams / ***l. p.*** B. Gleeson, A. Dunbar, S. McGinley, M. Doyle Kennedy.
THE NEPHEW, Ire., 106 mn, col, F / ***dir.*** Eugene Brady, ***w.*** J. O'Neill, S. P. Steele / ***l. p.*** H. Harper, A. McGuckin, P. Brosnan.

SOURCES:
K. ROCKETT, *The Irish Filmography, Fiction Films 1896-1996*, Dublin : Red Mountain, 1996, 776 pages.
International Movie Data Base, www.imdb.com
Irish Film Board Film File, www.ireland.iol.ie/filmboard

TABLE OF CONTENTS

10 Education

11 Culture and the Media

12 Religion

13 Ireland and the World

14 Ireland on the Move

The Famine,
by Edward Delaney (see p. 15)
Ph. © B. Fitzgerald.

CHAPTER ONE

Place and People

The island of Ireland is made up of 32 counties (see map, p. 21).

Since 1921 it has been divided in two:

• the Republic of Ireland – often called Ireland, or by the Irish language (Gaelic)* name of Éire – which today is a sovereign state composed of 26 of the 32 counties,

• Northern Ireland, situated in the north east, which is part of the United Kingdom* and comprises the 6 remaining counties. The term Ulster is often used to designate Northern Ireland though the actual province of Ulster has 9 counties – the 6 Northern counties and Donegal, Monaghan and Cavan.

Many people in Ireland hope to see soon an increase in the political and economic links between North and South (see Chapters 6 and 14).

In order to get to know this island, one must begin with the fundamental aspects of its geography and its population.

GEOGRAPHY

As the map, p. 21, indicates, Ireland is situated on the western maritime fringe of Europe between latitude 51.5 ° and 55.5 ° north, and longitude 5.5 ° and 10.5 ° west. Between Malin Head, the most northerly point, and Mizen Head, the most southerly, there are 486 km, and between Howth Head, on the east coast, and Slyne Head, on the west, there are 275 km. The total surface is 84,40 km^2 – England: 131,76; Scotland: 78,77; Wales: 20,76; (France: 547,02). The Republic's share, which accounts for 73% of the whole, is 70,28 km^2, and that of Northern Ireland, 14,12 km^2.

The island is also situated on the western geological fringe of the European continent. It is, in fact, a structurally detached fragment of the continental mainland, separated by shallow seas. A 100 m sea drop would establish a land link with Wales and a further 200 m drop would see France and Ireland become one. The actual edge of the continent is to be found at about 300 km off the west coast.

1 MOUNTAINS AND RIVERS

The European character of the island is further reinforced by the fact that two continental mountain systems converge there. On one hand, originating in Scandinavia, descending through Scotland and ending in the north and west of Ireland, one finds the Caledonian mountain system. The sedimentary and metamorphic rocks and the granite of the mountainous landscapes of Donegal, Mayo and Galway find their origins in that system. On the other hand, there is the Armorican system which, originating in Central Europe, includes the Alps, Britanny, and South West England, and ends in the sandstone of the south of Ireland.

These mountains – or maybe one should say hills since the highest mountain in the island, Carrauntuohil, is only 1,041 m high – form a discontinuous rim around a broad central lowland which is dotted with many lakes and bogs. Narrow plains break the continuity of the hills and allow the numerous rivers to run into the sea. These rivers took on a particular importance for the Vikings* and the Anglo-Normans* when they came to choose sites for their future towns. Such is the case, to mention only the most important towns and rivers, of Dublin on the Liffey, Belfast on the Lagan, Cork on the Lee, Limerick on the Shannon and Waterford on the Suir.

2 CLIMATE

Thanks to the ocean waters of the Gulf Stream, the island has a mild and equable climate. The different ranges of temperature are quite low. Along the west coast a range of only 8 °C separates the average winter temperature (7 °C), from that of summer (15 °C). On the east coast the variation is 11 °C, between 4.5 °C and 15.5 °C. The difference between the extreme south and the extreme north is also particularly small, 2.5 °C on average. A steady stream of depression moving across the Atlantic from west to east means that in the west and the north of the island low pressure is very frequent with persistent strong westerly winds bringing with them rain in abundance. Such are the principal geographical factors which explain the scenic beauty of the western regions of the island.

3 AN ATLANTIC CULTURE

Ireland is also part of Europe in its sensibilities, its religions and its culture. It has much in common with the other countries and regions which face the Atlantic, from Portugal and Galicia, through Atlantic France, Highland Scotland, the Orkneys and the west of Norway. A wet, mild Atlantic climate, the existence of populations who now form cultural minorities, and disadvantaged peripheral economic positions in relation to dominant centres, are some of the traits which they share.

4 RESOURCES

The soil

About 70% of the surface of Ireland is improved land with pasture accounting for the biggest share. The remaining area is composed essentially of peat bogs from which turf, the traditional fuel of the country, is extracted. Cattle constitute the principal output in the two parts of the island followed in importance by milk, crops (mainly barley), pigs, poultry, sheep and horses.

Minerals

From the late 1950s onwards particular attention began to be paid to mineral resources. New legislation and tax incentives were introduced in an effort to encourage exploration which, in turn, was aided by new technological developments in mining. A major lead-zinc*-deposit is located near Navan, Co. Meath.

Energy

In the Republic, from 1921 on, the development of energy sources and the discovery of minerals were to occupy the minds of successive governments.

• The Electricity Supply Board (ESB) was established in 1925 with responsibility for the generation and distribution of electricity. A hydro-electric scheme was opened (1929) but today the principal source of generated electricity all over Ireland is imported fuel.

• In the 1940s the domestic activity of turf exploitation was industrialised.

In the six counties the Northern Ireland Electricity Service for the generation transmission and distribution of electricity.

• Since the 1970s exploration for oil and gas has been undertaken on a considerable scale. The only significant commercial discovery made to date has been that of gas off the coast of Kinsale in County Cork. Gas began to be piped ashore in 1978.

INFLUENCES

It is believed that Ireland was not inhabited until the post-glacial period. Around 8000 BC the first inhabitants entered the island through the northeast coming from Scotland and leaving traces of occupation along the Bann valley.

Around 4000 BC, there seems to have been a major opening up of migrations from Europe with the arrival of many neolithic settlers whose tombs or court cairns are still to be seen in the northern part of the central plain. The best example of what are called megalithic tombs, is the "passage-grave" of Newgrange in Meath.

Those settlers were followed by megalithic peoples. They left a variety of monuments, notably their tombs (wedge-shaped galleries), sites of which can also be seen today.

1 CELTIC INFLUENCE

It was not until around 600 BC that the first Celts* or Gaels* began to arrive from Europe. The contribution of Celtic culture was to be of great importance, though most specialists today underline the substantial cultural input of pre-Celtic peoples. Though the Celts inherited much from them, including their sacred sites, what they brought with them was also impressive: harrows, axes, iron ploughs, spades and oats. They also established a permanent sedentary culture, and by imposing place-names and family names they divided up the total territory of the island. The order, or the system, they created was to last for more than thousand five hundred years. It underwent change however due to the influences of foreign forces among them [???] of the viking at the end of the 8th century. Different traces of that order can be seen in the National Museum in Dublin.

2 OTHER INFLUENCES

Christianity

Between the Celts and the Vikings there were no further arrivals which means that Ireland escaped both the Roman conquest and the barbarian invasions. The influence of Rome was felt, however, in another way since Christianity was introduced among others by Saint Patrick into the country in the 5th century and seems, if one is to judge by the absence of martyrs, to have spread peacefully throughout the island. It is the founders of great monasteries in the 5th and 6th centuries whose names have survived – Colum, Cille, Ciarán, Brendan among the men, and Brigid, Moninne, Ita and Safann among women.

The Vikings

795 AD is given as the date of the first Viking descents. Their permanent settlement dates from the beginning of the 10th century. They are often remembered for their plundering attacks against monasteries but less so for their town-building (Dublin, Waterford, Wexford, Cork, Limerick), their use of stone, their minting of silver coins and their contribution to the growth of commerce and trade.

The Anglo-Normans

The middle of the 12th century saw the arrival of the Anglo-Normans. Unlike the Vikings they set out to conquer territory but like them they also contributed to the building of towns and boroughs, fortifications, manors and churches in Ireland.

The English and the Scots

The final major movement of people into the island was in the early 17th century when Protestant English speakers came to colonize Ulster. Many of them were Presbyterians,* sometimes called Dissenters.

3 THE ENGLISH-SPEAKING WORLD

Ireland through conquest became part of a wider colonial world created by England which spread beyond the confines of western Europe. In this it distinguished itself from its Atlantic neighbours. Its language, its territorial organisation, its land system, its legal and social systems became the victims of this colonialism. At a later period it established itself as an active member of the English-speaking world and due to massive emigration left a profound mark on that world and more particularly on the United States. Our own period has seen it turn again to Europe, thus reuniting itself with essential elements of its own past.

DEMOGRAPHY

Ireland participated in the European population growth which started in the mid-18th century. It is estimated that its population was 5.5 million in 1801 which can be compared to England's 9 million. It was not however until the census of 1841, which showed that the country had a population of 8.2 million people, that fully reliable information on the size and composition of the population was obtained.

An atypical model

Ten years later, the population of Ireland, in complete opposition to what was happening in other countries, had declined to 6.6 million. The reason for this was the Great Famine* which was caused by the land system and the failure of the potato crop through blight. The failure of the British government to intervene efficiently meant that directly or indirectly, between 1845 and 1849, it caused the death of around one million people in what was the worst catastrophe of modern Irish history, and at the same time forced another million to emigrate.

The most surprising thing about subsequent demographic developments is that the tragic decline which occurred between 1845 and 1851 was, though abated, to continue, practically uninterrupted for fifty years. For the following fifty years the population remained stable: 4.5 million (1901) and 4.3 million (1951).

In 1801 Ireland's population was about half that of Britain. Today, with a population of 5 million, the Irish are 11 times less numerous than the British or French. How can this exceptional situation be explained?

Counting the population

Once compulsory registration of births and deaths came into force in Ireland in 1864, precise statistics became available and allow us to study the reasons for the decline. From 1871 to today, the birth rate has always been higher than the death rate. The natural rate of increase has therefore been systematically positive over more than one hundred and twenty years. At the same time, over the same period, the migration balance, with the exception of the ten year period between 1971-1981, has been negative. In other words the single reason which explains Ireland's population decline is emigration.

1 EMIGRATION

Until the 1980s emigration* from Ireland was mainly a rural phenomenon, usually provoked by poverty, the absence of opportunity and the decline in the number of small holdings. It has been calculated that between 1801 and 1921 around 8 million Irish emigrated. The average emigrant was young and unskilled. For long periods in the 19th century and during the first years of the 20th more girls than boys took the emigrant boat.

Up to the First World War, America, and particularly the United States, was the principal destination. Afterwards Britain, which had always been the second most important destination, became the principal one and has remained so since then. Considerable numbers have also gone to other Commonwealth countries such as Australia, New Zealand and Canada.

The pattern of emigration was to change somewhat in the 1980s with the departure of young university graduates, a category of the population which previously had little or no difficulty in finding employment in the Republic of Ireland. From the 1980s onwards Protestant middle-class emigration was also to become a new feature of the demographic scene in Northern Ireland.

2 CONTEMPORARY TRENDS

Beginning in the 1980s, and becoming more accentuated in the 1990s, was the decline in the fertility rate. In Northern Ireland the gap between the traditionally higher Catholic fertility rate and the Protestant one began to narrow. The adoption of new attitudes towards fertility which are best illustrated by the expansion of family planning explains this change.

On the whole therefore, if one excludes emigration, Irish demographic patterns are now becoming closer to those of other European countries even to the extent of becoming, for the first time in three centuries a land of immigration.

FURTHER READING

FREEMAN, T. W., *Ireland*, London: Methuen, 1972.
GRAHAM, B. J., *A Historical Geography of Ireland*, London: Academic Press, 1993.
HUTCHINSON, W., *La Question irlandaise*, Paris: Ellipses, 1997.
MAIGNANT, C. *Histoire et Civilisation de l'Irlande*, Paris: Nathan, 1996.

1

The population of Ireland

Population figures constitute one of the main illustrations of the social and economic evolution of the territory.

Year	Millions	Republic of Ireland	Northern Ireland
1687	1.3*		
1712	2.8		
1788	3.8		
1791	4.2		
1805	5.4		
1821	6.8**		
1831	7.8		
1841	8.2		
1845	8.7*		
1851	6.6		
1861	5.8		
1871	5.4		
1881	5.2		
1891	4.7		
1901	4.6		
1911	4.4		
1926	4.2	2.97	1.26
1936/37	4.2	2.96	1.28
1946	4.3*	2.95	1.35*
1951	4.3	2.96	1.37
1961	4.2	2.81	1.43
1971	4.5	2.97	1.54
1981	5.0	3.40	1.50
1991	5.1	3.52	1.59
1996	5.3	3.62	1.65

* = Estimate (1687-1805) /
** = Censuses of Population (1821-1991).

questions

1. What are the main demographic tendencies?
2. Significant population changes occurred at particular periods in Ireland's past. What were these and how can they be explained?

2

The Famine, by Edward Delaney

See p. 8.

This sculpture, commemorating the Great Famine of the 1840s, is situated in the very heart of Dublin, in St Stephen's Green.

questions

1. Why is it important that the Famine be commemorated?
2. What is the approach of the artist to that tragedy?

3
Population statistics

The migration factor is central to Ireland's demographic experience.

questions

1. Birth, death and migration are the components of population growth or decline. How did they evolve in Ireland?
2. Study the reasons for demographic change.

Average annual births, deaths, natural increase and estimated net migration for each intercensal period, 1926-1996

Period	Total births	Total deaths	Natural increase	Change in population	Estimated net migration
1926 - 1936	58	42	16	0	-17
1936 - 1946	60	43	17	-1	-19
1946 - 1951	66	40	26	1	-24
1951 - 1956	63	36	27	-12	-39
1956 - 1961	61	34	26	-16	-42
1961 - 1966	63	33	29	13	-16
1966 - 1971	63	33	30	19	-11
1971 - 1979	69	33	35	49	14
1979 - 1981	73	33	40	38	-3
1981 - 1986	67	33	34	19	-14
1986 - 1991	56	32	24	-3	-27
1991 - 1996	50	31	18	20	2

Census 96. Central Statistics Office. July 1997.

4
19th-century emigration

The Great Famine opened the floodgate of emigration.

questions

1. Where did the Irish emigrants go to?
2. How can their choice be explained?

Population of Ireland (32 counties) and geographical distribution of Irish-born persons, 1841-1901

thousands

	1841	1851	1861	1871	1881	1891	1901
Population:	8,175	6,552	5,799	5,412	5,175	4,705	4,459
of which Irish-born:	8,141	6,502	5,721	5,307	5,062	4,581	4,327
Irish-born persons living in :							
USA	*	962	1,611	1,856	1,855	1,872	1,615
Canada	122	227	286	223	186	149	102
Australia	*	*	*	*	213	227	184
England and Wales	289	520	602	567	562	458	427
Scotland	126	207	204	208	219	195	205
Total for countries above:	*	*	*	*	3,035	2,901	2,533

*Not available.

Population Trends, n° 39, London: OPCS.

5

Irish and European population trends

Ireland's population trends diverge considerably from those of her neighbours.

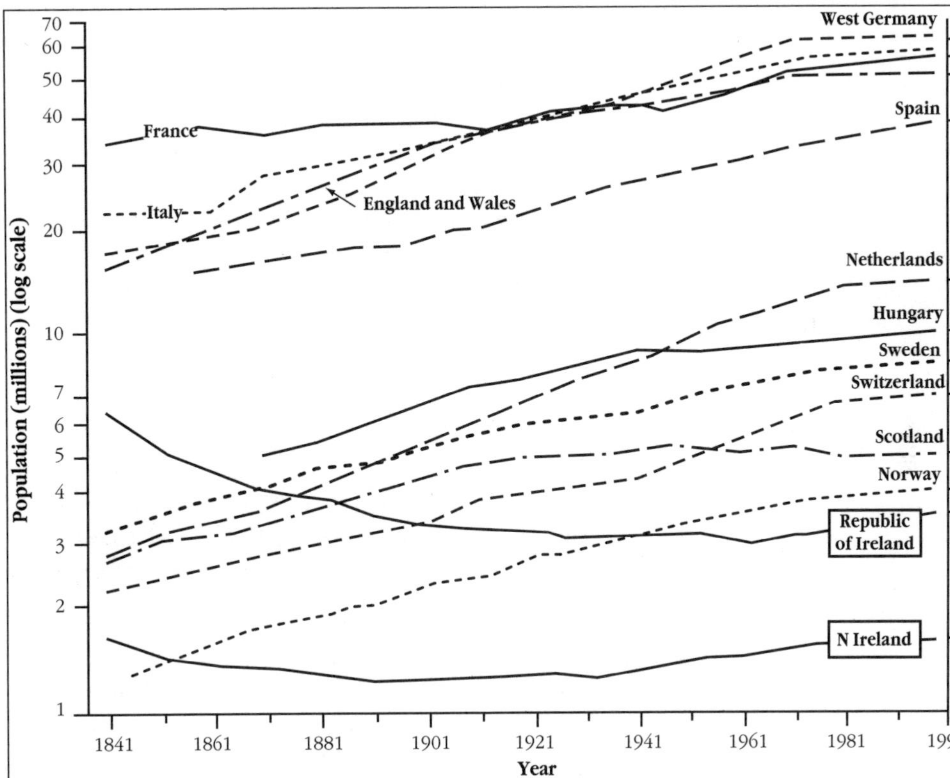

Population Trends, n° 39, London: OPCS.

questions

1. How unique is Ireland's demographic experience?
2. How different is the situation between Northern Ireland and the Republic?

6

Jail journal

John Mitchell, 1815-1875, a Presbyterian from Co. Londonderry

In 1846 came the Famine, and the "Relief Acts" advancing money from the Treasury, to be repaid by local assessment; and of course there was an aggravated and intolerable Poor-rate to meet this claim. Of which Relief Acts, only one fact needs to be recorded here – that the Public Works done under them were strictly ordered to be of an →

and an ardent Republican, was a member of the Young Ireland Movement. During the Great Famine he advocated that the peasantry should withhold the harvest and payments, resist eviction and arm themselves. He was sentenced to fourteen years transportation to Tasmania.

unproductive sort – that is, such as would create no fund to repay their own expenses. Accordingly, many hundreds of thousands of feeble and starving men were kept digging holes, and breaking up roads – doing not only no service, but much harm. Well, then, to meet these Parliamentary advances there was nothing but *rates*: and, *therefore*, there was the higher premium to landlords on the extermination, that is the slaughter, of their tenantry. If the clearing business had been active before, now there was a rage and passion for it; and as if the Cheap Ejectment Acts were not a speedy enough machinery, there was a new Poor-law enacted containing amongst other clauses, the "Quarter Acre clause," which provided that if a farmer, having sold all his produce to pay the rent duties, rates and taxes, should be reduced, as many thousands of men were, to apply for public out-door relief, he should not get it until he had first delivered up all his land to the landlord. Under that law it is the able-bodied idler only who is to be fed – if he attempt to till but one rood of ground, he dies. This simple method of ejectment was called "passing paupers through the workhouse" – a man went in, a pauper came out.

Under these various Poor-laws and Relief Acts, there were at least 10,000 government offices, small and great; looking and canvassing for these were 100,000 men; a great army in the interest of England.

At the end of six years, I can set down these things calmly; but to see them might have driven a wise man mad. There is no need to recount how the Assistant Barristers and Sheriffs, aided by the Police, tore down the roof-trees and ploughed up the hearths of village after village – how the Quarter Acre clause laid waste the parishes, how the farmers and their wives and little ones in wild dismay, trooped along the highways – how in some hamlets by the seaside, most of the inhabitants being already dead, an adventurous traveller would come upon some family eating a famished ass – how maniac mothers stowed away their dead children to be devoured at midnight – [...] – how the "law" was vindicated all this while; how the Arms Bills were diligently put in force, and many examples were made; how starving wretches were transported for stealing vegetables by night; how overworked coroners declared they would hold no more inquests; how Americans sent corn, and the very Turks, yea, negro slaves, sent money for alms; which the British Government was not ashamed to administer to the "sister country"; and how, in every one of these years, '46, '47 and '48, Ireland was exporting to England, food to the value of fifteen million pounds sterling, and had on her own soil at each harvest, good and ample provision for double her own population, notwithstanding the potato blight.

John Mitchell, *Jail Journal*, 1854.

questions

1. What was the government's policy when faced with the Famine?
2. What were some of the popular reactions to the Famine?

7

The Irish in Britain

The Irish emigrants arriving massively in British cities experienced the worst possible conditions there.

Irish settlers were caught up in the fears and anxieties surrounding the urban crisis that dominated early Victorian Britain. It was a tragic coincidence that an awareness of acute urban problems in the 1830s and 1840s occurred at the same time as the rising tide of Irish immigration into the cities of mainland Britain. The Irish became a target for denunciation by reformers and officials alike. As numerous investigations and commissions of enquiry revealed the alarming scale of urban squalor, crime, drunkenness and epidemic disease, an explanation was found in the presence of an alien people. The horrific details uncovered were in truth part of an old problem. Slums had existed long before in London and elsewhere but the problems were now perceived to be of epic proportions. The burgeoning cities lacked the administrative and legislative capacities to deal with the crisis and, even if they had been in place, there was no recognition in contemporary understanding of the economic forces that created a slum district. What was seen as a social evil was interpreted as the product of moral degeneracy.

The wretched inhabitants of early Victorian slums were regarded as outcasts from respectable society and, as many such districts were labelled "Irish colonies" or "little Irelands", the association between Irish immigrants and slum conditions became established in a crisis atmosphere. More significantly, what was to prove a temporary condition and one that affected only part of the Irish community was to carry a stigma that took on a long-lasting and universal application. The image of the Irish in the ghetto exerted a powerful influence, fuelling both English prejudice and an Irish sense of injustice. That influence remains a dominant force in shaping modern attitudes on both sides of the Irish Sea. The theme recurs in some recent work on Irish settlement in Victorian cities, depicting an outcast mass of poor migrants, huddled together in squalid ghettos and subject to the hostility and prejudice of the host community in terms of race, religion, politics and employment. Moreover, discussion of anti-Irish racism, depicting the Celt as a sub-human, ape-like creature, allied to Irish appraisals of their own national character, accepting the much advertised features of stupidity, drunkenness and violence, tended to confirm the well-established "Paddy" stereotype. Taken altogether, this reinforces the contemporary view that Irish fecklessness, allied to the fatalism induced by Roman Catholicism, created a poverty-stricken people destined to fester in the slums of Victorian cities.

Graham Davis,
The Irish in Britain (1815-1914),
Dublin: Gill & Macmillan, 1991.
By kind permission.

questions

1. To what extent were the immigrant Irish treated as scapegoats?
2. What was the image of the Irish in England ?

8
The Irish in America

The Irish had been emigrating to America for a long time but because of population growth at home the number began to reach impressive totals by the late 1820s. By the mid 1830s the figure was 30,000 annually and increased to unprecedented heights during the Famine.

Flight from Ireland

Those who could reach the seaports fled the stricken land. American and Canadian ships, having discharged their grain cargoes, replaced them with humans. Twice as many emigrants left in 1847 as in the year before. Now the terrified Irish risked whatever of life remained to them on the once-feared winter crossing. In this crisis for the first time emigrants left without sea stock. Many of them never made it to the New World. Famine and fever (and occasional shipwreck) got them first. It was estimated that almost one in six died at sea or at ports of debarkation.

In some Irish parishes from 10 to 17% of the population left for North America in the spring of 1847. Galway villages lost nearly one-third of their people. In the desolate scene the famine "lay upon them and it rubbed a wet wisp across the place." Of the overseas emigrants driven by famine to the western hemisphere, 75% went to the United States.

Even during the hysterical flight of 1847 some 25% of the emigrants belonged to a superior group. In the next year or two the latter contributed a larger proportion to the number of departures. Malignant nature and misgoverning Englishmen were too much to contend with. Many in the emigration of 1849 were described as "of those people [...] whom one would wish to keep; [...] farmers with £1 or £200 in their pockets. They cut the corn on the Sunday, sell it on Monday morning, and are off to America in the evening, leaving the waste lands behind them and the landlords without rent." Irishmen spoke of people surrendering their land and "taking the emigration".

A starving time occurred again in 1848, accelerating the departure of tens of thousands more. Emigration was the topic of universal discussion, even without the compulsive pressure of famine. Irishmen succeed in America, it was said, "Why do they not thrive at home?" In America, came the answer, they are on a level with their neighbors. There "they are industrious and reap the fruits of their industry;" in Ireland the laborer "earns a bare subsistence by precarious employment at low wages, with but little hope of improvement, and consequently but little stimulus to exertion."

Michael Kraus, *Immigration, the American Mosaic*, New York: Van Nostrand Reinhold, 1966.

questions

1. Who were the emigrants?
2. Did the Irish succeed in America?

MAP OF IRELAND (1999)

The executed leaders of 1916 (see p. 31)

Seated: P.H. Pearse, J. MacBride, T. Clarke, E. Ceannt, J. Connolly, J. Plunkett

Standing: W. Pearse, T. MacDonagh, S. Heuston, M. Mallin, S. MacDermott, M. O'Hanrahan, E. Daly, C. Colbert

Inset: R. Casement, T. Kent

CHAPTER TWO

Nationalist Ireland

The process of nation-building preceded that of state-building in Ireland.* This implied the elaboration of a nationalist ideology and the adoption of that ideology by the majority of the inhabitants of the country. Irish nationalism is essentially a product of the 19th century but was also drawn from earlier political thought and from Irish Protestant nationalism of the 18th century. It was founded on an opposition to England inspired by the latter's political and cultural conquest of Ireland and its religious persecution of the Catholics. Once national consciousness was sufficiently developed, the demand for independence, already put forward in the 1790s reemerged. From 1922 on, with the beginning of state building, the application of the ideals which nationalism had nurtured became part of the global nationalist project.

From the arrival of the Anglo-Normans* in 1169 on, the distinction between the "native" Gaels* and the "colonists" became a permanent feature of Irish life. From as early as 1297 statutes were passed to prevent assimilation. The most famous are the Statutes of Kilkenny (1366), which forbade marriage between the English and the Irish and the fostering of children, and condemned those who abandoned the English language in favour of Irish. By the late middle ages the hostility between the two nations was firmly rooted in cultural identity.

Protestant Nationalism in the 18th Century

Early in the 17th century the last traces of the old Gaelic* political order disappeared to be replaced by country-wide Protestant ascendancy control closely supervised by London. The first to react against this state of things were, curiously enough, members of the Protestant ruling class. Whenever some of its members felt that their interests were being attacked by London they advanced the claim to the right of self-government for Ireland. This claim constitutes the very foundation of Irish nationalism. As far back as 1698 William Molyneux,* and later Jonathan Swift* affirmed Ireland's constitutional rights, its status as a kingdom, and denied that Ireland was ever a conquered country. The nationalism or the patriotism of those Protestants was one of place, not of race, and assumed major proportions during the latter part of the 18th century. One of its principal leaders was Henry Grattan* who led the battle in favour of parliamentary reform. He and his followers were, however, confronted with the major problem of the composition of the political nation. Were Catholics part of it or not?

A second leader drawn from the ranks of the Irish Protestants of that time was Wolfe Tone,* who, heavily influenced by the American and French revolutions, answered that question positively, and this led him to seek to achieve the unity of all Irishmen – Catholics, Protestants and Dissenters. This, according to the United Irishmen Society* which he helped create, could only be achieved by severing the link with England and proclaiming the Republic.* Hence the birth of Irish Republicanism. The armed rising of 1798 for which the Society was responsible was an unsuccessful attempt to achieve that aim. The direct consequence of that rising, which had French backing, and of the military danger which it represented for England itself, was the Act of Union* which, by suppressing the Dublin Parliament,* joined Ireland and Britain together in 1801 in the United Kingdom* under the legislative control of the Westminster* Parliament. Henceforth, while small groups or individuals from among the Protestants did participate in the nationalist effort, their collective commitment, as will be seen in Chapter 3, was finally to lie in defending the union with Britain, in other words in unionism.*

NATIONALISM IN THE 19TH AND EARLY 20TH CENTURIES

While borrowing some elements from the 18th century, Irish nationalism, in the 19th century, was to adopt specific traits of its own. It elaborated a dynamic and powerful ideology which consisted above all in a coherent version of the history of the island. While this history was, to a large extent, founded on fact, it underwent, in the course of its elaboration, a process of mythicising, the aim of which was to use the past as an instrument to give a cohesive explanation of the present, to overcome the different divisions within Irish society, whether regional, class, religious or other, and to fix the direction of the collective effort for the future –to create, in reality, a comprehensive Irish nation.

According to this version of history the Gaels, or the Goidelic Celts,* were the fathers of the Irish race. By the 8th century their descendants were widely admired for their learning, and Irish monks were winning back Europe to Christianity after the barbarian invasions. This period, which they called the Golden Age, ended with the first Viking* invasions at the very end of the 8th century. Henceforth decline set in and was confirmed by a second invasion, that of the Anglo-Normans in the middle of the 12th century. The latter was the starting point of the English conquest which was to be completed by Queen Elizabeth's armies in the 16th century, by the plantation* or the colonization of Ulster* at the beginning of the following century, by the massive confiscation of land in the 17th and 18th centuries and by the passage of particularly severe anti-Catholic laws in the 18th century. This led to a situation where power and wealth were in the hands of a small Protestant minority.

A more objective view of history would rectify this version of Ireland's past. It would point out that the island was inhabited before the arrival of the Gaels, which meant that the fathers of the Irish nation had also been invaders. It would underline not only the negative side of the Viking and Anglo-Norman presence on the island, but also the positive contribution they made. But then the nationalists were not historians; they set out to build a nation, and Irish nationalism in its three dimensions, the political, the religious and the cultural, was the cement they used to achieve their task.

1 POLITICS

The task the Irish nationalists set themselves in the 19th century was extraordinarily ambitious. They aimed at undoing the conquest. This meant winning back political power for the Irish people, undoing the whole land settlement, abolishing all anti-Catholic measures and, more globally, putting an end to England's cultural invasion. To achieve such a task the Irish, according to the nationalists, needed to be convinced of their prestigious origins, of the fundamental wickedness of the invaders and of their own great destiny.

Two charismatic leaders

Under the leadership of two charismatic figures, the Catholic Daniel O'Connell,* for the first half of the 19th century, and the Protestant Charles Stewart Parnell* from 1880 to 1890, Irish nationalism became a mass movement, which helps to explain the democratic character which it has retained up to our own times. The demand for political autonomy in the 19th century was expressed by O'Connell in his call for the repeal of the Act of Union and later by Parnell in his call for Home Rule.* But autonomy was refused by the Parliament of Westminster, first in 1886 and then in 1893, though it did introduce fundamental change by transferring the ownership of the land from the landlords to the tenants.

Easter 1916

But then, during the 1914-1918 war, seeking independence rather than autonomy, a group of young republicans, taking the United Irishmen's call for a complete break with England as their model, organized an armed rising* in Dublin on Easter Monday, 1916. Risings had already been attempted by Republican movements in the 19th century, by the Young Ireland movement in 1848 and by the Fenians in 1867. While initially a failure from a military point of view, the 1916 rising, because of the execution of its idealistic leaders and the ensuing upsurge of sympathy for them, was a success. Their followers, after the general elections of December 1918, created a Parliament in Dublin in January 1919, called the Dáil* and once it convened, they declared Ireland an independent and sovereign Republic.

The war of independence

Such a unilateral decision was rejected by London. The direct consequence was what came to be called the War of Independence* (sometimes called the Black and Tan War*). It lasted from 1919 to June 1921 when a ceasefire was declared. A treaty was signed between Dublin and London in December 1921. The Anglo-Irish Treaty,* which was refused by the republicans because of the limited independence it granted, obtained nevertheless a majority in the Dáil. It accorded dominion status to Southern Ireland, London having previously bowed to unionist pressure and, in application of the Government of Ireland Act* (1920), created Northern Ireland* from the six counties of the north-east of the island. The Treaty officially came into force in 1922. Nationalist Ireland had at last achieved its goal, at least partially, though it failed to unite in one nation all the people of the island. But seventy-six years later, in 1998, the Good Friday Agreement has opened up new possibilities in that direction (see Chapter 14).

2 RELIGION

A further relevant characteristic of 19th-century Irish nationalism, in sharp contrast to its 18th-century predecessor, was its Catholic content. Because of massive land confiscation and with the passage of the Penal laws,* sometimes called the Popery Code, early in the 18th century which allowed Catholics few or no legal rights, no means to educate their children openly, no right to organize their Church, and deprived them of practically all property rights, the Catholics of Ireland built up within themselves an acute antagonism towards Protestants. It is not unduly surprising therefore that Catholicism penetrated Irish nationalism. Indeed, the first major political campaign led by O'Connell, with the support of the masses, was on the theme of Catholic emancipation.* Catholics were unable to sit in Westminster and the aim of the campaign was to put an end to this situation. Its victory, in 1829, reinforced Catholic cohesion.

3 CULTURE

As will be seen in Chapter 11, Irish nationalism also had a cultural dimension. In order to give new life to the Irish language and to Irish culture, revivalists began, as early as the 18th century, to create the foundations for an authentic Irish civilization which would be distinct from that of England. The revival of the Irish language was one of its dimensions. Another is to be found in the literary revival which gave birth to such great names as Yeats,* Lady Gregory,* Synge,* Joyce* and O'Casey.*

To what extent did the achievement of independence in 1922 correspond to the carrying into effect of nationalist projects and ideals? On the political level, two principal obstacles hindered the realisation of the nationalist plan. The first one was that dominion* status, which accorded a considerable amount of power to the new Dublin government, did not however correspond to national sovereignty. Secondly, the whole of the island did not accede to even dominion status since Northern Ireland remained fully part of the United Kingdom.

Soon after the creation of the new state, Catholicism emerged stronger than ever before. The initial project as embodied in the 1922 Constitution* was to create an essentially secular state. However, the political influence of the Catholic hierarchy soon began to be brought to bear on a consenting government. The logical consequence of such cooperation between Church and state was a new Constitution in 1937 which incorporated the essential elements of Catholic social teaching. Just as Northern Ireland had a Protestant Parliament for a Protestant people, so Southern Ireland, by 1937, had become a Catholic State for a Catholic people.

On the cultural level, confronted with the continuing decline of the use of Irish, many now believed that it was up to the state to assure the gaelicization* of the country. But the early governments refused to assume such a responsibility. Éamon De Valera,* a language enthusiast himself, who came to power in 1932 at the head of the Fianna Fáil Party* which claimed to be the party of the Gaelic tongue, believed that the revival could not be achieved by the state or by public institutions. According to him only one person could save the language and that was the individual citizen. The English-speaking individual citizen, though remaining well disposed towards the Irish language, refused in turn to assume the responsibility, so the decline continued.

FURTHER READING

George BOYCE, D., *Nationalism in Ireland*, London: Routledge, 1991.
LYONS, F.S.L., *Ireland since the Famine*, London: Weidenfeld & Nicolson, 1971.

1
The Protestant nation

Henry Grattan, in a speech in the Irish House of Commons in favour of legislative independence, traces the progress made by Ireland from a position of total subjection to that of a free nation.

Mr Grattan rose, and spoke as follows:

"I am now to address a free people: ages have passed away, and this is the first moment in which you could be distinguished by that appellation.

I have spoken on the subject of your liberty so often, that I have nothing to add, and have only to admire by what Heaven-directed steps you have proceeded until the whole faculty of the nation is braced up to the act of her own deliverance.

I found Ireland on her knees, I watched over her with a paternal solicitude; I have traced her progress from injuries to arms, and from arms to liberty. Spirit of Swift! spirit of Molyneux! your genius has prevailed! Ireland is now a nation! in that new character I hail her! and bowing to her august presence, I say, *Esto perpetua*![1]

She is no longer a wretched colony, returning thanks to her governor for his rapine, and to her king for his oppression; nor is she now a squabbling, fretful sectary, perplexing her little wits, and firing her furious statutes with bigotry, sophistry, disabilities, and death, to transmit to posterity insignificance and war.

Look to the rest of Europe, and contemplate yourself, and be satisfied. Holland lives on the memory of past achievements; Sweden has lost liberty; England has sullied her great name by an attempt to enslave her colonies. You are the only people – you, of the nations in Europe, are now the only people who excite admiration, and in your present conduct you not only exceed the present generation, but you equal the past. I am not afraid to turn back and look antiquity in the face: the revolution – that great event, whether you call it ancient or modern I know not, was tarnished with bigotry: the great deliverer (for such I must ever call the Prince of Nassau) was blemished with oppression; he assented to, he was forced to assent to, acts which deprived the Catholics of religious, and all the Irish of civil and commercial rights, though the Irish were the only subjects in these islands who had fought in his defence. But you have sought liberty on her own principle: see the Presbyterians of Bangor petition for the freedom of the Catholics of Munster. You, with difficulties innumerable, with dangers not a few, have done what your ancestors wished, but could not accomplish, and what your posterity may preserve, but will never equal: you have moulded the jarring elements of your country into a nation, and have rivalled those great and ancient commonwealths, whom you were taught to admire, and among whom you are now to be recorded: in this proceeding you had not the advantages which were common to other great countries […]."

Henry Grattan, speech in the Irish Parliament, 16 April 1782.

1. Latin for "Let her be eternal!"

questions

1. According to Grattan, what was England's role in Ireland?
2. How has Ireland become a nation?

2
The birth of Irish republicanism

England dominated Ireland by opposing one religion to another and by convincing the Catholics that it was their ally.

questions

1. How was the disunion between the great religions achieved?
2. What vision of the Ireland of tomorrow is suggested?

The dominion of England in Ireland had been begun and continued in the disunion of the great sects which divided the latter country. In effectuating this disunion, the Protestant [Episcopalian] party were the willing instruments, as they saw clearly that if ever the Dissenters and Catholics were to discover their true interests and, forgetting their former ruinous dissensions, were to unite cordially and make common cause, the downfall of English supremacy, and, of course, of their own unjust monopoly, would be the necessary and immediate consequence. They therefore laboured continually, and, for a long time, successfully, to keep the other two sects asunder, and the English Government had even the address to persuade the Catholics that the non-execution of the penal laws, which were, in fact, too atrocious to be enforced in their full rigour, was owing to their clemency; that the Protestants and Dissenters, but especially the latter, were the enemies, and themselves, in effect, the protectors of the Catholic people. Under this arrangement the machine of government moved forward on carpet ground, but the time was, at length, come when this system of iniquity was to tumble in the dust, and the day of truth and reason to commence.

The Autobiography of Theobald Wolfe Tone, vol. 1: Dublin, 1893.

3
The sources of Irish democracy

Many influences combined in the Ireland of the first half of the 19th century to promote democracy. The most important were the work of Daniel O'Connell and the political convictions of the Catholic clergy.

March 1829 had seen the passage of Catholic Emancipation in London and also the triumphant popular inauguration of Andrew Jackson as President in Washington. Jacksonian democracy, like O'Connellism, spelled the end of the easy ascendancy of the elite ruling classes: the day of the multitude had dawned. In the new democratic era, with the creation of the broadly-based national organisation, power was not imparted from above but was built up from the ground. Tocqueville and Beaumont believed that the future of European society lay with democracy; people were "beginning to get the idea that they, too, could take part in government". Beaumont examined with great clarity the causes by which Ireland tended "to become a democratic country": amongst the main causes was the political organisation which developed from the Catholic struggle, Daniel O'Connell's leadership, as well as the development of the Irish middle class.

Both Tocqueville and Beaumont reflected on the "democratic" tendency of the Catholic clergy in Ireland. In July 1835 Tocqueville dined with some Irish bishops and priests and he noted his impressions:

"The feelings expressed were extremely democratic. Distrust and hatred of the great landlords; love of the people and confidence in them. Bitter memories of past oppression. An air of exaltation at present or approaching victory. A profound hatred of the Protestants and above all of their clergy. Little impartiality apparent. Clearly as much the leaders of a party as the representatives of the Church."

In the 1820s O'Connell, Doyle and MacHale had given the Catholic Church a new vital sense of its potential influence in political affairs. The priests had been essential lieutenants assisting the local organisation of the Catholic Association. Given the Association's policy of exerting the maximum moral force in favour of Emancipation the personnel of the Catholic Church were an obvious mainspring for O'Connellite organisation: O'Connellites had cultivated a coincidence of purpose with the Catholic Church.

Beaumont identified the Ulster Presbyterians as another possible democratic influence in Ireland; he noted that the democratic nature of their organisation could be compared with the Constitution of the United States. While Catholicism proceeded from a principle of authority Presbyterianism proceeded from a principle of liberty yet, according to Beaumont, in Ireland both had a common democratic effect which was a "remarkable phenomenon". He observed the division of Irish Presbyterians into those who saw some political interests in common with Catholics and those who saw only religious barriers between themselves and Catholics. Both liberal Presbyterians and Catholics were opposed to the aristocracy – the first because they saw an Anglican Establishment and the Catholics because it was Protestant and anti-national. The tendency towards democracy in Ireland could derive immense power from the union between these interests but Beaumont realistically posed the question: "Is not this alliance between the Presbyterians and Catholics factitious and transitory?" He certainly believed that it was – the gap between "the Scotch Puritan of the North" and the Catholic was too great. Beaumont had visited Ulster in July 1837 and was a witness to "hateful passions". He concluded that Ulster "[…] might be supposed constantly on the eve of a civil war".

F. O'Ferrall, *Catholic Emancipation*, Dublin: Gill & Macmillan, 1985.
By kind permission.

questions

1. What were the different origins of Irish democracy?
2. What role did the Catholic Church play in the development of that democracy?

4
A nationalist vision of a golden age

"The Island of Saints and Scholars"

The success of St Patrick's mission was not more remarkable than the great outburst of religious zeal which followed it, and which continued for centuries. Easy as had been the conversion of Ireland, it was profound. St Patrick was immediately followed by many disciples of →

An extract from a textbook used in secondary schools in former times.

sanctity and fervour, and these again were succeeded by numerous others, who devoted their lives to religion and learning. During the three centuries after Patrick's death the history of the country is mainly devoted to the records of spiritual and intellectual work – for to such work were the energies of the Irish people almost entirely devoted. It was the era in which Ireland won the title of "*Insula Sanctorum et Doctorum*."

During this period, Christianity and civilization were nearly swept out of Europe. The barbarian tribes had finally destroyed the Empire of Rome (A.D. 476), and settled upon its territories. Ignorance reigned over most of Western Europe, and it was in Ireland that the torch of learning was kept alive. Ireland was "the intellectual head of Europe": Armagh was "the Metropolis of Civilization."

M. Hayden and G. Moonan, *A Short History of the Irish People*, Part I, Dublin: Educational Company of Ireland, 1950. By kind permission.

questions

1. Does the description of Ireland after the arrival of Saint Patrick correspond to historical reality?
B Was the part Ireland played in European history as important as suggested here?

5
The proclamation of the Republic

Having taken over the General Post Office on Easter Monday, 1916, Padraig Pearse proclaimed the Irish Republic.

POBLACHT NA H'ÉIREANN

The Provisional Government of the Irish Republic to the people of Ireland

IRISHMEN and IRISHWOMEN: In the name of God and of the dead generations from which she receives her old tradition of nationhood, Ireland, through us, summons her children to her flag and strikes for her freedom.

Having organised and trained her manhood through her secret revolutionary organisation, the Irish Republican Brotherhood, and through her open military organisations, the Irish Volunteers and the Irish Citizen Army, having patiently perfected her discipline, having resolutely waited for the right moment to reveal itself, she now seizes that moment, and, supported by her exiled children in America and by gallant allies in Europe, but relying in the first on her own strength, she strikes in full confidence of victory.

We declare the right of all the people of Ireland to the ownership of Ireland, and to the unfettered control of Irish destinies, to be sovereign and indefeasible. The long usurpation of that right by a foreign people and government has not extinguished the right, nor can it ever be extinguished except by the destruction of the Irish people. In every generation the Irish people have asserted their right to national freedom and sovereignty: six times during the past three hundred years they have asserted it in arms. Standing on that fundamental right and again asserting it in arms in the face of the world, we hereby proclaim the Irish Republic as a Sovereign Independent State, and we pledge our lives and the lives of our comrades-in-arms to the cause of its freedom, of its welfare, and of its exaltation among the nations.

The Irish Republic is entitled to, and hereby claims, the allegiance of every Irishman and Irishwoman. The Republic guarantees religious and civil liberty, equal rights, and equal opportunities to all its citizens, and declares its resolve to pursue the happiness and prosperity of the whole nation and of all its parts, cherishing all the children of the nation equally, and oblivious of the differences carefully fostered by an alien government, which have divided a minority from the majority in the past.

Until our arms have brought the opportune moment for the establishment of a permanent National Government, representative of the whole people of Ireland and elected by the suffrages of all her men and women, the Provisional Government, hereby constituted, will administer the civil and military affairs of the Republic in trust for the people.

We place the cause of the Irish Republic under the protection of the Most High God, Whose blessing we invoke upon our arms, and we pray that no one who serves that cause will dishonour it by cowardice, inhumanity, or rapine. In this supreme hour the Irish nation must, by its valour and discipline and by the readiness of its children to sacrifice themselves for the common good, prove itself worthy of the august destiny to which it is called.

Signed on the Behalf of the Provisional Government,

THOMAS J. CLARKE, SÉAN MacDIARMADA, THOMAS Mac DONAGH, P. H. PEARSE, ÉAMONN CEANNT, JAMES CONNOLLY, JOSEPH PLUNKETT.

Dublin, 24 April 1916.

questions

1. How was the Rising justified?
2. What rights and what principles does the Proclamation defend?

6

The executed leaders of 1916

See p. 22.

A montage of the executed republican leaders of the Easter rising of 1916

questions

1. What does the *montage* suggest?
2. Fill in the leaders' background.

—7—

The centenary of the Gaelic League

One hundred years after the creation of the Gaelic League, one can examine what it has achieved.

"It is arguable that the current uncertainty in the Republic about what events of the past to celebrate and how, reflects serious uncertainty about the present and no vision for the future," wrote the Trinity College, Dublin, theology lecturer, Dr Terence McCaughey, in his recent book, *Memory and Redemption*.

The lacklustre celebration of the centenary of the founding of the Gaelic League illustrates his contention well. For, even more than the Easter Rising of 1916, the league is widely regarded as providing the inspiration and the leadership for an independent Irish state. As Patrick Pearse put it: "When the Gaelic League was founded in 1893, the Irish revolution began."

The marginal and largely ornamental place of the Irish language in Irish national life probably accounts for the widespread neglect of the centenary. But, as analysts such as Dr Kieran Kennedy of the ESRI[1] and Dr Joe Lee of UCC[2] remind us again and again that our performance as an independent State has, by any European standard, been mediocre, the legacy of the Gaelic League is a resource we can ill afford to ignore.

For the central insight of Douglas Hyde, expressed in his famous lecture on *The Necessity for De-Anglicising Ireland*, which led directly to the league's founding, was that Ireland would never develop to its full potential until its people learned a sense of self-confidence and self-respect. For this, he argued, restoring Irish was essential. If this did not happen, he feared Ireland would remain "a nation of imitators [...] lost to the power of native initiative and alive only to second-hand assimilation."

The Gaelic League was a key agency in sparking such creativity in the first decade of the century. It was a time of robust debate, carried on through such papers as Arthur Griffith's *United Irishman*, D. P. Moran's *The Leader* and W. P. Ryan's *The Irish Peasant*, and was far more pluralist, practical and diverse than anything taking place today. And, amid all this ferment of ideas about Irish development, Hyde did his utmost to keep the league and the Irish language as a meeting ground for nationalists and unionists.

Yet the creative promise of those years was snuffed out. Some blame clericalist forces, others the takeover of the league by political revolutionaries. What is certain is that the foundation of the State robbed the language movement of much of its popular dynamism. The State was now expected to complete the task begun by the league and did so by imposing the burden of language revival on the nation's children.

In the process, Irish became identified with Catholic nationalism in a way it never was throughout the 19th century. As such, it became a largely ornamental badge of identity as Catholicism remained, in practice, the real distinguishing mark. And Hyde's key insight into the importance of the language as a unifying and regenerative element in Irish life was lost.

1. Economic and Social Research Institute
2. University College Cork

What can be salvaged from this failure is a potential that urgently requires to be built on with imagination and energy. The revival effort has made the language a truly twentieth-century medium of communication and ensured that many Irish people have a basic knowledge of it. Goodwill towards the language, sorely tested at the height of the revival, has returned. And, as Catholicism declines as a badge of Irish identity, so do people turn more to the language.

If the last century has taught us anything, it is that the revival is too serious a matter to leave to the State. The popular dynamism of the first decades of the revival is being rekindled, as can be seen from the burgeoning of *naionrai* and *gaelscoilcanna*[3] throughout the State. Local communities, often with high levels of social deprivation such as Tallaght, Clondalkin and Ballymun, are active in this cause.

The Irish Times, August 2, 1993.

3. Infant schools and schools using Irish

questions

1. Why has Ireland not achieved the aim set by the Gaelic League?
2. Why is it time for a second revival?

8

An anti-British protest in Derry (1979)

Ph. © Steele-Perkins/Magnum

questions

1. Analyze the steps in the campaign. 2. What background information are we given?

Dublin Castle,
by James Malton, 1792 (see p. 39)

Northern Ireland: established under the Gov of Ireland Act (1920) It is part of the U.K and made up of 6 of the 32 counties of Ireland. The 1920 Act was later modified by the Northern Ireland Constitut Act (1973) and the N.I Act (1979).

Act of Union: passed (1800), came into force (1801) creating the UK by supressing the Irish Parliament & placing Ireland under the control of Westminster

UK: England, Scotland, Wales, N.I.

CHAPTER THREE

Unionist Ireland

Irish unionism,* just like Irish nationalism, is a product of 19th-century Ireland. Its roots go back, however, to when the first ties were established between England and Ireland. Later the term «unionist» came to be used to designate those in favour of the Act of Union* (1801). In post-1920 Ireland unionists are those who defend the 1920 partition of the island, the creation of Northern Ireland,* the maintenance of its union with Britain within the United Kingdom,* and who oppose unification with the South.

unionism : political ideology founded on maintenance of link between Ireland & Britain -

1 THE UNION

For hundreds of years, after the arrival of the Anglo-Norman* barons in Ireland in 1169, the nature of the union between Ireland and England varied considerably. Its closeness, or its looseness, was dependent on the strength of the three major actors on the Irish scene: the Gaelic* chiefs, the descendants of the Anglo-Norman lords, often called the Anglo-Irish,* and the English king. They fought intermittently, intrigued and established alliances to obtain the supremacy of the island. By the beginning of the 17th century the Tudor* kings and queens had considerably advanced their strategy of colonization through plantations and centralization, which were the hallmarks of their policy of conquest of Ireland. The Stuarts,* Oliver Cromwell* and William of Orange* were to bring this strategy to a successful conclusion.

Plantations

Plantations* were used as a colonization strategy by the English in Ireland. James I* planted Ulster* after the defeat of the O'Neills in 1607. He planted Donegal, Londonderry, Armagh, Tyrone, Fermanagh and Cavan. The two north-easterly counties of Antrim and Down were also planted. It has been reckoned that over 200,000 English-speaking Protestants, Scots Presbyterians* but also English Anglicans*, came to settle in the northern part of the island. In the following years, by using military and legislative measures the conquerors continued the transfer of land ownership into Protestant hands so that by the end of the 18th century only about 5% of the land of the island remained in the ownership of Catholics.

Centralization

As for centralization it sought to eliminate all local resistance to the English monarchy. Its aim in Ireland was to maintain the land settlement, to perpetuate the established order and to assure, by the domination of the island, the military control of the western approaches to Britain. A London appointed executive, at the head of which were a Lord Lieutenant and a Chief Secretary, working from Dublin Castle,* (the centre of England's government in Ireland as early as 1260) were the agents of this centralization. Between 1297 and the Act of Union (1801) a Parliament sat in Dublin. Throughout

*Penal law: The 1st anti catho law was voted by Irish parliam' (1695) and followed by other, notably by the 1704 Act creating an anti-Catholic code of an extraordinary repressive nature.

the entire 18th century no Catholic sat there. Thus the majority of the inhabitants of the island were deprived of all representation. Most historians would agree that up to the latter part of the 18th century Ireland was consistently governed in England's interest.

2 THE BIRTH OF MODERN IRISH UNIONISM

A new order seemed to be emerging at the end of the 18th century in Ireland. Revolt simmered among Protestants. The causes were numerous. England's interference in the government of Ireland began to be severely resented. The revolutions in America and in France helped considerably in the spread of new ideas among the rising middle class. The Presbyterians of the north began to espouse republicanism, prompted by the egalitarian nature of their own religion; prompted also by the disabilities from which they too suffered, though to a lesser extent than the Catholics, under the 1704 Act which introduced the Penal laws.* They were joined by a number of Catholics within the United Irishmen Society.* As has been seen in Chapter 2, a common group of Catholics and Protestants now existed which favoured the unity of all Irishmen, regardless of their religion. According to them unity could only be achieved by setting up an independent Irish Republic. As stated above, the failure of the 1798 rising and the passage of the Act of Union put an end to those emerging patterns. The five hundred year-old Irish Parliament was suppressed. Ireland and Britain became constitutionally one within the United Kingdom. The unity between Catholic and Protestant failed to materialize. It was replaced by a strong alliance of the Presbyterians and the Anglicans in favour of the Union. How did this come about?

A reaction to Irish nationalism

Unionism, as it developed in the 19th and early 20th centuries was, to a large extent, though not exclusively, a reaction to Irish nationalism. Its justification was to be found in three main areas, the religious, the economic and the political. Although it became part of the United Kingdom conservative tradition in the 19th century, unionism in Ulster gained its autonomy in the early years of the next century.

Growth of sectarianism

The Protestants of Ireland, notably the Presbyterians of the north-east turned away from Irish nationalism partly because of its developing Catholic nature and the increasing assimilation between "Catholic" and "Irish". The Presbyterians, some of whom had espoused the cause of Irish republicanism in the 1790s, felt alienated from this form of Irish nationalism. At the same time, within Protestantism itself, beginning in the 1820s, religious revivalism made considerable progress. Catholicism became the object of persistent attacks on the part of revivalist ministers for its false doctrines and its neglect of the revealed truth which was to be found in the Bible. Later in the century those positions were to be vigorously defended by Presbyterian ministers such as Hugh Hanna.* A growth of sectarianism and bigotry accompanied this renewal. Such developments contributed in no small way to the first Catholic-Protestant sectarian riots which broke out in Belfast in the 1830s and which have been a feature of the life of that city since then.

Belfast

The distinctiveness of the north-eastern part of the island was to be further accentuated in the 19th century as a consequence of the economic development of Belfast and its region. Thanks to the expansion of two industries, linen and shipbuilding, the city on the Lagan river became a hive of economic activity. Given the restricted market that the island of Ireland represented for the products of these industries, Belfast became heavily dependent on the much larger British market. Such economic considerations could not but reinforce political unionism, and all the more so in the early 20th century when Irish nationalism, under the influence of the Sinn Féin* political movement, began to favour economic protectionism as a means to create an industrial basis in the south.

Sinn Fein = wee ourselves - Developed from 1905 on, it finally became the republican political party which it still is today

Reaction to Home Rule

= political autonomy for Ireland. 3 H.r. bill = 1886, 93, 1912 were presented to the H. of Common.

The unionist reaction to the nationalist demand for Home Rule* in the 1880s was to give political substance to those differences. By then the country was divided between the south which, under the leadership of the nationalist Parnell,* was calling for Home Rule, and the north which was resisting this demand and, by putting their confidence in the conservatives, the Protestant unionists hoped to maintain the established constitutional order. But in 1906 when the liberals returned to power, the probability of Home Rule becoming a reality prompted the unionists to strengthen their own forces in Ulster in case the conservatives might, one day, be tempted by a political stance contrary to their interests. Hence the unionist party was created and, while it was linked to the conservative party, it had its own organization, its own structures and above all its own territory to defend. Unionism was not, however, limited to Ulster, or rather, to be precise, to the six counties which later became Northern Ireland. One could find unionists all over the country. But elsewhere in the island they only formed a small, even in some places a tiny, minority of the population.

The UVF

Given the chance of success for Home Rule in the House of Commons, the unionists began mobilizing in Ulster in 1912, when the third Home Rule bill was introduced and finally adopted in 1914. At their head were Edward Carson* and James Craig.* Refusing to accept the possibility of being governed by a Dublin parliament they decided they would create a provisional government for Ulster if Home Rule were adopted and set up an illegal army, the Ulster Volunteer Force (UVF)* and in 1914, in the famous Larne gun-running* expedition, they imported 35,000 rifles from Germany. The most amazing aspect of this whole affair was that the Ulster unionists obtained the full backing of the Conservative party led by Bonar Law* in Britain and the sympathetic support of practically the whole Establishment. Given the force of the opposition to the will of Parliament, many people believed the country to be on the brink of civil war for the first time since the 17th century.

Partition

However, the outbreak of the First World War in August 1914 put an end, for the moment, to the crisis since the application of Home Rule was suspended for the duration of the hostilities. The war offered to the men of the UVF the opportunity to redeem themselves, notably during the battle of the Somme. By the end of the war the positions were so far apart between the Ulster unionists and the southern nationalists that compromise seemed impossible. That, at least, was London's conclusion which led it to decide to partition the country and in 1920 to pass the Government of Ireland Act creating Northern Ireland.

3 NORTHERN IRELAND UNIONISM

Now, for the first time, unionists held political power. How were they to exercise it over a territory which contained roughly two thirds Protestants and one third Catholics? How were they to define themselves both politically and ideologically? The unionist party governed Northern Ireland on its own without interruption for half a century. Unionism, throughout that period, consisted, above all, in a defence of the union with Britain within the United Kingdom. It also consisted in maintaining Protestant cohesion. This meant elaborating a strategy allowing for the creation of an all-class alliance between Protestants. Thirdly, in order to conform to the two preceding characteristics, unionism also consisted in the practice of discrimination against the nationalist minority. Added to that, the unionist party refused to accept Catholic members. Unionist political logic was perfectly clear-cut – one could not have confidence in a community, the vast majority of which was opposed to the constitution, or to the very existence of Northern Ireland.

Apart from the firm belief that their interests lay in the continuation of the union with Britain, unionists shared a common broad-based ideology. Given the very numerous theological divergences between different forms of Protestantism and notably between Anglicanism and Presbyterianism, the existence of such an ideology was all the more necessary to maintain Protestant cohesion. Whatever the theological differences might be between the Protestants of Northern Ireland, the opposition encapsulated in the historical slogan "Home Rule is Rome Rule" summed up their persistent common profound opposition to nationalism and catholicism. The signing of the Good Friday Agreement by the Ulster Unionist party in 1998 suggests change in unionist attitudes.

The Orange Order

The Orange Order organized, perpetuated and cemented this opposition. Protestants of every background – men only, since women have always been excluded from it – were bonded together by their common membership of this association which dates back to 1795 and which was created in opposition to reform in favour of Catholics and to the United Irishmen. A further aim was to defend the monarch and heirs to the monarchy as long as they support the Protestant ascendancy. Catholics naturally were and are forbidden to join, and while many members of the Order would claim to bear no grudge against individual Catholics, they all profess a shared hostility to the Catholic religion. It is the Orange Order which is the main organizer of the marches which take place every year all over Northern Ireland in July, particularly on July 12, to celebrate the victory of the Protestant King William III* over the Catholic King James II* in 1690 at the battle of the Boyne.*

FURTHER READING

BANDON, J., *A History of Ulster*, Belfast: Blackstaff, 1993.
HUTCHINSON, W., *L'Irlande du Nord: l'imaginaire unioniste*, Caen: Presses universitaires, Caen, 1999
LEE, J. J., *Ireland 1912-1985*, Cambridge: Cambridge University Press, 1989.

1

The unique nature of the plantation of Ulster

In application of its strategy of conquest, London confiscated the land of Ulster, and having transferred ownership to English colonists, settled the province with planters from Britain.

By 1703, […] only 14% of the land in Ireland remained in the hands of the Catholic Irish, and in Ulster the figure was 5%. But these figures are not a real measure of the changes introduced within the Plantation of Ulster. What made it unique in Irish plantations was the comprehensive attempt made to attract, not only British gentry, but colonists of all classes, and the fact that the colonists were Protestant and represented a culture alien to Ulster. This policy of comprehensive colonization […] was an attempt to replace one entire community with another. The Catholic Irish remained, of course, but in conditions which emphasized their suppression. They were relegated to a state below servility, because the Planters were not allowed to employ the native Irish as servants in the new towns which they built. The towns themselves were unashamedly fortresses against the armed resentment of the Irish. Outside the town they were banished from the land they had owned and worked, and were confined to the boggy and mountainous regions. The reality differed from the intention, however. There were simply not enough settlers to achieve comprehensive control […].

The sum of the Plantation then was the introduction of a foreign community, which spoke differently, worshipped apart, and represented an alien culture and way of life. It had close commercial, cultural and political ties with Britain. The more efficient methods of the new farmers, and the greater availability of capital which allowed the start of cottage industries, served to create further economic differences between Ulster and the rest of Ireland, and between Catholic and Protestant within Ulster. The deep resentment of the native Irish towards the planters, and the distrustful siege mentality of the planters towards the Irish, is the root of the Ulster problem.

John Darby (ed.), *Northern Ireland: The Background to the Conflict*, Belfast: Appletree Press, 1983. By kind permission.

questions

1. To what extent did the reality of the plantation strategy reflect the initial strategy?
2. What were the Catholic reactions to the plantation?

2

Dublin Castle

See p. 34.

This is a benign 18th-century view of Dublin Castle, the seat of British power in Ireland between the 13th and 20th centuries.

questions

1. Historically, is Dublin Castle's bad reputation justified?
2. What mission did London confide to its executive at the end of the 18th century?

3
The Act of Union

In 1800 the two Parliaments of Ireland and of Great Britain voted in favour of uniting the two former kingdoms, thus creating the United Kingdom.

Whereas in pursuance of H.M.'s most gracious recommendation to the two Houses of Parliament in Great Britain and Ireland respectively, to consider of such measures as might best tend to strengthen and consolidate the connection between the two Kingdoms, the two Houses of the Parliament of Great Britain and the two Houses of the Parliament of Ireland have severally agreed and resolved that, in order to promote and secure the essential interests of Great Britain and Ireland, and to consolidate the strength, power and resources of the British Empire, it will be advisable to concur in such measures as may best tend to unite the two Kingdoms of Great Britain and Ireland into one Kingdom, in such a manner, and on such terms and conditions, as may be established by the Acts of the respective Parliaments of Great Britain and Ireland.

And whereas, in furtherance of the said Resolution, both Houses of the said two Parliaments respectively have likewise agreed upon certain Articles for effectuating and establishing the said purposes, in the tenor following:

ARTICLE FIRST. That it be the first Article of the Union of the Kingdoms of Great Britain and Ireland, that the said Kingdoms of Great Britain and Ireland shall, upon the 1st day of January which shall be in the year of our Lord 1801, and for ever after, be united into one Kingdom, by the name of The United Kingdom of Great Britain and Ireland; and that the royal style and titles appertaining to the Imperial Crown of the said United Kingdom and its dependencies; and also the ensigns, armorial flags and banners thereof shall be such as H.M., by his royal Proclamation under the Great Seal of the United Kingdom, shall be pleased to appoint.

ARTICLE SECOND. That it be the second Article of Union, that the succession to the Imperial Crown of the said United Kingdom, and of the dominions thereunto belonging, shall continue limited and settled [...] according to the existing laws, and to the terms of union between England and Scotland.

ARTICLE THIRD. That it be the third Article of Union that the said United Kingdom be represented in one and the same Parliament, to be styled The Parliament of the United Kingdom of Great Britain and Ireland.

ARTICLE FOURTH. That it be the fourth Article of Union that four Lords Spiritual of Ireland by rotation of sessions, and 28 Lords Temporal of Ireland elected for life by the peers of Ireland, shall be the number to sit and vote on the part of Ireland in the House of Lords of the Parliament of the United Kingdom; and 100 commoners (two for each County of Ireland, two for the City of Dublin, two for the City of Cork, one for the University of Trinity College, and one for each of the 31 most considerable Cities, Towns and Boroughs) be the number to sit and vote on the part of Ireland in the House of Commons of the Parliament of the United Kingdom [...].

ARTICLE FIFTH. That it be the fifth Article of Union, that the Churches of England and Ireland, as now by law established, be united into one Protestant Episcopal Church, to be called, The United Church of England and Ireland; and that the doctrine, worship, discipline and government of the said United Church shall be, and shall remain in full force for ever, as the same are now by law established for the Church of England; and that the continuance and preservation of the said united Church, as the Established Church of England and Ireland, shall be deemed and taken to be an essential and fundamental part of the Union.

2 July 1800.

questions

1. What was the political project behind the Act of Union?
2. What was the effect of the union to be on some institutions in existence until then?

4

The Hillsborough speech

Delivered in 1834 by the Rev. Henry Cook, it sealed the alliance between the Presbyterians and the Anglicans in defence of their common Protestantism.

A

[...] There are two departments of politics where I hold it to be the bounden duty of every minister to interfere. The first department embraces the teaching of the relative duties of rulers and subjects. This is well defined and permanent. It forms an integral part of the Gospel commission, and has equally been discharged by prophets and apostles. The second is of a more indefinite and uncertain character, and I endeavour to explain it thus: a minister may, and must, interfere with politics whenever politics interfere with religion. Such a crisis, I believe, has now arisen; and I pity the faithless watchman who sees the enemy coming in like a flood, and will not blow the trumpet and rouse the sleeping garrison. The thoughtless may wonder, the incredulous may deny, the bold may disregard, and the abettors of anarchy may affect to despise, when I declare it to be my deliberate and fixed opinion, that never, in the history of Ireland, was Protestantism in greater danger than at this hour.

I have made my election to serve under the banners of our common Protestantism; and this declaration will require me to explain how I, as a Presbyterian, and standing by all the religious and political principles of my Puritan fathers, can in anywise undertake the defence of a Church not governed by presbyters, but by prelates. I know it is possible that by some my attempt at explanation, or, if you will, vindication, will be supposed hopeless. Let me bespeak their candour and their patience; and, above all, I entreat them to open that old almanac, history, and read to learn, and wait to judge, before they pronounce sentence.

→

questions

Text A

1. What is the Rev. Henry Cook's view on the link between religion and politics?
2. Why is Protestantism in danger?

B

First, then, allow me to state, that I stand here as a Presbyterian, supporting and adhering to every principle of Presbyterianism, in doctrine and Church government. Were my appearance here to imply my surrender of one jot or tittle of the doctrines of the Church of Scotland, I should hold myself unworthy to be called her son. Did my appearance here imply that I surrendered the humble temple of Presbyterianism to ruinous dilapidation, or more splendid reconstruction, I should hold myself unworthy of a sentinel's post upon the lowest of her venerable watch-towers. But I surrender not my own post, I betray not my own charge, while I cheer forward another column of our noble Protestant army, who, though differently officered and differently dressed, yet wield the same weapons of truth, and serve under the same banners. *(Cheers)* And if any one condemn me for affording them that cheer; if any one think I should leave them to their fate, without sympathy for their sufferings, or encouragement in their conflict, I would again entreat such an one to recur to the old almanac of history; and, before he condemn me for uniting in defence of our general and common Protestantism, ask himself would he condemn our Presbyterian forefathers for uniting in a similar defence within the walls of Derry, or at the passes of Enniskillen? Common danger produced that union. [...] Presbyterians, I speak to you. The days are gone by when in Ireland Wentworth unleashed his bloodhounds on the track of your fathers; when Laud[1], papist at heart, forged chains at once for their consciences and their liberties. The days are gone by when a Lauderdale plotted and, upon the mountains of Scotland, a Dundee executed, the purposes of a bloody and heartless tyranny. Let us thank God that these days are gone by; and let us not stand, like moody magicians, conjuring up the ghosts of departed jealousies or injuries; but let our common faith, and our common dangers, unite us for common protection; and, united thus, though the powers of earth, and the powers of darkness, frown with equal hate upon our compacted ranks, they will never make a breach in our array; but they will flit around us as fierce, yet as innocuous, as the Chasseurs of Napoleon galloped round the irongirt squares of Wellington upon the memorable field of Waterloo.

Rev. Henry Cooke, 1834.

1. William Laud (1573-1645), archbishop of Canterbury and religious adviser to Charles I, tried by the Long Parliament and executed.

questions

Text B

1. Why does Henry Cook speak of the Church of Scotland?
2. What changes have taken place in the relations between the Church of Laud and the Church of Scotland?

A line -

— 5 —
The unionist Proclamation

Hundreds of thousands of Ulster unionists signed this covenant, some in their blood, to manifest their total opposition to Home Rule, which they assimilated to Rome Rule.

Ulster's solemn league and covenant

Being convinced in our consciences that Home Rule would be disastrous to the material well-being of Ulster as well as of the whole of Ireland, subversive of our civil and religious freedom, destructive of our citizenship, and perilous to the unity of the Empire, we, whose names are underwritten, men of Ulster, loyal subjects of His Gracious Majesty King George V, humbly relying on the God whom our fathers in days of stress and trial confidently trusted, do hereby pledge ourselves in solemn Covenant throughout this our time of threatened calamity to stand by one another in defending for ourselves and our children our cherished position of equal citizenship in the United Kingdom and in using all means which may be found necessary to defeat the present conspiracy to set up a Home Rule Parliament in Ireland. And in the event of such a Parliament being forced upon us we further solemnly and mutually pledge ourselves to refuse to recognize its authority. In sure confidence that God will defend the right we hereto subscribe our names. And further we individually declare that we have not already signed this Covenant.

The above was signed by me at

"Ulster Day", Saturday, 28th September 1912.

GOD SAVE THE KING

questions

1. What is the religious content of the covenant?
2. Can it be said that the content is seditious?

— 6 —
Ian Paisley and his beliefs

The Rev. Ian Paisley has come a long way. From being a marginal preacher in the 1960s, he has topped the polls at every European election in Northern Ireland, and is today a member of the House of Commons in Westminster.

No one, of course, took him seriously. He was a throwback, a raving, outrageous, somewhat uncouth religious zealot out of the backwoods of Ulster. He was the lunatic preacher, the simple-minded bigot, the often belligerent buffoon whose hellfire fulminations were cause for amusement, good for pub conversation. His bizarre antics were sometimes repulsive, like his staging of a mock mass in Ulster Hall in 1959, or comical, like his journey in 1963 to the Vatican ("Harlot City" in his words) to protest the ecumenical council, or even embarrassing, like his illegal march on Belfast City Hall later the same year to protest the City's decision to fly the Union Jack at half-mast when Pope John XXIII died.

But today few are laughing, and none take the Reverend Dr Ian Paisley lightly. Of the major Protestant leaders who came to prominence in Northern Ireland in the late 1960s and the early 1970s, he alone remains at centre stage. He brought down three Prime Ministers – Terence O'Neill, James Chichester-Clark, and Brian Faulkner. He destroyed →

the hegemony of the Unionist Party, which had stood as the sole voice of Protestant opposition to a united Ireland since 1892. And he claims, with some justification, to be *the* leader of the Protestant people of Northern Ireland since 1979, when he topped the polls for a seat in the European Parliament.

His success does not surprise him. Says Paisley: "We are traditional Unionists, walking completely in the Carson mould, and in the Carson stand. The Official Unionist Party has changed its coat too many times. It has gone in for the denial of democracy in the power-sharing Executive; it has gone in for the Sunningdale Agreement and the united Ireland concept; it changes as often as its leaders change."

"Traditional Unionists," on the other hand, do not change. They are loyal above all else only to [...] the Williamite Revolution Settlement Act, which guarantees civil and religious liberties for all men, and to the Protestant monarchy because, as the Act says, it has been seen that it is not good for a nation to be controlled by a Roman prince, whose first loyalty is to a foreign monarch, that is, the King of the Vatican, that is, the Pope.

Padraig O'Malley, *The Uncivil Wars*, Belfast: Blackstaff Press, 1983.

questions

1. What is Paisleyism?
2. How can the success of Paisley's political action be explained?

7
The many hues of the Orange Order

The Orange Order, founded in 1795, has a sinister reputation among Catholics. Yet, according to one of its leaders, it is little different from a golf or football club.

The world is a hostile place for the Orange Order in the 1990s, but its members are maintaining a brave face. They will don Sunday suits and sashes today and take to the streets of the North to parade what they see as their Protestant birthright.

To the outsider, the Orangemen appear strange creatures, caught in a time warp. White-gloved, carrying meticulously rolled umbrellas with military precision, they march in the utter certainty of their own rightness. Bowler hats, symbols of a privileged elite abandoned even by the City of London, continue to grace Orange heads.

In an increasingly complex society, the Order's primary goal remains unshakeably simple – to stop the spread of "Popery" by all lawful means. Membership is determined strictly by religion: Roman Catholics cannot join and attendance at Catholic services is forbidden.

Formed in 1795 after sectarian clashes in Co. Armagh, the Order is both a religious and political organization. It aims to preserve

Protestantism, which it believes is best achieved by maintaining the Union, and it swears loyalty to the British monarch so long as he or she remains a Protestant.

However, Mr George Patton, the Order's executive officer, insists that it is no threat to Northern Catholics and would "never want to deny anyone the right to worship according to their conscience". It is the Catholic religion – not the people – that the Order opposes, he says, and its rules advise members to be courteous to their Catholic neighbours.

Last year, Orange marchers chanted pro-UFF slogans and made five-fingered gestures outside the bookmaker's office in the lower Ormeau Road in south Belfast where, a few months earlier, five Catholics had been murdered by loyalists. Mr Patton concedes that sometimes trouble may be caused by "a few yobbos".

According to the Order's rules, Orangemen should be regular churchgoers and Bible-readers, and should avoid swearing and the company of wild characters. Yet a desire for scriptural studiousness or fear of God do not seem to have motivated many young people to join. Although Orangemen are urged to strive for sobriety, many stagger home from the Field on the Twelfth behind temperance banners. "Some of our members do not live up to our expectations and hopes," says Mr Patton, shaking his head sadly.

There are about 1,500 lodges in Ireland, the vast majority of which are in the North. Some Orange sources claim that the Order has 100,000 members but this figure is grossly over-optimistic, according to outside observers. The Order is unashamedly sexist: women cannot join.

The Ladies' Orange Association concentrates mainly on raising funds. It is separate but equal, says Mr Patton, using the phrase favoured for years by white American apologists for segregation.

The Orange Order condemns sectarian killings but lodges have in the past placed sympathy notices in newspapers for dead UVF men. The deceased may have been "a great member of the lodge and a terribly decent fellow", Mr Patton says, and it may be natural to pay one's last respects without "associating oneself with an illegal organisation". The Order's rules forbid membership of any paramilitary group, he adds.

Orange lodges are often viewed as sinister places where conspiracies are hatched, but Mr Patton says that meetings are mundane and non-ritualistic, opening with a hymn or prayer before addressing political, security or religious issues. The secrecy surrounding the Order is no different from that attached to a football or golf club, he says.

→

The Order cannot be dismissed as a lunatic fringe: clergymen from all the Protestant churches are members. Most unionist MPs are also members: this is still beneficial – although not a prerequisite – for an aspiring politician. The Order maintains institutional links with the Ulster Unionist Party, holding a statutory number of seats on its executive.

During 50 years of Stormont government, when it is believed that only two cabinet ministers were not Orangemen, the Order's influence was pervasive.

Jobs, council houses and mortgages (many bank managers were members) were all believed to be under its control. Although this power has waned since the introduction of direct rule in 1972, the Order still plays an important part in Northern politics, uniting the diverse strands of unionism. DUP and Ulster Unionist members, paramilitary supporters, integrationists and devolutionists march side by side in a cross-class alliance.

The Order's historical record is far from progressive. It opposed Catholic emancipation, the secret ballot and Catholic membership of the Unionist party.

Today, its literature bemoans the increase in divorce and opposes abortion and homosexuality. Mr Patton regrets the increasingly secular, materialistic nature of society and the growth of a hedonistic culture. Leaving politics aside, he says, he respects the devout Catholic more than the non-believing Protestant. He points to the similar views on abortion shared by the Order's Grand Master, the Rev. Martin Smyth, and the SDLP MP Dr Joe Hendron.

The Irish Times, July 12, 1993.

questions

1. What are the main functions of the Orange Order?
2. Why may Catholics feel threatened by the Orange Order?

8
The rise in loyalist violence

In this report of what 3,000 people in 554 written and taped submissions said about ways forward for Northern Ireland in 1992-93, a North

"There has been a hardening of attitudes among Protestants," the North Belfast women told us.

They feel under siege and see all Catholics as legitimate targets. It comes down to territory. Ardoyne is bulging, but you can't move the peace wall and therefore the territorial boundary. With peace walls, young people don't meet and are taught to fear and hate the other side. Young loyalist paramilitaries are not motivated by politics, but by sheer sectarianism. Protestants believe their numbers are in the balance. Their areas are emptying, becoming derelicts. Nationalists perceive themselves as the future, and loyalists feel their backs are up against the wall. There are two perceptions: an ascending Catholic community, growing in confidence and power, and a beleaguered, isolated, diminishing Protestant one. No one represents Protestants. Protestants would like to replicate the community structures you have in Catholic areas. But there's a low spirit among Protestants – maybe since the Anglo-Irish Agreement. They feel almost apologetic about being Protestant.

A Citizens' Inquiry, The Opahl Report on Northern Ireland, ed. by Andy Pollack. Dublin: The Lilliput Press Ltd, 1993.

Belfast woman talks about attitudes among Protestants.

question

What is the loyalist perception of Catholics and of themselves?

9

Marching Unionism

The Orangemen are marching here, as they do every year, to celebrate the Battle of the Somme.

Ph. © C. Steele-Perkins/Magnum

questions

1. What is the significance of the Battle of the Somme?
2. How important is ritual for unionists?

(A)

(B)

CHAPTER FOUR

The Political Systems

We have seen how the Government of Ireland Act* (1920) changed the Act of Union* (1801) by creating a separate Parliament for the six north-easterly counties of the island. The Anglo-Irish Treaty* (1922) led to the setting up of the Irish Free State.* Henceforth Ireland possessed two political entities with two sets of political institutions:

- the first, the independent Free State, initially retained a link with Britain. The proclamation of the Republic* in 1949 put an end to that link;
- the second, the autonomous province of Northern Ireland,* still remains united to Great Britain within the United Kingdom* and is likely to do so for some time though developments since 1985 have opened the door to collaboration with the Republic (see Chapter 14).

THE REPUBLIC OF IRELAND

1 THE CONSTITUTIONS

The first Constitution (1919)

When the first Dáil* met in Dublin on 21 January 1919, it adopted a new Constitution* composed of four documents:

- a Declaration of Independence,
- a Message to the Free Nations of the World,
- the Constitution, and
- the Democratic Programme.

It is interesting to note that this draft was founded on the principle that all legislative, executive, administrative and judicial power had its source in the people. The republican revolutionaries had thus clearly opted in favour of democracy.

Two seats of power (see p. 61)
(A) Leinster House, Dublin, Republic of Ireland
Ph. © R. Gardner/Rex
(B)The Parliament building, Stormont, Northern Ireland.
Ph. © Herbert/Archive Photos

The 1922 Constitution

The Anglo-Irish Treaty was adopted by the Dáil in January 1922. To meet the requirements of the new situation the Irish Free State government set about writing a new Constitution. In keeping with the Treaty, it incorporated among other elements an oath of fidelity to the King. Executive authority was symbolically invested in the English monarch. Such a restriction on Irish sovereignty explains republican hostility to the Constitution, hence the intention of the republicans to change it once the opportunity arose. Other aspects of the 1922 text are often neglected. It was a secular Constitution. It also aimed at encouraging popular participation in politics through its provisions for proportional representation, the referendum and popular initiative.

The 1937 Constitution

The weak points of the 1922 Constitution, in the eyes of the republicans, were to lead to its replacement in 1937 after De Valera and his Fianna Fáil* party came to power in 1932. The new Constitution, still in force, eliminated all references to the British monarch and created the office of President of Ireland. This gave a *de facto* republican status to the state which became a *de jure* one in 1949. Though highly respectful of democracy and human rights it was, nevertheless, fundamentally a Catholic document. Divorce for instance was forbidden. Another point is that it laid claim to the territory of Northern Ireland. Change however was brought about in the 1995 Constitutional Referendum which allowed divorce and in the 1998 Good Friday Agreement (see Chapter 5, 6 and 14).

2 THE INSTITUTIONS

The President

At the head of the state, therefore, there is a President, elected for a period of seven years. The President of Ireland, who carries out formal acts of government, is not the Head of Government.

The Oireachtas

• The lower house of Parliament or of the Oireachtas,* is called the Dáil and is the principal legislative body. Its composition has varied from 128 to 166 members. According to the Constitution there must be a deputy for every 20,000 to 30,000 electors and there must be a revision of the constituencies at least every twelve years to take into account population changes. Today the country is divided into 41 multi-member constituencies. The life-span of each Dáil is a maximum of five years and it has three sessions a year. Its work can be fitted into four principal categories:

– it examines legislation initiated by ministers or by private members;
– it considers expenditure proposals;
– it debates motions, and
– it is a forum in which questions may be addressed to members of the government.

• The upper house, the Senate – called Seanad Éireann – has 60 members. Its function is to check, redraft and amend legislation. It may organize debates on important questions. The structure of membership of the Senate is inspired by the vocationalism* which was particularly popular among European Catholics in the 1930s. In fact, political parties control the actual election of senators who are chosen from vocational panels.

The government

The government, according to the Constitution, consists of not less than seven and not more than fifteen members. At the head of the government is the Taoiseach,* or Prime Minister. Unlike in many other European countries, all members of the government must be members of the Oireachtas. They are selected by the Taoiseach and appointed by the President. The executive power of the state is exercised by the government which is responsible to the Dáil. It meets and acts as a collective authority and its powers, duties and functions are provided for by the Constitution and by law.

Local government

Local government was inherited from the old UK. There are 5 county boroughs: Dublin, Cork, Limerick, Waterford and Galway (see map, p. 21). The rest of the state is divided into 28 county council areas. Each local government authority is made up of elected councillors and a manager. Local government is responsible for housing, roads, water supply, sanitary services, development control and environmental protection. It is less powerful than local government authorities in most other EU countries and has been further weakened since 1978 when it was deprived of its local source of income, i. e. when rates were abolished.

3 The Electoral System

For all elections, a form of proportional representation by the single transferable vote (STV) is in force. For Dáil elections, there are multi-member constituencies and each constituency returns a minimum of three deputies. Throughout the 1980s and into the 1990s, the maximum was five, though at an earlier period in the history of the state the number could be much higher.

The percentage number of seats won by political parties in Ireland corresponds, more or less, to the percentage number of votes they get. The system does, however, give a small advantage in terms of seats to the largest parties.

4 The Legal System

The new Irish state gave citizens cheaper access to the law through a system of

- District and Circuit Courts. Above these courts, one finds
- the Court of Criminal Appeal,
- the High Court, and
- the Supreme Court* to which appeal can be made from the decisions of lower courts. The High Court and the Supreme Court can also decide whether legislation is in accordance with the Constitution.

The law which these courts administer is that elaborated by Westminster* during the period of the Union and, prior to that, by the Irish Parliament.* To which, of course, must be added all new laws, all additions and all amendements made by the Oireachtas since its creation in 1919.

NORTHERN IRELAND

1 THE CONSTITUTION

The Government of Ireland Act (1920) provided the framework of the Constitution of Northern Ireland. The Crown and two Houses of Parliament comprised the legislature. Matters, such as the Army, foreign affairs, taxation and currency, were reserved to Westminster as were all matters relating to the superior courts of justice. In accordance with the 1920 Act the Northern Ireland Parliament had power to make laws for the peace, order and good government of Northern Ireland in matters relating exclusively to Northern Ireland, subject to the supreme authority of Westminster. Any Act passed in Parliament, generally called Stormont* because of its location in that town on the outskirts of Belfast, could, in theory, be refused by Westminster. This, in fact, never happened.

Westminster never interfered until 1969, i.e. after the beginning of the troubles. In 1972, at the height of the violence, due to the unionist government's failure to find an early solution to the conflict, it put an end to the existence of Stormont and took over the direct government of the province. The constitutional framework was modified. Once Northern Ireland came under the direct control of Westminster a new situation emerged. Since then the Northern Ireland Constitutional Act (1973) and the Northern Ireland Act (1974) have largely replaced the 1920 Government of Ireland Act.

2 THE INSTITUTIONS

Stormont

• The House of Commons of the Northern Ireland Parliament, consisting of 52 members, was elected by universal suffrage.

• The second House, the Senate, was composed of 26 members elected by the House of Commons.

Westminster

While those two institutions represented Northern Ireland's autonomy, the union with Great Britain within the United Kingdom was assured by a representation in Westminster –13 MPs under the 1920 Act, but reduced to 12 in 1948 when university seats were abolished. Since direct government has been introduced, the number has been increased to 18.

The government

The reality of governmental power was in the hands of the Executive or Cabinet which included the Prime Minister and all the ministers, the number of which was less than ten.

Local government

As for local government, there were

• 2 county boroughs: Belfast and Londonderry,

• 6 administrative counties: Antrim, Armagh, Down, Fermanagh, Londonderry and Tyrone,

• 10 boroughs,

• 24 urban districts and

• 31 rural districts.

They assumed responsibility, for example, in the areas of local housing and employment, two factors which were to take on considerable importance in the initial stages of the conflict in the late 1960s.

Westminster, since 1972, if one excepts a five-month period of Belfast rule in 1974, has legislated for Northern Ireland. The number of Northern Ireland seats in Westminster was increased to 17 for the 1983 General Election and to 18 for that of 1997. The post of Secretary of State for Northern Ireland, with Cabinet rank, was also created in 1972. Appointed by the Prime Minister, and surrounded by a number of junior ministers, the Secretary of State heads the government of Northern Ireland. Local government has also been changed as a result of the conflict. Its powers have been diminished, as far as housing is concerned for example, and its electoral system has been modified.

3 THE ELECTORAL SYSTEM

It was not the first time that the electoral system was changed. Northern Ireland inherited, for local government elections, the system of proportional representation. The Government of Ireland Act (1920) imposed the same system for elections to the Belfast Parliament. In 1922, however, the unionist government abolished this system for local elections and replaced it by the British system. It repeated the same measure in 1929 for Northern Ireland parliamentary elections. Half a century later, the British government, in an attempt to reintroduce fair representation for the minority, restored a form of proportional representation for all elections in the province with the exception of those to Westminster.

4 THE LEGAL SYSTEM

Throughout the period of the existence of the Northern Ireland Parliament (1921-1972), superior court judges were appointed by the Crown. Lower court judges, however, were appointed by the Belfast government. Throughout its history the judiciary of the province had, for most of the time, been openly associated with the unionist Party. It must also be added that the 1922 Civil Authorities (Special Powers)* Act conferred on the Minister of Home Affairs and on the police unrestricted power to make regulations which had the force of law, notably powers of arrest, questioning, search, detention and internment.

THE EUROPEAN UNION

Ireland became a member of the European Economic Community* on 1 January 1973. The United Kingdom also became a member at the same time. This meant that Northern Ireland and the Republic, since that date, share a common membership of a supranational organization. After 1973, the Rome Treaty, as amended, became part of the Irish and British Constitutions and the exclusive law-making power of the two respective Parliaments was removed. European law is now part of the legal systems of the two states. Since several articles of the Irish Constitution were incompatible with Community membership three referendums were organized in order to adapt to the new situation: the first (1972) dealing with the question of membership, the second (1987) ratifying the Single European Act and the third (1992) ratifying the Maastricht Treaty.

The referendum results, to which can be added the results of successive European parliamentary elections, showed an Ireland deeply committed to the construction of the Union. Its adoption of the Euro further reinforced that commitment. This of course can be explained, to a large extent, by the direct monetary benefits which membership won for the island, as well as the indirect benefits coming from the existence of a market of 370 million people to which the multinationals, which had set up in Ireland, had access. But Ireland's convergence towards European levels of prosperity means that in the coming years the direct benefits will be reduced. Will Irish enthusiasm for Europe resist the new reality? It is too early to say since the absence of a serious debate on the evolution of Europe in the new millenium is striking. When positions have been taken, for instance on regionalism, on duty-free allowances and on company taxation, they have systematically been short-term defensive ones. Such issues, as well as the enlargement of the Union, foreign policy and defence and security will have to be debated if Ireland wishes to play a dynamic role in the forthcoming developments of the Union.

FURTHER READING

CHUBB, B., *The Government and Politics of Ireland,* London: Oxford University Press, 1971.
DOONEY, S. & O'TOOLE, J., *Irish Government Today,* Dublin: Gill & Macmillan, 1992.
LAWRENCE, R.J., *The Government of Northern Ireland,* London: Oxford University Press, 1965.
L'Irlande politique et sociale: L'Irlande et l'Europe, vol. 4, Paris: PSN, 1992.

—1—
Message to the free nations of the world

During the December 1918 General Election campaign, Sinn Féin proposed a withdrawal from Westminster and the establishment of an independent Irish Parliament. When swept to power, it adopted the Message when the 1st Dáil met for the first time.

Dáil Éireann address to the free nations of the world, 21 January 1919

To the Nations of the World! Greeting.

The Nation of Ireland having proclaimed her national independence, calls through her elected representatives in Parliament assembled in the Irish Capital on January 21st, 1919, upon every free nation to support the Irish Republic by recognising Ireland's national status and her right to its vindication at the Peace Congress.

Nationally, the race, the language, the customs and traditions of Ireland are radically distinct from the English. Ireland is one of the most ancient nations in Europe, and she has preserved her national integrity, vigorous and intact, through seven centuries of foreign oppression: she has never relinquished her national rights, and throughout the long era of English usurpation she has in every generation defiantly proclaimed her inalienable right to nationhood down to her last glorious resort to arms in 1916.

Internationally, Ireland is the gateway of the Atlantic. Ireland is the last outpost of Europe towards the West: Ireland is the point upon which great trade routes between East and West converge: her independence is demanded by the Freedom of the Seas: her great harbours must be open to all nations, instead of being the monopoly of England. To-day these harbours are empty and idle solely because English policy is determined to retain Ireland as a barren bulwark for English aggrandisement, and the unique geographical position of this island, far from being a benefit and safeguard to Europe and America, is subjected to the purposes of England's policy of world domination.

Ireland to-day reasserts her historic nationhood the more confidently before the new world emerging from the War, because she believes in freedom and justice as the fundamental principles of international law, because she believes in a frank co-operation between the peoples for equal rights against the vested privileges of ancient tyrannies, because the permanent peace of Europe can never be secured by perpetuating military dominion for the profit of empire but only by establishing the control of government in every land upon the basis of the free will of a free people, and the existing state of war, between Ireland and England, can never be ended until Ireland is definitely evacuated by the armed forces of England.

Minutes of Proceedings of the First Parliament of the Republic of Ireland, 1919-1921.

questions

1. How did the Dáil justify Ireland's claim to national independence?
2. What was Ireland's importance in the international scene?

2

The Government of Ireland Act 1920

The Government of Ireland Act passed in 1920 established Northern Ireland with its own parliament. It also made provision for a Council of Ireland which, in fact, never met.

les unionistes ne voulaient pas de pouvoir : voulaient être gouvernés directement de Londres ≠ B.
leur a donné 1 pouvoir a eu pr verrouiller la situation constitutionnelle
→ difficile pr Londres d'interférer
⇒ politique discriminatoire des Unionistes.
→ pr eux atout énorme. leur a donné 1 pouvoir t. stable pdt 50 ans (→ ce que la minorité se révolte) les unionistes contrôlaient ~~tt~~ le syst (les anglais finançaient)

questions

Text A

1. What was the extent of the powers of the Northern Ireland parliament?
2. What weaknesses appear in the arrangements proposed?

A

The original scheme of government

The main points of the Act of 1920 as it came into force in Northern Ireland were as follows:

(i) It provided for the establishment in Belfast of a bicameral Parliament, consisting of a 52 member House of Commons elected by Proportional Representation, and a Senate of 26 Members, 24 elected by the Members of the Northern Ireland House of Commons and two (the Lord Mayor of Belfast and Mayor of Londonderry) sitting ex officio.

(ii) This Parliament was given a general power to make laws for "the peace, order and good government" of Northern Ireland, subject to certain specific reservations, conditions and safeguards. In particular:

(a) The Act specifically reserved to the Parliament of the United Kingdom certain powers principally relating to the Armed Forces, the Crown, and international matters.

(b) The fiscal powers of the Northern Ireland Parliament were severely restricted by the reservation to the Parliament of the United Kingdom of power to levy income tax and customs and excise duties.

(c) The Northern Ireland Parliament was specifically prohibited from making laws and the Northern Ireland Government from taking administrative action other than on a basis of religious equality.

(d) Section 75 of the Act provided that:
"the supreme authority of the Parliament of the United Kingdom shall remain unaffected and undiminished over all persons, matters and things in [Northern] Ireland and every part thereof".

(iii) The Governor of Northern Ireland, in whom the executive powers of the Northern Ireland Parliament were vested, was "aided and advised" by the executive committee of the Privy Council, or Cabinet consisting of Ministers of Northern Ireland.

(iv) Northern Ireland was to be represented in the Parliament of the United Kingdom by 12 members for territorial constituencies and one for the Queen's University of Belfast.

(v) Northern Ireland was to make towards "Imperial liabilities and expenditure, a "just" contribution having regard to the relative taxable capacities of Northern Ireland and the United Kingdom as a whole.

B

The Act also made provision for a Council of Ireland, whose purpose was defined in the Explanatory Memorandum to the Government of Ireland Bill in the following terms:

"Although at the beginning there are to be two Parliaments and two Governments in Ireland, the Act contemplates and affords every facility for union between North and South, and empowers the two Parliaments by mutual agreement and joint action to terminate partition and to set up one Parliament and one Government for the whole of Ireland. With a view to the eventual establishment of a single Parliament, and to bringing about harmonious action between the two Parliaments and Governments, there is created a bond of union in the meantime by means of a Council of Ireland, which is to consist of 20 representatives elected by each Parliament, and a President nominated by the Lord Lieutenant. It will fall to the members of this body to initiate proposals for united action on the part of the two Parliaments and to bring forward these proposals in the respective Parliaments."

The Act reserved certain specific but limited matters to the Council, provided that the Belfast and Dublin Parliaments might confer additional functions upon it by identical legislation, and charged it with the specific duty of considering what further matters might, in the general interest of the whole of Ireland, best be administered on a central basis rather than by the two separate administrations.

The Future of Ireland, Belfast: H.M S.O. 1972.

questions

Text B

1. Why was there a need for a Council of Ireland?
2. What sort of "united action" could have been taken by the Council?

Constitu° de la Rep. of I

3

Bunreacht na hÉireann

The 1937 Constitution, sometimes called De Valera's Constitution, replaced the 1922 Free State one. The latter, in the eyes of De Valera and his followers, did not contain an acceptable affirmation of national sovereignty.

Preamble

In the Name of the Most Holy Trinity, from Whom is all authority and to Whom, as our final end, all actions both of men and States must be referred,

We, the people of Éire,

Humbly acknowledging all our obligations to our Divine Lord, Jesus Christ, Who sustained our fathers through centuries of trial,

Gratefully remembering their heroic and unremitting struggle to regain the rightful independence of our Nation,

And seeking to promote the common good, with due observance of Prudence, Justice and Charity, so that the dignity and freedom of the individual may be assured, true social order attained, the unity of our country restored, and concord established with other nations,

Do hereby adopt, enact, and give to ourselves this Constitution.

→

République proclamée en 49.

how cette loi va ê rentrée grâce à accord Angl/Irlandais.

nature démocratique
& indépendent. Pays sorti du
colonialisme
bases théoriques -
importance de la tradit°: relation
avec langue, identité.

THE NATION

Article 1

The Irish nation hereby affirms its inalienable, indefeasible, and sovereign right to choose its own form of Government, to determine its relations with other nations, and to develop its life, political, economic and cultural, in accordance with its own genius and traditions.

Article 2

The national territory consists of the whole island of Ireland, its islands and the territorial seas.

Article 3

Pending the re-integration of the national territory, and without prejudice to the right of the Parliament and Government established by this Constitution to exercise jurisdiction over the whole of that territory, the laws enacted by that Parliament shall have the like area and extent of application as the laws of Saorstat Éireann and the like extra-territorial effect.

THE STATE

Article 4

The name of the State is Éire, or in the English language, Ireland.

Article 5

Ireland is a sovereign, independent, democratic state.

Article 6

1. All powers of government, legislative, executive and judicial, derive, under God, from the people, whose right it is to designate the rulers of the State and, in final appeal, to decide all questions of national policy, according to the requirements of the common good.

2. These powers of government are exercisable only by or on the authority of the organs of State established by this Constitution.

Article 7

The national flag is the tricolour of green, white and orange.

Article 8

1. The Irish language as the national language is the first official language.

2. The English language is recognised as a second official language.

3. Provision may, however, be made by law for the exclusive use of either of the said languages for any one or more official purposes, either throughout the State or in any part thereof. […]

Constitution of Ireland (extracts), Dublin: Stationery Office, 1937.

questions

1. What is the basis of power in this document?
2. How is the national territory designated?

4
Voting in the Republic

The aim of the Irish electoral system is to reflect, to a large extent, all shades of political opinion in the country.

questions

1. What effects does such a system (A) produce in Parliament?
2. To what extent did the Galway West results (B) in seats reflect the results in votes?

A

Voting is by secret ballot and on the system of proportional representation, each elector having one transferable vote. The names of the candidates appear in alphabetical order on the ballot paper. The voter indicates the order of his choice by writing 1 opposite the name of his first choice and, if he so wishes, 2 opposite the name of his second choice, 3 opposite the name of his third choice, and so on. He then places the ballot paper in a sealed ballot box. In this way the voter gives instructions to the returning officer to transfer his vote to the candidate of his second choice if the candidate of his first choice receives more than the quota of votes necessary for election or if his first choice is eliminated (through receiving so few votes as to have no chance of election). If the same applies to his second choice, the vote may be transferred to his third choice, and so on.

S. Dooney & J. O'Toole, *Irish Government Today*, Dublin: Gill & Macmillan, 1992. By kind permission.

B

Counting and transfer of votes in Galway West, 1989 general election

Electorate: 77,178 Valid votes: 49,339 Number of seats: 5
Quota: 8,224

	1st count	2nd count Transfer of Molloy's surplus		3rd count Transfer of O'Connor's & Shanley's votes		4th count Transfer of Brick's votes		5th count Transfer of Higgins's surplus		6th count Transfer of Ó Cuív's votes		7th count Transfer of Fahey's surplus	
Brick, Jimmy (WP)	1555	+ 30	1585	+ 38	1623	– 1623							
Coogan, Fintan (FG)	5297	+ 204	5501	+ 18	5519	+ 204	5723	+ 352	6075	+ 253	6328	+ 229	6557
Fahey, Frank (FF)	8010	+ 44	8054	+ 7	8061	+ 68	8129	+ 48	8177	+ 2152	10329	– 2105	8224
Geoghegan-Quinn, Máire (FF)	5902	+ 39	5941	+ 8	5949	+ 47	5996	+ 47	6043	+ 2272	8315		8315
Higgins, Michael Daniel (Lab)	7727	+ 181	7908	+ 67	7975	+ 1155	9130	– 906	8224		8224		8224
McCormack, Pádraic (FG)	5987	+ 131	6118	+ 12	6130	+ 49	6179	+ 152	6331	+ 380	6711	+ 211	6922
Molloy, Bobby (PD)	8917	– 693	8224		8224		8224		8224		8224		8224
O'Connor, Paul Ollie	84	+ 3	87	– 87									
Ó Cuív, Eamon (FF)	5733	+ 59	5792	+ 25	5817	+ 36	5853	+ 63	5916	– 5916			
Shanley, Dermot (Non-Party)	127	+ 2	129	– 129									
Non-transferable papers		+ 0	0	+ 41	41	+ 64	105	+ 244	349	+ 859	1208	+ 1665	2873
TOTAL	49339		49339		49339		49339		49339		49339		49339

Elected: Molloy, Bobby (PD); Higgins, Michael D. (Lab); Fahey, Frank (FF); Geoghegan-Quinn, Máire (FF); McCormack, Pádraic (FG).

Official results, Dublin, Stationery Office, 1989.

5

The Good Friday Agreement (10 April 1998)

Here one finds the Declaration of Support which is the preamble of the document. Its official name is Agreement Reached in the Multi-Party Negotiations. It was signed on 10 April 1998, on Good Friday, hence the common name. With the exception of Ian Paisley's DUP and its satellite party the United Kingdom Unionist Party (UKUP) all the Northern Ireland political parties signed the agreement.

Both loyalist & Republic ready to use force when needed.

questions

1. What concessions did the different sides make?
2. How is one to understand "the commitment to exclusively democratic and peaceful means"?

Agreement Reached in the Multi-Party Negotiations

Declaration of support

1. We, the participants in the multi-party negotiations, believe that the agreement we have negotiated offers a truly historic opportunity for a new beginning.

2. The tragedies of the past have left a deep and profoundly regrettable legacy of suffering. We must never forget those who have died or been injured, and their families. But we can best honour them through a fresh start, in which we firmly dedicate ourselves to the achievement of reconciliation, tolerance, and mutual trust, and to the protection and vindication of the human rights of all.

3. We are committed to partnership, equality and mutual respect as the basis of relationships within Northern Ireland, between North and South, and between these islands.

4. We reaffirm our total and absolute commitment to exclusively democratic and peaceful means of resolving differences on political issues, and our opposition to any use or threat of force by others for any political purpose, whether in regard to this agreement or otherwise.

5. We acknowledge the substantial differences between our continuing, and equally legitimate, political aspirations. However, we will endeavour to strive in every practical way towards reconciliation and rapprochement within the framework of democratic and agreed arrangements. We pledge that we will, in good faith, work to ensure the success of each and every one of the arrangements to be established under this agreement. It is accepted that all of the institutional and constitutional arrangements – an Assembly in Northern Ireland, a North/South Ministerial Council, implementation bodies, a British-Irish Council and a British-Irish Intergovernmental Conference and any amendments to British Acts of Parliament and the Constitution of Ireland – are interlocking and interdependent and that in particular the functioning of the Assembly and the North/South Council are so closely inter-related that the success of each depends on that of the other.

6. Accordingly, in a spirit of concord, we strongly commend this agreement to the people, North and South, for their approval.

Implications for the Future

The presidential election held in Ireland on 7 November 1990 was significant in a number of ways. The success of Mary Robinson made Ireland only the second European country (after Iceland) to elect a woman as its head of state. Moreover, the victory of a long-standing and prominent campaigner for liberal reform, after the apparent reaffirmation of a traditional Catholic ethos in two referendums in the 1980s, caused widespread surprise. It generated considerable speculation as to whether the vote was merely the outcome of a number of specific short-term factors or whether it could herald a fundamental realignment of Irish politics, with major implications for the party system. Some felt that her success heralded a new dawn for the Irish left, or at the very least for Irish liberalism. It was argued both that the election was a signal that the electorate was changing, and that the clear existence of a sizeable liberal constituency would bring about more change in the future, a process that the presence of Mary Robinson in Áras an Uachtaráin could only assist. It was also suggested that her election, by showing that being a woman was not necessarily an electoral handicap and could in some circumstances be an asset, might boost the prospects of women seeking party nominations to run for political office. Others felt that the significance of it all was being exaggerated, arguing that a majority still voted for traditional candidates.

Ronald J. Hill & Michael Marsh, *Modern Irish Democracy*, Dublin: Irish Academic Press, 1993. By kind permission.

6
The 1990 presidential election

Mary Robinson was elected President of Ireland on November 7, 1990. She was the first woman ever to hold such a position in Ireland.

questions

1. Given the powers of the President of Ireland, how significant was Mary Robinson's election?
2. To what extent do the arguments advanced here apply to the 1997 presidential election?

7
Two seats of power

See p. 48.

Leinster House – the former residence of the Duke of Leinster, now the Oireachtas and Dublin government buildings (photo A), and Stormont – the Northern Ireland Parliament building opened in 1932 by the Prince of Wales (photo B)

question

How satisfactory, in terms of symbols, are the two buildings?

Mary McAleese accepting her seal of office
as President of Ireland, 11-11-1997
Ph. © Sipa Press

CHAPTER FIVE

Political Change

There has been a sharp contrast in the politics of the two parts of Ireland* since the early 1920s. The South, after an initial moment of violence, settled into a long period of stagnation, to be followed, in turn, by rapid modernization. The background to change always remained one of political stability. In the North, it would seem retrospectively that the first fifty years were just a preparation for the following twenty-five years of political violence. 1994 opened a new perspective for that part of the island with the Catholic and Protestant paramilitary organisations declaring ceasefires. Having restarted its campaign in February 1996, the IRA called a new ceasefire in July 1997. Since then the search for peace dominates Northern politics. (see Chapter 14).

The Republic of Ireland

1 A New State

The principal traits which dominated politics between 1921 and 1927 were the creation of the Irish Free State,* the Civil War* and the boycott of the Dáil* by the republicans. The success of the first task depended entirely on the victory of the new government over the republican forces. At the same time the legitimacy of the new state depended on the integration of the republicans into the political system.

The Anglo-Irish Treaty

The Anglo-Irish Treaty* was adopted by a majority in the Dáil in January 1922. However a minority, made up of republicans led by De Valera,* opposed it. A General Election which followed showed that a majority in the country was in favour of the political compromise that the Treaty represented. The pro-Treaty party, Cumann na nGaedheal,* set about forming a government. However the Sinn Féin* party, i.e. the republican minority, though continuing to present candidates at General Elections, decided that from then on it would refuse to sit in the Dáil. Its refusal to submit to the will of the majority sparked off the Civil War.

The Civil War

The war was to last eleven months and like most civil wars it was particularly atrocious. The superior military force which the new government disposed of, the low level of support for the republicans among the people and the total opposition of the Catholic hierarchy to those who opposed the Treaty are the essential factors which explain the republican defeat.

Fianna Fáil

A split in the ranks of the republicans in 1925 led to the founding of a new political party, called Fianna Fáil,* by Éamon De Valera. Recognizing the fact that the government was winning the political battle and that, henceforth, the contest would have to be fought from within the existing political institutions, De Valera and his new party took their seats in the Dáil in 1927. This move by Fianna Fáil was to herald in a period of remarkable political stability which, on the whole, has continued since then.

2 STAGNATION

Fianna Fáil domination

The 1932 general election was to see Fianna Fáil take over the reins of power and the fact that it was able to retain that power for two exceptionally long periods of sixteen years, from 1932 to 1948 and from 1957 to 1973, shows how successful it was in moving from its former position to constitutional politics. During the period between 1932 and 1973 a Fine Gael*-led coalition, that being the new name adopted in 1933 by the old Cumann na nGaedheal party, came to power for two 3-year terms. It headed governments composed of Labour and a number of minor parties. The political scene was therefore largely dominated by Fianna Fáil. Fine Gael came a poor second, and was followed by the much smaller Labour party. The first two were catch-all parties while the Labour party, in spite of the weakness of class politics in the country did on the whole defend a centre-left position. The Irish party system was, in fact, deeply rooted in the divisions of the Treaty and the Civil War.

Conservatism

Major events of international or national importance did not bring with them any significant political cleavages during this period. The 1937 Constitution,* largely the work of De Valera himself, once adopted, was the object of a general consensus. The country's neutrality during the second world war obtained all-party agreement as did the proclamation of the Republic* in 1949. Because of the protectionism imposed by Fianna Fáil during the 1930s, because of the country's neutrality during the war and because of the excessive emigration and unemployment of the late 1940s and 1950s, the whole period is one of political conservatism and stagnation. It is not surprising therefore that the new economic strategy developed by the Fianna Fáil government in the late 1950s met with little opposition.

3 CHANGING TIMES

Modernization

Since the 1960s the process of modernization has engendered a number of minor crises. These have brought with them changes in the economic and financial fields, in the party system, the constitution, church-state relations, the country's place in the world and the role of the president. A greatly increased number of elections and referendums in the 1980s and 1990s correspond to the attempts made to adapt to new realities.

The troubled 1980s

The 1980s were to see the end of the prosperity of the 1960s and 1970s brought about by the largely successful policy of industrialization and the country's membership of the European community. By 1981 inflation had risen to 20%. On the employment level, the same period witnessed the beginning of the decline in the numbers at work and an increase in the numbers of unemployed. The financial situation worsened and borrowing requirements increased. Between 1978 and 1981, public sector expenditure increased from 49.6% to 69.8% of GNP. The principal explanation for this was to be found in the rising cost of public service provision and in the increasing costs of social security and foreign debt repayments.

Into the 1990s and the 2000s

The dissatisfaction with the treatment by successive governments of those problems contributed to the emergence of new political parties. In 1982 the official Sinn Féin party, which was a product of a split within Sinn Féin over the Northern Ireland* conflict in 1969, became the Workers' Party*. In 1992 a further split occurred within this party, between the more traditional socialist elements and the Democratic Left* who advocate a western type of parliamentary socialism. In 1998 the Democratic Left integrated the Labour Party. In 1986, some Fianna Fáil dissidents, soon joined by others from Fine Gael, created a new party on the right, the Progressive Democrats,* whose initial inspiration was clearly thatcherite. At the end of the decade, still another party, the Green Alliance, gathered some weight and won a seat in the Dáil* in 1989 and in 1992 and in the European elections in 1994.

In the 1992 elections the Labour party took on a new momentum. It became the second partner in a two-party coalition government with Fianna Fáil in 1993. As a result of an internal crisis it was replaced by a Fine Gael Labour-led coalition in December 1994. The 1997 general election gave a majority to a Fianna Faíl - Progressive Democrats coalition led by Bertie Ahern. Pressure groups have also emerged as powerful forces in the Ireland of the 1980s and 1990s, reflecting present day preoccupations with such questions as business, the Irish language, environmental protection, pollution and the Third World.

Church and state

Constitutional change and church-state relations were compounded during this period. In 1983, church and state seemed to be of one mind on the question of abortion. Both wanted it to be forbidden by the constitution. Their aim was achieved in a referendum. Three years later disagreement surfaced. The government wished to introduce divorce. The Catholic Church strongly dissented and in the subsequent referendum was followed by the electorate. However in 1995 in a new referendum a majority voted in favour of divorce. But even earlier than that, in 1992, expressions of Catholic morality were to be negated when in further referendums the right to travel abroad to obtain an abortion and the right to be informed on abortion facilities were adopted. The 1990s was therefore a period when the traditional political influence of the Catholic Church began to decline visibly. The country's adapting to its membership of the European community; its adoption of European norms, particularly in the area of women's rights help to explain the change.

A woman president

The election of Mary Robinson,* as President of Ireland, in 1990 was to symbolize those changes. She was the first woman to occupy the post and though the political functions of the office are largely ceremonial she has succeeded in investing public life with a new meaning and in giving importance to groups and causes which, hitherto, were excluded or marginalized. She was succeeded in 1997 by another woman, Mary McAleese from Northern Ireland.

NORTHERN IRELAND

Political violence

Political violence also marked the first years of the existence of Northern Ireland. In 1920, the IRA* mounted a military campaign in the border counties. The unionists responded by forming the Ulster* Special Constabulary, which became the "B Specials".* The "Specials" were to remain a feature of life in the province for practically half a century, hated by the Catholics because of their use against the IRA and because, according to them, it was the armed militia of the unionist party. The province also had a regular police force, the Royal Ulster Constabulary* (RUC). Early 1922 saw a renewal of IRA activity which led to a new wave of violence. In order to meet what it saw as a threat to its very existence, the Belfast government passed the Civil Authorities (Special Powers)* Act which set up a special court with wide powers, laid down particularly stiff penalties for certain offences and gave extensive new powers to the Minister of Home Affairs who, in turn, could delegate them to any police officer. These measures, to which must be added the outbreak of the Civil War in the South, had the effect of quietening the turmoil in Ulster. For 1922 alone, 232 people were killed, two-thirds of whom were Catholics, over 1,000 were wounded and more than £3 million worth of damage was caused. The situation in the province remained relatively calm until the first riots in the 1960s.

Unionist control

The unionist party, at every election but one to the Northern Ireland Parliament, between 1921 and 1972 – when that Parliament was prorogued – won an absolute majority of votes. It was thus in a position to exercise complete political control over the province.

Behind the exceptional immobility that Protestant control of the political system seemed to produce and that repeated unionist party electoral victories imposed, change, nevertheless, was not entirely absent. Protestant unity behind the unionist party was in sharp contrast to Catholic disunity. The minority was divided between support for the nationalist party and for the republican Sinn Féin party. The nationalist party was, however, to become the principal representative of the minority community after 1925, and some of its MPs even integrated Stormont* after boycotting it initially.

London pays the bill

A further area where change occurred was in the relations with London and in the distribution of power between Whitehall* and Stormont. According to the Government of Ireland Act (1920), Northern Ireland was to finance itself. But this soon became impossible if the same standards were to be maintained as in the rest of the United Kingdom.* When the Welfare State was implemented in Britain by the Labour government after the Second World War, it was decided that London would subsidize the new provisions in Northern Ireland. Henceforth the people of Northern Ireland won the same advantages as in Great Britain. The exercise of the new powers that those measures entailed was in the hands of Stormont since a strategy of non-intervention had been adopted by London as early as the 1920s and was continued by the Labour government after the war. In other words London paid the bill without scrutinizing its contents. But the growth of a civil rights movement within the minority community in the 1960s and the outbreak of political violence in the province soon obliged the British government to abandon its policy of non-intervention (see Chapter 6).

FURTHER READING

COAKLEY, J., & GALLAGHER, M., (ed.), *Politics in the Republic of Ireland*, Galway: PSAI Press,1992.
HARKNESS, D., *Northern Ireland since 1920*, Dublin: Helicon, 1983.

—1—
The Republic declared, 1948

The Taoiseach, speaking during the second reading of the Republic of Ireland Bill in the Dáil on 24 November 1948, renounced membership of the British Commonwealth and declared the Republic.

This Bill will end, and end forever, in a simple, clear and unequivocal way this country's long and tragic association with the Institution of the British Crown and will make it manifest beyond equivocation or subtlety that the national and international status of this country is that of an independent republic. It is necessary for me to state what I believe to be the effect of this Bill as clearly and as emphatically as possible so that there can be no arguments in the future, no misunderstandings, no suggestions that lurking around the political structure of this state there is some remnant or residue of that old institution and that politicians might be able to seize upon that for their own purposes, for the purposes of vote-catching or for the purposes of evoking again the anti-British feeling which has been fruitful ground on which politicians have played for many years past. [...]

[...] Nothing that can be done by this measure will in any way be a retrograde step in our relations with that country. Our people pass freely from here to England. We have trade and commerce of mutual benefit to each other. We have somewhat the same pattern of life, somewhat the same respect for democratic principles and institutions. The English language in our Constitution is recognized as the second official language of this nation. But we have still stronger ties than even those. Our missionary priests, nuns and brothers have gone to England and have brought the faith there, and are giving no inadequate contribution to the spiritual uplift which is so necessary in the atheistic atmosphere of the world today. We have our teachers there, lay and religious; we have our doctors and professional men there; we have our working men and our craftsmen and our girls who have gone over to earn a living there.

[...] But no people can be expected willingly and permanently to accept as part of their political institutions the symbol of the British Crown, when fidelity to the Catholic faith, the faith of the vast majority of our Irish people, was throughout the years regarded as disaffection and disloyalty to the British Crown, when love of country became treason to the British Crown, when every attempt to secure personal rights and national liberty was deemed rebellion against the Crown. [...]

Dáil Debates, CXIII, pp. 347-90, 24 November 1948.

questions

1. How does the Taoiseach see relations with Britain?
2. What justification does he give for the measure announced?

2

Direct Rule

In 1972, London ended the existence of the Northern Ireland Parliament and imposed direct rule on the province.

The principal purpose of imposing direct rule from London was to replace the divisive Stormont regime by a patently fair and efficient system of government, both for security and for the distribution of governmental resources for housing, job creation and other such matters. In the short term it was hoped that this would reduce communal support for the IRA and other paramilitaries and increase the prospects of a ceasefire. In the longer term it was hoped that it would enable a new and more generally acceptable structure for devolved government to be established. After more than twelve years of direct rule neither of these objectives has been achieved. Why?

The answer given by the Forum Report is that the British Government has never got further than crisis management. That is unfair. Certain clearly defined policies have been consistently pursued: on the security front the policies of criminalization (treating terrorists as if they were ordinary criminals) and Ulsterization (handing over as much responsibility for security as possible to the locally recruited RUC and UDR); on the political front a policy of attempting to persuade local party leaders to agree on some form of internal "power-sharing"; and on the socio-economic front measures to eliminate all forms of discrimination. The real problem is that none of these policies has worked because none of them has fully recognized the extent of the communal division in Northern Ireland and the need to accept the legitimacy of both traditions.

Kevin Boyle and Tom Hadden, *Northern Ireland: A Positive Proposal*, Harmondsworth: Penguin, 1985. © K. Boyle and T. Hadden, 1985.

questions

1. Why was direct rule imposed?
2. How successful has the British government been in following clearly defined policies?

3

The President of Ireland

See p. 62.

Mary McAleese was elected President in 1997.

questions

1. What do you know about Mrs Robinson?
2. Constitute a *dossier* on the 1990 Presidential elections.

4
Women in government

Irish women's involvement in political life started rather late as compared to other European countries. However, they seem to be catching up on their European sisters.

Women in government in the Republic of Ireland, 1979-93

		Ministers		Junior ministers	
Period	Administration	Total	Women	Total	Women
1979-1981	Fianna Fáil	15	1	10	0
1981-1982	Fine Gael-Labour	15	1	14	1
1982	Fianna Fáil	15	0	10	0
1982-1986	Fine Gael-Labour	15	1	15	1
1986-1987	Fine Gael-Labour	15	1	15	2
1987-1989	Fianna Fáil	15	1	15	1
1989-1992	Fianna Fáil-Progressive Democrat	15	1	15	2
1992-1993	Fianna Fáil-Progressive Democrat	15	1	15	2
1993	Fianna Fáil-Labour	15	2	15	3
1994	Fine Gael-Labour Democratic Left	15	2	17	4

Compiled from official sources.

questions

1. Has there been much progress in the representation of women in government?
2. Are there any major differences in this area between the parties?

5
Ireland and the external environment

In spite of setbacks, the European Community is in a sound position in the 1990s and Ireland's fate is more and more intertwined with its future.

European integration is characterized at present by an intense period of constitution-building and the Community is faced with the prospect of a sizeable increase in the number of member states.

This represents a remarkable transformation in the fortunes of the European Community if we recall its weak institutional and political capacity during the 1970s and early 1980s. The literature on integration in the early 1980s portrayed the European Community as an organisation that was largely irrelevant to the problems of its member states. This was not too harsh a judgement if we recall that it took the Community's legislative system five and a half years to agree the noise levels allowed for lawn mowers. Yet within a decade Western Europe was experiencing renewed confidences and exercising a new assertiveness. At the beginning of the 1990s the European Community has emerged as the core regional organisation for the continent as a →

questions

1. What are the main stepping stones in the building of the European Union?
2. How has Ireland been affected in its domestic and foreign policies by its membership of the Union?

whole. The economic and political fortunes of its members states and of its neighbours are bound up with developments in European integration.

Increasingly Irish politics, too, are intertwined with developments in Europe. The Community's treaties and legal system amount to an external constitution. Significant areas of economic policy, notably monetary policy, are fashioned in Europe. Irish ministers and civil servants participate in an intensive system of joint policy making with their counterparts in other members states. European elections have added a further occasion for party competition. Membership of the European Community is not just a matter of foreign policy but bites deeply into the domestic arena and domestic politics.

R. J. Hill and M. Marsh, *Modern Irish Democracy*, Dublin: Irish Academic Press, 1993. By kind permission.

6

Election results in the North

The suppression of Stormont and the political violence have provoked major changes in election results.

Northern Ireland: House of Commons, 1921-1969

Election year	Unionist MPs	Unionist vote %	Nationalist MPs	Nationalist vote %	Other MPs	Other vote %
1921	40	67	12	32	0	1
1925	36	64	12	29	4	7
1929	40	64	11	13	1	22
1933	39	65	11	27	2	7
1938	42	86	8	5	2	10
1945	35	55	10	9	7	35
1949	39	63	9	27	4	10
1953	39	60	9	16	4	24
1958	37	53	8	18	7	30
1962	34	49	9	15	9	36
1965	36	59	9	8	7	33
1969	39	67	6	8	7	25
Mean	38	63	10	15	5	21

Electoral support in the British House of Commons, 1970-1992 (%)[2]

1970	59	22	19
1974[1]	64	24	12
1974[2]	60	25	14
1979	53	23	23
1983	57	33	10
1987	50	33	18
1992	48	33	20
1997	50	40	10

Compiled from official sources.

1. All candidates who gave priority to defending the union are grouped under the term "unionist". All candidates who opposed the union, notably nationalist and Sinn Féin candidates, are grouped together under the term "nationalist".

2. Given the small number of Northern Ireland seats in the House of Commons in Westminster this table excludes the results in seats.

questions

1. To what extent did the unionists dominate the Northern Ireland parliament?
2. How has unionist representation evolved?

See table of Dáil results (1923-1992), next page.

questions

1. What are the principal political forces?
2. Taken collectively, how have small parties fared?

7

Election results in the South

Year of Election	Total Seats	Fianna Fáil (Anti-Treaty to 1927)		Fine Gael (Cumann na nGadlheal to 1937)		Labour		Farmers	Other Parties* and Independents	Government	Taoiseach (President of Executive Council to 1937)
		Seats	% Votes	Seats	% Votes	Seats	% Votes	Seats	Seats		
1923	153	44	27.6	63	38.9	14	12.4	15	17	C na nG	W. T. Cosgrave
06. 1927	153	44	26.1	47§	27.5	22	13.8	11	29	C na nG	W. T. Cosgrave
09. 1927	153	57	35.2	62§	38.7	13	9.5	6	15	C na nG	W. T. Cosgrave
1932	153	72	44.5	57§	35.3	7	7.7	4	13	FF	E. De Valera
1933	153	77§	49.7	48	30.5	8	5.7	–	20	FF	E. De Valera
1937	138	69§	45.2	48	34.8	13	10.3	–	8	FF	E. De Valera
1938	138	77%	51.9	45	33.3	9	10.0	–	7	FF	E. De Valera
1943	138	67§	41.9	32	23.1	17	15.7	14	8	FF	E. De Valera
1944	138	76§	48.9	30	20.5	12§§	11.5	11	9	FF	E. De Valera
1948	147	68§	41.9	31	19.8	19	11.3	7	22	Inter-Party	J. A. Costello
1951	147	69§	46.3	40	25.7	16	11.4	6	16	FF	E. De Valera
1954	147	65	43.4	50	32.0	19§	12.0	5	8	Inter-Party	J. A. Costello
1957	147	78	48.3	40	26.6	12§	9.1	3	14	FF	E. De Valera to 1959 S. Lemass
1961	144	70	43.8	47	32.0	16§	11.6	2	9	FF	S. Lemass
1965	144	72	47.8	47	33.9	22§	15.4	–	3	FF	S. Lemass to 1966 J. Lynch
1969	144	75§	45.7	50	34.1	18	17.0	–	1	FF	J. Lynch
1973	144	69§	46.2	54	35.1	19	13.7	–	2	Coalit. (FG/Lab)	L. Cosgrave
1977	148	84	50.6	43	30.5	17§	11.6	–	4	FF	J. Lynch to 1979 C. J. Haughey
1981	166	78§	45.3	65	36.5	15	9.9	–	7	Coalit. (FG/Lab)	G. FitzGerald
02. 1982	166	81	47.3	63	37.3	15	9.1	–	4§	FF	C. J. Haughey
11. 1982	166	75	45.2	70	39.2	16	9.4	–	3§	Coalit. (FG/Lab)	G. FitzGerald
1987	166	81	44.2	51§	27.1	12	6.4	–	19	FF	C. J. Haughey
1989	166	77	44.2	55	29.3	15	9.5	–	14§	Coalit. (FF/PD)	C. J. Haughey to 1992 A. Reynolds
1992	166	68	39.1	45	24.5	33	19.3	–	20§	Coalit. (FF/Lab) (FG/Lab/DL)	A. Reynolds to 1994 J. Bruton
1997	166	77	39.3	54	28	17	10.4	–	18	FF/PD	B. Ahern

*** Other parties**

06. 1927: National League 8, Sinn Féin 5
09. 1927: National League 2
1933: Centre Party 11, later merged with Fine Gael
1948: Clann na Poblachta 10
1951: Clann na Poblachta 2
1954: Clann na Poblachta 3
1957: Sinn Féin 4, Clann na Poblachta 1
1961: National Progressive Democrats 2, Clann na Poblachta 1
1981: SFWP 1, SLP 1
02. 1982: SFWP 3
11. 1982: WP 2
1987: PD 14, WP 4, DSP 1
1989: WP 7, PD 6, DSP 1
1992: PD 10, DL 4
1997: PD 4, DL 4, Ind. 6, Green 2, Sinn Féin 1, Socialist 1

§ includes outgoing Ceann Comhairle returned without contest.
§§ includes National Labour 4. In 1943 Labour divided with Labour and National Labour.

Nealon's Guide to the 27th Dáil & Seanad, Election '92, Dublin: Gill & Macmillan, 1993. By kind permission.

8

"No," to Europe

The 1992 Maastricht referendum was the occasion for those who were opposed to Europe since 1973 to renew their campaign.

Ph. © Nahassia/Sipa Press

questions

1. What forces oppose Europe? **2.** How successful have they been?

9

The end of Fianna Fáil domination?

General elections: Republic of Ireland, 6 June 1997

Party	Fianna Fáil	Fine Gael	Labour	Progressive Democrats	Democratic Left	Green	Sinn Féin	Others
% vote	39,3	28	10,4	4,7	2,5	1,5	1,5	6,1
seats	68	45	33	10	4	2	1	6
% seats	41	27	20	6	2	0,6	0	3

Adapted from P. Brennan, "L'Irlande en 1997", A. Grosser (dir.), *Les Pays d'Europe occidentale*, éd. 1998. Paris: La Documentation française.

questions

1. What global conclusions do the results impose?

2. Do such conclusions confirm recent trends?

Daily fear (see p. 84)
Ph. © C. Steele-Perkins/ Magnum

CHAPTER SIX

Conflict in Northern Ireland

The violent conflict which erupted in Northern Ireland* in 1968 was until the second Republican ceasefire of 1997, a running sore in the life of the island. At its origin, one finds, of course, the past, but one also finds contemporary political, social and economic factors. At different times throughout nearly thirty years a number of attempts were made to solve it.

Origins

1 Political Differences

In 1920 the Catholic nationalists of the north east of the country were opposed to the partition of the island, and the Protestant unionists,* hostile to any form of political independence or autonomy for Ireland, considered that they had a basic right to opt out of the new state. The former continued to seek some link with the Republic* of Ireland, whereas the latter systematically refused any institutional relation with the South. They favour retaining the union with Britain within the United Kingdom.* This fundamental constitutional disagreement is the political cause of the conflict. A further cause was unionist discrimination against nationalists. As long as unionists, nationalists and Republicans are not working together for a common future, political discord will continue.

2 Social Differences

The differences between the two sides also took on a pronounced social dimension which was to lead to a quasi-permanent separation between the two communities who, nevertheless, shared a common territory. In the 19th and 20th centuries separation often became institutionalized. To attendance at different churches was added attendance at different schools. From infancy on, members of each community were socialized into one form or another of distrust of the other side.

3 ECONOMIC DIFFERENCES

There was also an economic dimension to the separation. Globally speaking, Protestants were better off. Not only did they control the political system, but they owned the best land, held the best jobs and possessed most of the wealth. Unemployment and emigration were systematically higher among Catholics than among Protestants.

Those different levels of separation made for a situation of latent conflict but once the initial violence which had accompanied the creation of Northern Ireland had abated, and with the exception of short periods in the 1930s and 1950s, the conflict never took a violent turn until the late 1960s.

THE BEGINNINGS OF THE CONFLICT

The stirrings of post-war change contributed to the first attempts to modify the *status quo* in Northern Ireland. Change engendered hope for a better future among Catholics. For this hope to take form concretely, all previous forms of blatant discrimination had to be eliminated. To achieve this the Northern Ireland Civil Rights Association* was created in 1967 with the aim of obtaining "one man, one vote" in local elections, the removal of gerrymandered* electoral boundaries, laws against discrimination by local government, the provision of machinery to deal with complaints, the allocation of public housing on a points system, the repeal of the Special Powers Act,* and the disbanding of the B-Specials.* Prompted by London, the Belfast unionist government reacted favourably to those demands. Such was not the case, however, among all strands of unionism. A group of ultra-Protestants or loyalists, under the leadership of a minister called Ian Paisley,* founder of the Free Presbyterian Church,* seized every opportunity to oppose the demands put forward by the Catholic minority.

1 VIOLENCE

Rioting and Protestant mob attacks against Catholic areas in Belfast were the most dangerous forms of this opposition. The rioting by Catholic youths in Derry* which followed a unionist traditional celebration revealed the incapacity of the police to control the situation and led directly, in August 1969, to the introduction of the British army on to the streets of Northern Ireland. Previously the Catholics, convinced that they would not be defended by the police, summoned up the IRA*. Once this latter body had the personnel, the money and the arms it launched into what it called a war against the British presence in Northern Ireland.

The IRA

The IRA considers itself the legitimate heir of all those republicans who, since 1798, have taken up arms to fight the British. It sees itself therefore as a real army and organizes itself as such in the utmost secrecy. Its soldiers, men and women, are volunteers. Generally they are young, come from a working class background, have no criminal record and often have families with a strong republican past. In August 1994, they decided on a complete ceasefire and in alliance with Sinn Féin* aim at achieving their ends by political means. After a further period of violence in 1996 a new ceasefire was declared in 1997.

The UDA and the UVF

The Ulster Defence Association (UDA)* emerged in 1971 and was an amalgamation of Protestant vigilante groups which first came into existence in 1969 with the aim of defending Protestant areas. Like the IRA, its members are working class. The Ulster Volunteer Force, (UVF),* is another Protestant paramilitary body. It surfaced in 1966 in order to resist the republican fiftieth anniversary commemoration of the 1916 Easter rising.* In October 1994 the Protestant paramilitaries put an end to their violent campaign. Dissident groups, such as the LVF have however emerged now and then.

2 ACTION

The activities carried out directly or indirectly by the paramilitaries fall into three categories: the waging of war, prison protest, and politics. Between 1969 and 1997 over 3,000 people were killed as a direct result of the violent conflict in Northern Ireland. The number of wounded is much greater and the material damage has been huge. The majority of those killed were innocent civilians. Those responsible for most of the killings are the paramilitaries, with the IRA heading the list.

A global outline of the violent action shows changing patterns over time. There was a greater concentration of paramilitary activity and of killings during the first six years of the conflict. The early 1990s saw a stepping up of a Catholic assassination strategy on the part of the UDA. Another changing pattern has been the choice of place. At first the war was waged on Northern Irish soil. But the republicans were soon to extend their activities further afield to Britain and even to continental Europe, tracking down the British army in different NATO countries. Now and then the IRA also succeeded in hitting the world headlines with particularly spectacular attacks. The killing of Lord Mountbatten (1979) was one such example, the bomb attack against the Grand Hotel in Brighton* (1984) where Margaret Thatcher was staying during the conservative conference was another.

In the area of prison protest, the IRA is again to the forefront. The most notable example of this kind of action was the 1981 hunger strike* carried out to the death by Bobby Sands* and ten other republicans. The sympathy created by the hunger strike prompted the republicans to abandon their traditional opposition to the electoral process and soon Sinn Féin, the political party of the republican movement, was presenting candidates at all elections both in Northern Ireland and in the Republic.

3 RESOURCES

Paramilitary activity costs money. Where did this money come from? For both Protestant and Catholic paramilitaries, it is believed that the main source of finance is racketeering and protection money. But for many years the principal source of funding for the republicans was certainly to be found among the descendants of Irish emigrants in the United States, though this source dried up during the latter years of the conflict. A further source, before the necessary precautions were taken, was bank and post-office robberies.

As for arms and explosives, major consignments from the United States came into the country, as did a number originating in Eastern Europe and passing through Arab hands. The persistence of the violent conflict has had profound effects on the life of the province. Several attempts have been made to find some form of solution, the most promising one being the 1993 Joint Dublin-London Declaration*, the 1994 paramilitary ceasefires and the 1998 Good Friday Agreement (see Chapter 14).

4 EFFECTS

The area of law and order, understandably so, was to be particularly affected by the conflict. An initial period of reform – reform of the police, repeal of repressive legislation – was followed by new measures introduced in application of the principle that exceptional situations require exceptional measures. The British authorities, once they took over the government of Northern Ireland in 1972, had two new repressive pieces of legislation adopted. The first is the Northern Ireland (Emergency Provisions) Act* (1973) and the second the Prevention of Terrorism Act* (1974) which is applicable all over the United Kingdom.

In the realm of law and order, some legal decisions, some political decisions, and behaviour by the security forces were to lead to a number of dramatic and even tragic situations. The cases of the Guilford Four,* the Maguire Seven*, and the Birmingham Six,* in which it was revealed that innocent Irish Catholics had been condemned in British courts to spend long years in prison for terrorist crimes which they had not committed, are one such set of examples. At the same time, in a particularly difficult situation, the role of the army in security duties was reduced and that of the police increased, while a serious effort to transform the RUC* into a professional police body met with a certain amount of success. The result is that today the Northern Ireland police is somewhat more acceptable to the Catholic population than it was in the early days of the conflict.

The conflict has probably accentuated the Protestant-Catholic divisions. This is not surprising if one considers the atrocities committed against each community by the paramilitaries of the opposite side. Yet many groups are making strenuous efforts to heal the divisions. At the same time a very serious attempt has been made by successive British governments to remedy the disadvantages under which Catholics laboured for so long. For example, little or no criticism is made today on the minority side as to how public housing is distributed.

5 SOLUTIONS

The conflict has pushed the politicians to try to find a solution to this tragic and complex problem. London, Dublin, the European Community and Washington have all been involved in the search. In 1973 the conservative government of the time advanced two concepts which, under one form or another, have remained at the basis of all the attempts made to solve the problem. The first is that of power sharing. This meant that there would be no return to majority rule in the province; in other words, if Northern Ireland wished to govern itself, its majority would have to accept the principle of sharing power with the minority. The second is the Irish dimension which, in turn, meant that the government of the Irish Republic would have to be associated with any new political arrangement.

Sunningdale (1973) and Hillsborough (1985)

A first failed attempt was made in 1974 in application of the Sunningdale Agreement* to put those ideas into pactice. The next really serious attempt took place in 1985 when the Anglo-Irish Agreement, or Hillsborough Agreement,* was signed by the Taoiseach,* Garret Fitzgerald, and the Prime Minister, Margaret Thatcher. This agreement gives priority to cooperation between Dublin and London in governing Northern Ireland, while maintaining the principle of power sharing if the province's political parties could agree. This they could not do.

The Joint Declaration (1993)

A series of new political talks in 1992 and 1993 led to a major Anglo-Irish Declaration, called the Downing Street Declaration,* on 15 December 1993 (see Chapter 14). According to this declaration the British government reaffirmed that, having no strategic or economic interest in Northern Ireland, they would uphold the democratic wish of the people there on the issue of whether they preferred to support the Union or a sovereign, united Ireland. As for the Irish government, they accepted that the democratic right to self-determination of the people of Ireland as a whole must be achieved with the consent of a majority of the people of Northern Ireland.

The ceasefire (1994)

After the IRA ceasefire on 31 August 1994, the Protestant paramilitary one in October, and the publication of the Joint Framework Document on 22 February 1995, the Dublin and London governments, and the principal political forces in Northern Ireland, began lengthy negotiations to try to agree on the future relationship between the two communities within Northern Ireland, between Belfast and Dublin and between Ireland and Britain. However, due to the unionist refusal to negotiate until the IRA had disarmed, the latter put an end to their ceasefire in February 1996.

The Good Friday Agreement (1998)

The search for an agreement was to be facilitated by the 1997 May general election in Great Britain and the June general election in the Republic of Ireland both of which brought new parties to power. An IRA cease-fire in July 1997 further added an impetus to the negotiations which were to conclude with the signing of the Good Friday Agreement (10 April 1998). The principal political forces in Northern Ireland, in conjunction with the two sovereign governments, agreed on constitutional changes in Ireland and Britain, on the creation of democratic institutions in Northern Ireland, on a North-South Ministerial council, on a British-Irish Council and on a British-Irish Intergovernmental Conference as well as other measures relating to human rights, decommissioning of arms, security, policing, justice and prisoners.

FURTHER READING

BRENNAN, P., *The Conflict in Northern Ireland*, Paris: Longman, 1991.
GOLDRING, M., *Belfast*, London: Lawrence & Wishart, 1991.
L'Irlande politique et sociale, vols 1 and 3, Paris: PSN, 1984, 1986.
WHYTE, J., *Interpreting Northern Ireland*, Oxford: Clarendon Press, 1991

1
Ballybeg and Northern Ireland

Rosemary Harris, a social anthropologist, studied rural inter-community relations in the 1960s in a small village in Northern Ireland which she designated as Ballybeg.

I have stressed already that relationships between Protestants and Catholics were for the most part peaceful. It is also worth pointing out that paradoxically, just because of the cleavage between the religious groups, relationships between individuals belonging to different groups might be particularly "neighbourly".
An individual could afford, if he wished, to be brusque and awkward towards members of his own group who asked a favour. The same man towards members of "the other side" would be much more amiable for fear that any refusal to help might be put down to religious prejudice on his part. It is perhaps not surprising that I met Protestants who seemed genuinely to think that under normal conditions Catholics made the best neighbours, and Catholics who were as convinced of the same thing about Protestants – such people were speaking out of their own experiences. Perhaps it was partly just because it was the very best of neighbours who might turn hostile that the adjective "treacherous" seemed so appropriate.
It is also important to note just how careful the people were to try, in normal circumstances, to avoid any behaviour likely to cause hostility, in other words to keep the latent hostility latent. The display of pictures in every house, which told the chance visitor quite clearly to which side the inhabitants belonged, and the wearing of badges of one kind or another, which often revealed the allegiances of chance-met individuals, were useful not merely because they symbolised in-group unity. Just because they made loyalties clear they made it possible to use the appropriate behaviour patterns that made peaceful relationships possible.

Rosemary Harris, *Tolerance and Prejudice in Ulster*, Manchester: Manchester University Press, 1976. By kind permission.

questions

1. How can the friendly relationship between Catholics and Protestants be explained?
2. Give the content of the latent hostility.

2
Inequality and separation

The divide is a reality in daily life in Northern Ireland. After more than thirty years of reforms the two communities still remain separated.

There have been many studies of inequality – notably in terms of employment and economic prosperity – between members of the Protestant and Catholic communities. In political terms this is clearly the most significant equality issue. But there are many other forms of inequality in Northern Ireland within and across the two communities, notably in terms of poverty and prosperity, educational provision, gender and disability. There is also an increasing degree of residential and other forms of segregation.

Some progress has been made under the Fair Employment Acts in achieving a more equitable balance between Protestants and Catholics in the workforce in most major companies and public bodies. But there remains a substantial differential in the unemployment rates.

Fig. 1 Unemployment rates (economically active)
(Fair Employment Commission 1994)

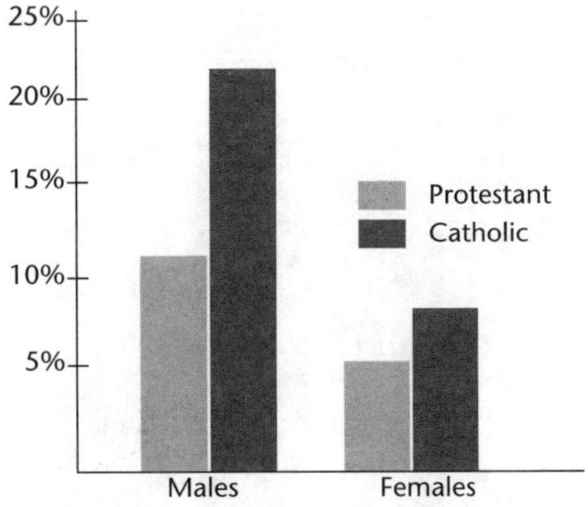

Fig. 2 Average gross weekly income (£) in 1995-1996
(Source: Family Expenditure Survey)

	Per household	Per person
Catholic	£293.2	£95.2
Protestant	£347.1	£135.6

But the analysis in *Figure 3* also shows similar levels of economic inequality, and thus of relative poverty, within each community.

Fig. 3 Percentage of households in each weekly income group
(Source: Family Expenditure Survey 1995-1996)

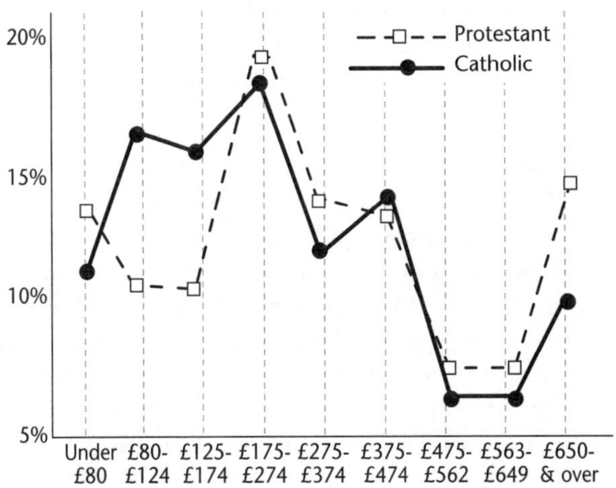

Communal segregation

There is also clear evidence of increasing levels of communal segregation in many areas of Northern Ireland. Detailed studies of the →

1991 Census have shown that the level of segregation in most electoral districts has increased substantially since 1971.

Fig. 4 Increases in communal segregation in West and East Belfast and L/Derry and Waterside 1971-1991 (*Source: Census*)

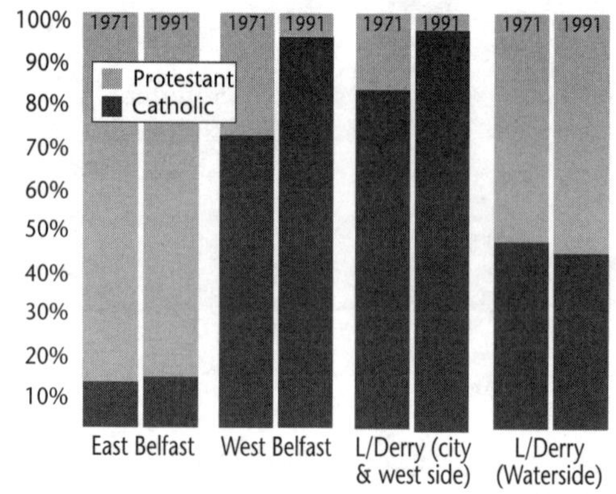

questions

1. What aspects of the separation are highlighted in the text?
2. Why has reform not achieved more?

3

A republican view of the conflict

Gerry Adams, the leader of Sinn Féin, gives his version of the Irish struggle for freedom.

The classic period of republican struggle, the period which is impressed upon one's mind as the definitive image of the IRA, is the Tan War, with its flying columns taking on the Black and Tans. At its height it was a military campaign with a background of incipient forms of alternative government apparatus functioning through the republican courts in certain parts of the country. The flying columns moved about as fairly self-contained units; they were fed and accommodated in sympathetic households or sometimes they commandeered Unionist houses and lived off the occupants.

In the 1930s and 1940s the IRA enjoyed no such background in the country, and their military actions took place in England, in the 26 counties and only in one or two places in the 6 counties. The 1950s campaign was restricted to the border counties – there was literally no activity in Belfast – and a lot of the IRA people involved came from the 26 counties and presumably worked around the border counties or maintained small flying columns based in Fermanagh, Tyrone and South Armagh. By the end this campaign like those before it consisted of just five or six active republicans skipping between five or six houses.

The current phase of armed struggle is different from any other, apart perhaps from a resemblance to the situation in the Black and Tan War in those areas that enjoyed some kind of governmental status. In the 1970s the struggle developed into a broad political and armed campaign, but even the military aspect developed its own politics of physical force.

What particularly characterises this phase is that the IRA/Óglaigh na hÉireann fights within the occupied area and exists cheek by jowl with the British forces, which have at their command a massive array of technological resources. The IRA today is one of the few guerrilla forces in the world which operates in and from within the occupied area, and despite the long duration of this phase of struggle, the IRA continues to enjoy unsurpassed community support.

I wish that physical force had never been part of the political struggle in my lifetime in Ireland. But a statelet which was born in violence has maintained itself throughout its more than sixty years of existence by violence and has been supported in so doing by the British army and government. [...]

From defensive origins the IRA campaign developed into an offensive against the state, and there is no denying the fact that innocent bystanders were killed and injured as a consequence of IRA actions. [...]

I deeply regret all the deaths and injuries which occur in the course of this struggle and although I have never tried to justify civilian casualties or fatalities of IRA actions I am challenged constantly by some journalists and television interviewers, imitating the attitudes of their political masters, with having placed myself and the whole republican movement outside the bounds of political debate by refusing to condemn the IRA, and the IRA is commented upon in an unreal way as if its motivation were the pursuit of violence for its own sake.

Gerry Adams, *The Politics of Irish Freedom*, Dingle: Brandon Books, 1986.

questions

1. Why is the republican struggle today different from that of yesterday?
2. How does Gerry Adams justify the armed struggle?

4
A murderous loyalism

Protestant paramilitary violence increased considerably after the signature of the Anglo-Irish Agreement in 1985.

The IRA is generally, and correctly, identified as the chief source of murder and violence in Northern Ireland, and as the main reason for the presence of British troops in the province. For that reason, the crimes of Protestant terrorists – such as Sunday night's murder of a Catholic snooker club owner and his son near Dungannon, the first sectarian killings of the new year – tend to receive less attention and sometimes appear to be less roundly condemned. It seems to be feared that to equate or compare so-called "loyalist" violence with the IRA's in some way diminishes the gravity of the latter.

That may be a natural anxiety, but it is not logical. It should be possible to condemn the one without in any way minimizing the other. The →

Northern Ireland Office does so very successfully, even though members of the security forces bulk large among the IRA's victims, whereas those of Protestant gunmen are typically Roman Catholic civilians. It is admirably even-handed and robust in its condemnation of all forms of sectarian murder.

The figures alone emphasise that republican terrorists have overall been the biggest killers. Since the present troubles began in the late Sixties, the IRA is reckoned to have accounted for around 1,740 victims, more than twice as many as loyalist groups. But the rate of killing by the Ulster Defence Association and the Ulster Volunteer Force has quickened considerably: in the past two years they have claimed 80 victims, more than the IRA. The acceleration is attributed to the signing in 1985 of the Anglo-Irish Agreement, which, to the disgust of many Protestants, acknowledged that the Republic of Ireland had a legitimate interest in Ulster's affairs.

That leads to another difficulty in discussing UDA/UVF terrorism: whereas the IRA is seen as the terrorist arm of a political organisation, Sinn Fein, the UDA and UVF are on their own. The IRA's so-called political agenda is bankrupt: to claim to use violence to get British troops out when the effect is the precise opposite is merely to add hypocrisy to criminality. Loyalist violence does not even bother to dress itself up in political clothes. Its twin aims are to kill off or delay any form of accommodation between the legitimate political parties and the governments in London and Dublin; and to demonstrate its ruthlessness, the better to enrich itself (as does the IRA) through protection rackets and the like. The IRA is a political organisation that became criminal; the UDA/UVF are criminals who became quasi-political.

The Independent, January 5, 1993.

questions

1. What developments occurred within the Protestant paramilitary movements?
2. What distinguishes the UDA/UVF from the IRA?

5

Daily fear

See p. 74.

The protected and the unprotected try to live their lives side by side in Northern Ireland.

questions

1. Give your impressions of the photo.
2. How true to real life is it?

6
Statistics of violence

Violence is one of the most striking and constant features of Northern Irish political life. The level of violence has, however, varied considerably over time.

Year	Shootings	Explosions and incendiaries	Armed robberies	Charged with terrorist offences	Firearms finds	Explosives finds (kgs)	Wounded	Deceased
1970	213	170	•	•	324	305	•	25
1971	1756	1515	489	•	716	1,25	2592	174
1972	10628	1853	1931	531	1259	18,819	4876	467
1973	5018	1520	1317	1418	1313	17,426	2651	250
1974	3026	1113	1353	1374	1236	11,848	2398	216
1975	1803	635	1325	1197	820	4,996	2474	247
1976	1908	1192	889	1276	736	9,849	2729	297
1977	1081	535	676	1308	563	1,728	1387	112
1978	755	633	493	843	393	0,956	985	81
1979	728	564	504	670	300	0,905	875	113
1980	642	400	467	550	203	0,821	801	76
1981	1142	529	689	918	357	3,419	1350	101
1982	547	332	693	686	288	2,298	525	97
1983	424	367	718	613	166	1,706	510	77
1984	334	248	710	528	187	3,871	866	64
1985	237	215	542	522	173	3,344	916	54
1986	392	254	839	655	174	2,443	1450	61
1987	674	384	955	468	206	5,885	1130	93
1988	537	458	742	439	489	4,728	1047	93
1989	566	420	604	433	246	1,377	959	62
1990	559	287	492	383	179	1,969	906	76
1991	499	367	608	404	164	4,167	962	94
1992	506	371		418	194	2,167		85
1993	476	289		372	196	3,944		84
1994	348	222		349	178	1,285		62
1995	50	2		440	118	0,005		9
1996	125	25	655	545	98	1,677		15
1997	225	53	621	405	105	1,258		22

Adapted from P. Brennan & R. Deutsch, *Une Chronologie du conflit irlandais, 1968-1992*, Paris: PSN, 1993.
By kind permission

questions

1. What are the main trends in the area of political violence?
2. How can one explain the outbursts of violence in the early 1970s, in 1981 and in the mid-80s?

7
Nobel Prize speeches

David Trimble, leader of the Ulster Unionist Party, and John Hume, leader of the Social Democratic and Labour Party were given the Nobel Prize to reward their efforts in favour of peace in Northern Ireland.

It is a truth universally understood that there is no such thing as a free lunch. That being so, John and I are obliged to sing for our supper. In short, some expect us to speak as experts and hand out advice on how to make peace. Some old hands say that there are two ways to sing for your supper. The first and the safest course, they say, is to make a series of vague and visionary statements. Indeed, are not vague and visionary statements much the same thing? The tradition from which I come, but by which I am not confined, produced the first vernacular Bible in the language of the common people, and contributed much to the scientific language of the enlightenment. It puts a great price on the precise use of words, and uses them with circumspection, so much so that our passion for precision is often confused with an indifference to idealism.

Not so. But I am personally and perhaps culturally conditioned to be sceptical of speeches which are full of sound and fury, idealistic in intention, but impossible of implementation; and I resist the kind of rhetoric which substitutes vapour for vision. Instinctively, I identify with the person who said that when he heard a politician talk of his vision, he recommended him to consult an optician. But, if you want to hear of a possible Northern Ireland — not a Utopia but a normal and decent society, flawed as human beings are flawed but fair as human beings are fair, then I hope not to disappoint you. [...] In the past 30 years of our conflict there have been many moments of deep depression and outright horror. Many people wondered whether the words of W.B. Yeats might come true:

Too long a sacrifice
Can make a stone of the heart.

Endlessly our people gathered their strength to face another day and they never stopped encouraging their leaders to find the courage to resolve this situation so that our children could look to the future with a smile of hope. This is indeed their prize and I am convinced that they understand it in that sense and would take strong encouragement from today's significance and it will powerfully strengthen our peace process.

Today also we commemorate and the world commemorates the adoption 50 years ago of the Universal Declaration of Human Rights and it is right and proper that today is also a day that is associated internationally with the support of peace and work for peace, because the basis of peace and stability, in any society, has to be the fullest respect for the human rights of all its people. It is right and proper that the European Convention of Human Rights is to be incorporated into the domestic law of our land as an element of the Good Friday Agreement.

Irish Times, 11-12-1998.

questions

1. How do the records of the two leaders compare as regards the search for peace in Northern Ireland?
2. What do the extracts reveal about the differences between the two leaders?

Ph. © O. Thomas/ Imapress

8
Support for the hunger strike

Women and children support the men on hunger strike in prison in 1981.

questions

1. What was the hunger strike?
2. What role did women and children play in the conflict?

(A)

(B)

Irish families (see p. 93)
(A) Ph. © P. Zachmann/Magnum
(B) Ph. Prod. By kind permission.

CHAPTER SEVEN

Irish Society

Irish society has changed rapidly and radically since the 1960s. Given the previous conservative nature of that society, both North and South, and the rural and Catholic nature of the Republic,* the change is particularly striking. The first forty years of existence of the two new Irish political entities were notable for continuity and isolation from the rest of Europe. In the late 1950s, in the Republic a social and economic crisis was at the origin of the decision to modify the direction of Irish affairs. In the late 1960s, in Northern Ireland* the political crisis contributed, in its turn, to change. Since then all social life there has been affected by the political conflict. In the South, the opening up of society to the winds of change from Europe, America and elsewhere has had repercussions in every walk of life.

One must nevertheless avoid the temptation of seeing Irish society today uniquely in terms of change. In reality continuity and change are blending to form a new pattern. The best way to follow this emerging pattern is to look at how society attempts to solve the problems that the individual may encounter throughout his or her existence. Is the family a stable and secure structure protecting the individual from the harshness of the outside world? How does society treat those who fall on hard times? Is society able to offer a job to everyone, thus allowing them to play a useful social role?

1 The Family

Since the 1970s, the issue of the family has been at the heart of a number of debates which have provoked lively controversy in the Republic. Northern Ireland, though in a less dramatic manner, has also been involved. Contraception, abortion, divorce and homosexuality were the objects of those debates. On the surface the outcome of the controversy which surrounded them has been to reaffirm the force of the traditional family model. Yet shifts and uncertainties have surfaced and reveal that all is not as it was in the past.

Legislation

No legislation governed the question of birth control in Northern Ireland. And although British legislation on abortion and homosexuality was not applied there the most intense debates on these issues took place in the South. The importation and sale of contraceptives were declared illegal there as early as the 1930s. However, in the early 1970s, the Supreme Court declared such legislation to be unconstitutional. It was not until the early 1990s that the final restrictions governing their distribution were lifted.

Victory of family values

Hence, over a period of nearly twenty years the defenders of what were called family values, aided and abetted by the Catholic church, were successful in delaying the liberalization of the legislation on the use of contraceptives. Among them was the Fianna Fáil* party, but also a number of pressure groups such as Family Solidarity and the Society for the Protection of Unborn Children. The same pressure groups succeeded in 1983 in having an amendment, adopted by referendum, added to the Constitution forbidding abortion. In 1986, they mobilized, once again in conjunction with the Catholic Church and Fianna Fáil, sufficient support to defeat an amendment to allow for the introduction of divorce. The 1980s could therefore be described as the decade of the victory of family values.

Abortion

The victory, though, was short-lived since in 1992 the Supreme Court decided, in a case dealing with the rape of a 14-year-old girl, that she had a constitutional right to an abortion on the grounds that her life was threatened by the suicidal tendencies arising from her pregnancy. The court ruling led to a triple referendum later in the same year on the question of abortion, the result of which showed a significant shift in the liberal direction. The right to travel abroad to have an abortion and the right to disseminate information in Ireland on legal abortion services in other countries were accepted, but a restrictive wording on abortion itself was rejected.

Liberalisation

Confirming the liberal trend the repressive legislation against homosexuality, in force since the 19th century, was revoked in 1993. Abortion was still in a legal limbo but divorce was finally accepted in 1995. Family values will still continue to be stoutly defended in the face of important liberal inroads. Nevertheless, today in Ireland, the family can no longer be considered as the haven of stability which its defenders claim it once was.

2 HEALTH AND WELFARE

The late 1940s saw the implementation of the Welfare State in Britain, soon to be followed by its extension to Northern Ireland. Initially opposition from the Catholic Church prevented any move towards a general welfare system in the Republic. The necessary modernization of society, revealed by the extent of the postwar crisis, was, however, to bring social as well as economic reform. Health was one area where improvements were badly needed, principally on account of the continuing tragic effects of tuberculosis. By the 1950s, this had been brought under control. The factors influencing health in contemporary Ireland are, of course, similar to those found elsewhere: atmospheric pollution, tobacco, abuse of alcohol, abuse of drugs, bad housing, homelessness, marital breakdown and unemployment. However, the framework in which those problems are treated there are specific to that country.

Health service

Over 35% of total government spending is devoted to health and social security in the Republic. The health services are administered by four health and social services boards in Northern Ireland and by eight regional health boards in the Republic. A total of 800 doctors in the North (1,500 in the South) have an average of 1,900 patients (900 in the South) on what are called their panels. Those patients have a right to free medical treatment. In the South, however, the system is not a universal egalitarian one since doctors can have private patients in addition to those whose care is funded by the state. This inegalitarian dimension is also to be found in the organization of hospitals. They are run by the health boards or by religious congregations or by private organizations. In all cases, whether private or public, they obtain state funding. Another feature of the health and welfare system of the Republic is its Voluntary Health Insurance scheme which provides an insurance system for health-care costs for those who are not entitled to benefit under the tax-based system. In other words a state system exists for the poorer and a subscription system for the middle class. The subscriptions of the latter to the Voluntary Health Insurance scheme are partially deductible for income tax purpose.

Social security service

The social security service is broadly similar throughout the island. It concerns different allowances, including those for old age, for children, for maternity leave, for absence from work in times of illness and in case of unemployment. Social insurance payments are the subject of reciprocal arrangements with other EU* member states. A system of supplementary benefits is in place to help those in particularly dire straits. But social assistance has not kept pace with need. Hence a high rate of poverty both in urban and rural Ireland.

Voluntary bodies

The failure of the states to meet the minimum needs of those who, for one reason or another, have fallen on hard times or who are faced with a particular problem explains the continuous need for voluntary bodies*. Their members are therefore doing necessary work to alleviate, for example, poverty and pain, to overcome different handicaps and to inform on birth control and abortion facilities. There has been progress in the area of social care. Yet it is not sufficient to alleviate the immense distress of a large number of people in Ireland generated by contemporary society, the most important source of which is unemployment.

3 UNEMPLOYMENT

Since its failure to industrialize sufficiently in the 19th century Ireland has been unable to create enough jobs to meet the needs of those coming on to the labour market. The consequences have been high emigration and high unemployment. The successful industrialization of the South, begun in 1958, and the equally successful industrial diversification in the North, at least until the early 1970s, which led to the creation of thousands of jobs, were not sufficient to match the decline in employment in agriculture and population growth. A further characteristic can be added to high unemployment and that is a high level of long-term unemployment. With the worsening of economic conditions, unemployment and more particularly long-term unemployment increases. With the improvement of economic conditions, notably in the 1990s, unemployment, underwent a dramatic decline. The multi-national industries are the first to benefit from any economic improvement and since they are all capital intensive their improved performance does not however always immediately translate itself into more jobs.

Manual unemployment

In the South, between 1921 and 1951, unemployment fluctuated between 5% and 8%. If one considers the high emigration rate and the fact that a large proportion of the work-force was made up of the self-employed, who, if unemployed, were not counted among the jobless, the percentage is particularly high. With the decline of that category, and more specifically of the numbers of small farmers, the unemployment figures increased. It is to be noted that unemployment, between 1921 and 1999 (6.6%), has been largely concentrated in the working class. This is particularly the case for the unskilled manual category. The unemployment rate among those workers has been, on average, around 30%. A high average duration rate of unemployment among the unskilled has led to the creation of an underclass which is heavily dependent on the state for welfare provision and which, in fact, lives in a situation of permanent poverty.

The demographic factor

Between the 1970s and the 1990s a number of factors combined to maintain a high unemployment level in the Republic. Young people leaving full-time education contributed every year to the growth of the labour force. A further factor was, curiously enough, immigration. The prosperity of the country in the 1970s, attributed largely to its successful industrialization, enticed a high number of former emigrants back home to fill skilled jobs in manufacturing. Their children, in the 1980s and 1990s, added further to the growth of the labour market.

Female employment

A third factor was the demand by women for jobs or rather their decision no longer to abandon their jobs on marriage. Married women's labour force participation is still low by OECD* standards, which probably indicates that, in the future, more and more of them will be staying on at work, and other women who have given up their jobs will wish to reintegrate the world of work. But what had Irish society to offer to all those who do not find work?

The traditional outlet was, of course, emigration. That is a possibility but it has always been highly dependent of the job situation in the host country. At home, in agriculture there is a long-term decline in the numbers at work and there is no reason to imagine that that situation will change. The indigenous sector of Irish industry, such as textiles, clothing and footwear, has been undergoing job losses since the 1970s. The largest area of employment growth has been and still is in the services or the tertiary sector.

Job creation

The policies of job creation in Ireland were not until the mid-1990s successful enough to reduce in any significant way the level of unemployment. When new jobs are created, which happened in some high-technology areas or in some branches of the services, it would seem that they benefit categories of people who previously were not on the unemployment register, such as married women or former emigrants. The late 1990s however witnessed a dramatic reversal of the situation which, in spite of increased female participation, net inward migration and continuing decline in agriculture employment, registered a sharp drop in unemployment.

FURTHER READING

CLANCY, P., et al. (ed.), *Ireland: A Sociological Profile*, Dublin: IPA, 1986.
PEILLON, M., *Contemporary Irish Society*, Dublin: Gill & Macmillan, 1982.

1

Family life in rural Ireland

Alice Taylor recalls family life in rural Ireland in the post-war years.

I suppose our farm originally would have been the biggest farm at that time, but it was divided up when different members of the family got married. [...] In a sense that made us a kernel of the town land. We felt very much that. My father felt that if anybody was on their own, or anybody wasn't able to cope, he should assume responsibility for them. I remember there was one old lady who lived near us on her own and when the snow was there he would visit her everyday and make sure she had milk or the messages. And it was no bother to him to send us, walking into town, three miles, to get something she needed and walk out again. You felt that if other people had problems they were your problems as well. [...]

The food was very simple. It all came off the farm, and there was no such thing as buying lemonade or cakes or anything like that. Our own wheat would have been the flour; we would have killed our own pig, that would have been meat; all the potatoes, vegetables, and eggs were our own. We made our own butter. Afterwards that came from the creamery. So everything came off the farm. There wasn't a thing from outside that could have any effect on us. The only two things that we bought were a gallon of paraffin oil for the lamps and the battery for the radio. Candles were counted as second-rate lighting. The lamp in the kitchen was the thing, so it was a terrible thing if you ran out of oil. You would have to walk across to the neighbours for a gallon of oil if you were stuck. My father had to have the radio going. If the battery ran out, it was a pure disaster. I mean my children today have the radios roaring all over the house. But then the radio was turned on, for the news, for different plays on Radio Éireann and different plays on BBC. My mother, if she heard something which she didn't think a hundred percent, she would turn it off. So we listened to the radio a lot.

Patrick O'Dea, *A Class of our Own*, Dublin: New Island Books, 1994.
By kind permission.

questions

1. What sort of social relationship is described here?
2. How idealized is the image of self-sufficiency given in this text?

2

Irish families

(See p. 88.) A Belfast republican taxi driver with his traditional Catholic family (A).*
The Snapper, *a different picture of a contemporary Dublin family (B).*

questions

1. Why is there no doubt as to the taxi driver's religious background? **2.** What are your impressions of *The Snapper?*

—3—
Women and abortion

A male-dominated Catholic pressure group, Pro-Life Amendment Campaign (PLAC), which promoted the introduction of an anti-abortion amendment to the Constitution, was successful due to the weakness of the women's rights movement.

On one level the answer is simple: it was a Catholic coup. In a country where a large majority are active, practising Catholics any group promoting what was essentially the Catholic ethos as applied to reproduction and other social issues was bound to win widespread support. And any group supported not just by the Catholic hierarchy and its network of priests and lay people but also by the largest political party in the state, Fianna Fáil, had a major headstart over their opponents.

In addition, the three general elections held between 1981 and 1983, the year of the abortion referendum, gave the Pro-Life Amendment Campaign unparalleled leverage as they played one party off against another. The presence of a conservative rump in both Labour and Fine Gael also ruled out the possibility of a united political front on the "liberal" side of the debate and enabled PLAC to target politicians in those parties vulnerable to conservative Catholic pressure.

But the conservative assault on Irish social legislation was successful also for less clear-cut reasons. The passage of liberal abortion and other social legislation in the United States of America and other countries came at a point when feminism had established a solid base in the political psyche of those countries. Abortion was recognised as a woman's right, not as a humanitarian gesture to women pregnant through rape, incest, or some other appalling circumstance.

The conservative lobby was successful in Ireland precisely because it struck before a feminist perspective on social legislation had taken hold. The country had not yet developed to a point where it could discuss such issues as contraception and divorce, never mind abortion, on the basis of the concept of a human right or more specifically of a woman's right. Contraception was viewed as a way to limit large families, not as a means through which women could control their fertility and therefore their public and private lives. Abortion in Ireland to this day is seen as acceptable only when the woman's life is at "substantial" risk or (and this line is taken only by a brave few), when she has become pregnant against her will. The idea that a woman should be allowed to choose for herself whether or not to go ahead with a life-changing pregnancy is still an alien concept, yet it is a cornerstone of feminist belief.

The widespread passive acceptance of the patriarchal nature of Irish society also enabled the conservative lobby to hold sway. Nothing threatens that system more than when women are enabled to take control of every aspect of their lives, public and private. And there is nothing more critical to the exercise of that control than the ability to decide how many children to have, if any, and when to have them.

E. O'Reilly, *Masterminds of the Right*, Dublin: Attic Press, 1992.

questions

1. Give a list of reasons to explain the success of the "Pro-Life" group.
2. How patriarchal is Irish society?

—4—

Church organization and control

Since the 19th century the Catholic Church has played a major role in social services.

Ever since the 19th century in Ireland, but earlier elsewhere in Europe, the Catholic Church has been concerned with the maintenance and care of people in terms of keeping them healthy and free from disease. Health and social welfare became a major point of conflict between the Church and the State, as spheres of power were at issue and, in particular, who was responsible for the care and supervision of people. It was a struggle that was vital to the very survival of the Church. The conflict culminated in the encyclical *Rerum Novarum* (1891) which was as much a dogma against the excessive interference by the State in social welfare as it was against class antagonism. As industrial society developed, the State became interested in creating the conditions of economic growth and political stability and, consequently, in disciplining and controlling people as well as keeping them healthy. It was central to the maintenance and development of the Church's power that social control be considered as a moral issue which came under its jurisdiction. One of the reasons why there is such a high level of adherence to the Catholic Church in Ireland is because the Church, as it had done in education, gained control of the health, care, and social welfare of the people. It was mainly nuns, working from the principle that it should be a Catholic doctor and nurse who looked after Catholic patients, who began to build the hospitals and homes in which Catholics were trained, and who eventually took control of what had been until then a State-sponsored Protestant system. As an indication of just how successful this process was, Ryan estimates that by the beginning of the 1970s: "Religious personnel either owned or had charge of 46 private hospitals, 25 nursing and convalescent homes, 32 geriatric homes, 35 homes for the mentally handicapped, 11 homes for the physically handicapped, 31 orphanages, 29 industrial schools and reformatories, 15 welfare hostels, and 20 student or business hostels." It was within these hospitals and homes that the vast majority of doctors and nurses got their training and practical experience. The departments of medicine within the universities became dominated by the Catholic code of medical ethics. Religious and medical discourse became interlinked. The physical health and social welfare for the people were not divorced from their spiritual welfare.

Tom Inglis, *Moral Monopoly*, Dublin: Gill & Macmillan, 1987.
By kind permission.

questions

1. Why did the Church become increasingly interested in people's health?
2. What kind of support did the Church offer to the Irish health system?

5
Where the Celtic Tiger does not roam

Ireland's recent exceptional economic results have created new wealth which has not been evenly redistributed in society. Children are often the victims of this new poverty.

Still remember my first encounter with poverty. It was only ten or eleven months ago, when, as a young journalist, I went out on my first assignment on Dublin's spiralling drugs epidemic. I still remember having to hold my breath for fear of inhaling the smell of stale urine as I climbed the stairwell up to the fourth storey; and the dank almost unfurnished flat where the young recovering addict lived with her three children; and, despite the genuine hospitality, the constant enquiry "Are you sure you won't have some tea?", the relief I felt as I got on my bike and cycled away from that place, ten minutes across town, to the leafy lung of middle-class Ranelagh.

The bright children – tiny slips of things aged between eight and ten – variously clung to "Mam" or happened in and out on rollerblades. She, aged about thirty, clearly doted on them and no doubt, had as high hopes for them as she once had for herself. As happy, shining, as enthusiastic about pleading "When are we going into town?" as any child anywhere might be, I thought of them some time later when speaking to Dermott O'Driscoll, a youth worker in the Summerhill Youth Action Project in the North Inner-City.

"There's something tragic about a kid from around here who's just as witty, confident and happy with life as any other at age eight, but who by age 12 has lost that. Something somewhere along the line snaps", he said. "By that age they've realised that society has not got the same plans for them as they had for themselves."

The figures bear tragic testimony to his summation. While 54% of the bright young things of Dublin 4 go to university, less than 4% of those in Dublin 3 do. Indeed the proportion of children from the Summerhill area leaving full-time education before the age of 15 has been put at 44% – significantly higher than the 27% in Dublin or the 29% in Ireland as a whole. A survey quoted recently in The Irish Times told that of the long-term unemployed, 74% had not completed second-level education.

In the same April this year that the Economic and Social Research Institute heralded ten more years of economic boom for Ireland, a survey released by the EU statistics agency, Eurostat, found that between 340,000 and 376,000, or 28% of Irish children were living in poverty. (Poverty is defined by the ESRI as living on less than 60% of the average industrial wage).

According to Barnardo's the situation has worsened rather than improved in the last 20 years. The risk for children of being in poverty has risen from 26% to 29%-40% in the last ten years.

Kitty Holland, *Ceíde*, Sept-oct. 1997.

questions

1. How can the poverty be accounted for?
2. What choices would have to be made to improve the situation?

6
The dole queue

The young and the less young are lining up for their unemployment benefit.

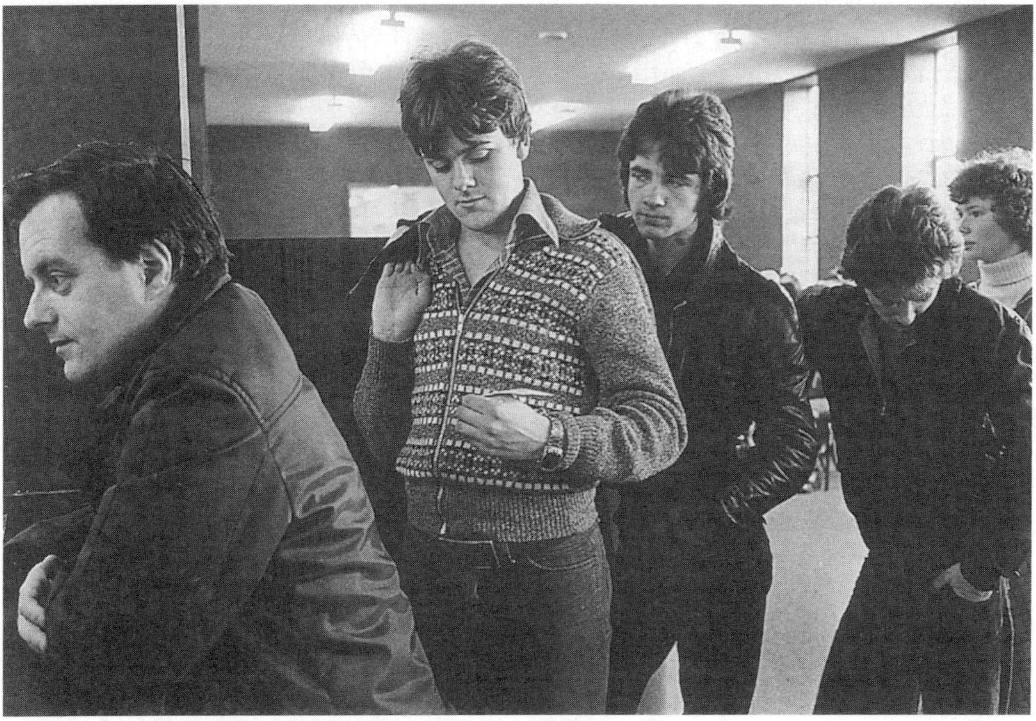

Ph. © Steele-Perkins/Magnum

questions

1. How serious is unemployment in Ireland?
2. Are there big differences between the North and the South in this area?

7
New drugs

Father Brendan Quinlan, administrator of Lourdes Parish in Dublin's north inner city, was officiating at the funeral of a young mother. She had died from AIDS after becoming infected from using a contaminated needle to inject heroin.

→

The wave of drug addiction in Dublin in the 1990s is different from that of earlier periods. The number of HIV virus carriers has greatly increased. Addiction starts at an earlier age and it is becoming more difficult to defeat the dealers.

She was one of the victims of a new wave of drug abuse which has been building up steadily since the start of the decade. It has been greeted with indifference by the wider society, many people in inner-city areas believe.

Yet the number of funerals still to come from the drug epidemic may have to be reckoned in hundreds if not in thousands. Estimates of the number of injecting drug-users in the greater Dublin area put the figure as high as 7,000 – enough to populate many an Irish town – with estimates of those among them carrying the HIV virus ranging from 11% to 35%.

As matters stand we can expect anything from 800 to 2,500 people in this group to die of AIDS in the coming years. Taking the most gloomy estimate, the current level of drug addiction in Dublin alone – where the heroin-injecting problem is largely concentrated – will kill roughly as many people as were killed in the conflict in Northern Ireland in the past quarter-century. [...]

There are important differences between the wave of addiction which afflicted many poor areas of the city in the 1970s and early 1980s and the current wave. "The age group is lower in regard to experimenting with drugs," Father Quinlan says. "I have known kids as young as 11 or 12 who are smoking hash on a fairly regular basis." Cannabis, he believes, is a "gateway to the hard stuff".

A community youth worker, Mr Paddy Malone, comments: "More young people are addicted now than in the 1980s. In the 1980s they would have been addicted at 18 or 19; now it's 13, 14, 15." [...]

Another difference between the problem now and the wave which subsided in the 1980s is "the pattern of dealing", according to Mr Mick Rafferty of the North City Centre Community Action Project. Dealing has become more dispersed instead of being concentrated in a small number of families, he says.

Consequently he does not believe that the kind of tactics used by the Concerned Parents groups in the 1980s would work this time. These tactics included forcing pushers to leave a particular area, but now, he says, "it's too widely going on in the community to simply knock on someone's door and say 'You are out'." [...]

Among a sample in a study of drug-abusers involved with the Merchants Quay Project in Dublin, almost one-third spent time in foster care or residential care when they were children. Almost half of their own children are living with relatives or in care.

The Irish Times, September 10, 1994.

questions

1. How has the drug scene changed since the 1970s?
2. How can the dealers be beaten?

8
Family Policy

In spite of the importance given to the family in the Constitution no specific family policy has been elaborated. The official Report "Strengthening Families for Life", of the Commission on the Family contains recommendations which ought to be at the centre of the Government's new family policy.

Strenghtening families for life

What is 'family policy'?

Family policy has never properly come into being in Ireland as a formal, separately identified segment of public policy – Ireland has never had a government department or office of the family and the term 'family policy' itself has only recently begun to be used in this country.

A change in designation of what formerly was the Department of Social Welfare to the Department of Social, Community and Family Affairs occured with the change in government in June 1997. The insertion of "family affairs" unto the department's title in this way marked a novel step for Ireland towards the formal identification of the family as a distinct area of responsibility in public administration, though the practical significance of that step is yet to emerge.

Though family policy traditionally has not existed in formal terms in Ireland, it may be identified in a less formal but nevertheless loosely structured way as an assortment of policy items drawn from a range of areas. These comprise both distributive measures, which provide supports to families in the form of income maintenance or services of various kinds (e.g. Child Benefit, One-parent family payments, housing supports, certain kinds of health services, etc.) and regulatory measures, which consist of laws that define what the family is and how family members can or should behave towards each other (as in the law on marriage, marital breakdown, family property, parents obligations to children, children's rights, along with constitutional provisions on the family, etc). The issues these measures touch on include not just 'family' in a general sense but also its component parts such as marriage, parenthood, childhood, reproductive matters, sexuality, housing, work in the home, family property, inheritance and so on.

Final report of the Commission on the Family to the Minister for Social, Community and Family Affairs, July 1998.

questions

1. Why is so much importance given to the family in the Constitution?
2. Why a report on the Family in 1998?

A multinational presence –
Analog Devices,
Limerick (see p. 111)
Ph. © IDA. By kind permission.

CHAPTER EIGHT

The Economy

Until 1921 the country formed one economic unit which, over time, had become increasingly dependent on Britain and had undergone uneven development within the island itself. The principal cause for the dependency was the increasing importance of the British market as an outlet for Irish products. Since the 1950s new economic policies and European membership have resulted in a profound transformation of the Irish economy

THE ECONOMY PRIOR TO PARTITION

English 17th century mercantilism was based to a certain extent on the necessity to control and restrict production in the neighbouring island of Ireland. The Cattle Acts (1663) and further legislation in 1667 placed heavy duties on animals imported from Ireland. The Navigation Acts (1663) obliged all Irish goods destined for the colonies to be shipped from England. Such restrictions were instrumental in imposing a dependency pattern on the Irish economy.

1 THE 18TH-CENTURY ECONOMY

The general picture, though, for the 18th century was one of sustained expansion and growth. Factory industry established itself. The textile industry was particularly successful. Large mechanized firms emerged in flour-milling which meant that expansion was not limited to textiles. In agriculture, the potato was to assume great importance. The increase of the total population was a further indication of an economic advancement which took place, however within the context of increased dependency. The best indication of this dependency is to be found in the proportion of Irish products exported to Britain which increased from 44% in 1720 to 85% on the eve of the Union, in 1801.

2 THE ECONOMY UNDER THE UNION

The project contained in the Act of Union* (1801) had an economic as well as a political content: free trade between Britain and Ireland. This solution was not to Ireland's advantage. The 19th century was one of global economic decline. Decline set in at the end of the Napoleonic Wars in 1815. It was dramatically and tragically illustrated by the Great Famine,* the principal economic effects of which were significant population decline, the increase in the size of landholdings, and a shift from tillage farming to pasture. Ireland became more and more a provider of cheap labour and agricultural products for Britain.

The north-east

Belfast was the exception. In the mid-19th century it distinguished itself from the rest of Ireland by building up two major industries: machine-woven linen and iron shipbuilding. Beyond Belfast and to a certain extent Derry, where shirt-making and tobacco-processing were major concerns, the remaining part of the northern province, being largely agricultural, had more in common with the greater part of the island. Like the rest of Ireland, it fully participated in the prosperity generated during the First World War, expressed by a heavy demand for ships, for linen, and for agricultural products.

Two distinct modes of production

On the eve of the creation of the two new political entities in Ireland, there were two quite different modes of production: the one in the south, with a limited industrial sector, was centred around farming, whereas the one in the north was centred around industry and skilled crafts. The conflictual political debate which was at the origin of partition contained equally conflicting economic positions. Nationalist protectionist ideas, put forward by Sinn Féin,* were totally rejected by the unionists,* for whom free trade was essential to maintain prosperity.

THE REPUBLIC OF IRELAND

The economy of the New State

The economy of the Free State* from 1922 to 1932 showed little or no change of economic policy from the past. No serious attempt was made to apply the protectionism advocated by Sinn Féin. The new government gave priority to agriculture. On the whole the economic policy of that first government was particularly cautious. It decided that the Irish pound would be maintained at an equal value with the pound sterling, thus keeping the country within the sterling area.

Protectionism

1932 heralded a new inward-oriented growth policy. This type of growth implied the production of home goods which, till then, had been imported. At the origin of the change in economic policy was the arrival to power of De Valera* at the head of Fianna Fáil* in 1932, committed to applying the Sinn Féin economic policy of self-sufficiency and to solving the problem of the land annuities* paid to Britain. De Valera, convinced that the annuities should be paid to the Irish Exchequer, refused to forward them to London, thus starting the Economic War,* in fact a battle of import duties. The six years which separated 1932 from 1938, when Dublin and London put an end to their quarrel, allowed the government to experiment with some of the ideas proposed by Sinn Féin. The measures were not severe enough to break the economic dependence on Britain. Yet they turned out, in the short term, to be wise measures in view of the needs in food of the population during the war. After the war unemployment increased. Emigration* soared. There was a balance of payments crisis in the mid-1950s. The nationalist protectionist policy was clearly a failure. It was time for change.

The opening up of the economy

This came in the form of outward-oriented growth. A series of Finance Acts introduced measures to favour exports. Grants were given for opening new factories. In 1958 the five-year Programme of Economic Expansion* was adopted. It aimed at channelling investment into increased production. The Control of Manufacturers Act* (1932), ensuring that control remained in Irish hands, was abolished also in 1958, reflecting the new belief that protection would have to go and be replaced by foreign investments and free trade. The two major steps taken to mark the end of protectionism were the Anglo-Irish Free Trade Agreement* (1965), and membership of the European Community* (1973). In spite of the global success of this economic policy, its fundamental weakness was heightened since Ireland became much more dependent on foreign trade and hence on international conditions. This meant that when the international economic crisis occurred in the 1970s, Ireland was not spared most of its effects.

Crisis

Four areas can be highlighted to examine those effects: production, trade, employment and finance. Agricultural production has undergone a long period of stagnation since the mid-1970s. The situation in manufacturing is, however, much brighter since production has more than doubled since the mid-1970s, particularly in electronics, chemicals, engineering and metals. Those industries are under the near exclusive control of foreign-owned firms. Those multinationals are capital-intensive and very inclined to withdraw their profits from the country. The fact that they do not put down solid local roots increases the dependent nature of the economy. Traditional Irish industry is, however, continuing to decline. Concentrated, to a large extent, on textiles, clothing and leather, those industries are very labour-intensive and have spin-off effects on the local economy. The performance of the multinationals means, however, that globally production has grown.

The increase in production was reflected in an increase in exports. Since 1985 the trade balance has been positive, which reveals the success of the country's industrial revolution but also reflected until the upturn of 1995 a decrease in imports caused by a decline in the demand for consumer goods (£18,000 million worth of exports as against £14,000 million worth of imports in 1993). In finance the major economic problem was the foreign debt. After 1973 borrowing increased to meet the needs of the public capital expansion programme but also to meet the current budget deficit. The tenfold increase in international oil prices was a severe blow to a country that imports 75% of its energy requirements. The increase in unemployment meant less revenue coming in and more benefits being paid by the state. The result by the mid-1980s was dramatic with the country indebted to the rate of one and a half times the GNP in 1987. By 1999 this had been reduced to a level which satisfied entry conditions to the Euro.

NORTHERN IRELAND

A good start

The particularly favourable war-time conditions outlived for some time the war itself which meant that when Northern Ireland* was created in 1921 it was done so in the best economic conditions possible. Belfast had the biggest shipbuilding industry in the world; linen and agriculture were prosperous.

Crisis

But immediate post-war conditions did not last. The 1920s, and above all the 1930s, were to be years of gloom. Unemployment averaged around 15% in the 1920s and moved up to 25% in the 1930s. In 1924 the linen industry employed almost 87,000 people. Ten years later the figure was reduced to 57,000. Over the same period the numbers in shipbuilding dropped from 20,000 to 2,000. The financial difficulties of the province were also accentuated during the same period. In 1938, London recognized that Northern Ireland was not only unable to continue paying the Imperial contribution but also to meet its own costs. It would have to be subsidized. Such has been the case since, with the result that the dependence of the province has greatly increased over time.

War time boom

The Second World War brought a halt to the situation of industrial decline. Shorts employed over 30,000 people in their aircraft industry. The shipyards were back to full production with 24,000 employed, and the linen industry, which was reoriented to meet wartime needs in clothing, had a workforce of over 60,000.

Post war gloom

The end of the war was, however, to see the repetition of the old difficulties for the staple industries of the North. An attempt at industrial diversification was made during the 1950s and 1960s. Goodyear, Michelin, Courtaulds, Dupont, ITT and ICI were among the transnational corporations which opened branch plants there. In spite of a decline in traditional local industry, the global result was one of increase in industrial employment.

New departures

This was a healthy development, given the fact that agriculture was becoming more and more capital-intensive. The jobs being lost there were being created in industry, but also in the service sector. In this latter sector jobs were created in the public services due to the extension to Northern Ireland of the Welfare State. However, a very high dependency continued to be the dominant characteristic of the economy during this period. The proportion of exports in relation to GNP was 70% in the mid 1960s, compared to 14% for the United Kingdom* as a whole. Another weak point to be mentioned was the branch-plant structure of the multinationals, which meant that they could close down any time and entirely abandon the province. Neither did they form many linkages with the rest of the economy.

Recession

Such weaknesses were to reinforce the impact of the world recession in the 1970s. The effect of the political violence though difficult to measure precisely, was also a contributory factor to the crisis which hit the province. Disinvestment, inflation, unemployment and de-industrialization were its hallmarks. Foreign investment since the 1970s has been only a shadow of what it was previously. Employment in industry, which accounted for 42% of all employment before the crisis, was reduced to 24% in the mid 1990s. Employment in agriculture over the same period declined from 16% to 6%. The services, however, have undergone a major increase, moving up from 42% to 70%. This of course is a very expensive operation for the government. When Northern Ireland was created it was able to pay its own way and contribute to the expenses of the empire. That is no longer the case today. The province is now being subsidized to the amount of £2,000 million a year.

Most economists would agree that the border between North and South constitutes a major hindrance to economic development in the two parts of the island. When one sees economic barriers being removed within the European Union, one would like to see greater economic collaboration, at least, develop between the Republic and Northern Ireland. The 1998 Agreement has opened up new possibilities in that area (see Chapter 14).

Even though there is much European and American backing, financial and otherwise, for economic recovery in Northern Ireland and for North-South economic cooperation, this will hardly give sufficiently satisfactory results until the political situation has been stabilized. As for the Republic of Ireland, it found itself, on the eve of the new century, in the position of being the country with the highest economic growth rate of all OECD countries.

FURTHER READING

KENNEDY, K.A., *The Economic Development of Ireland in the Twentieth Century*, London: Routledge, 1988.

KENNEDY, L. et al. (ed.), An *Economic History of Ulster*, Manchester: Manchester University Press, 1985.

MEENAN, J., *The Irish Economy since 1922*, Liverpool: Liverpool University Press, 1970.

TEAGUE, P., *Beyond the Rhetoric*, London: Lawrence & Wishart, 1987.

1
The Famine, a myth?

Some economic historians bend backwards to throw new light on the past. Because some of the trends which are described here emerged prior to 1845 the author justifies this approach.

The subject of the Great Famine of 1845-51 is of consuming interest to all who study Ireland's history. In the popular imagination this vast national calamity stands as the great divide; before the Famine there is the "old economy", and after it, the "new". The popular imagination views Ireland before the Famine as inhabited by small farmers who cultivated potatoes, grew some cereals, reared a pig or two, and, if they were affluent, owned a cow. These farmers lived at a bare subsistence level on milk and potatoes, selling their pigs and cereals to pay the rent and to earn cash for buying any other necessities. In the years prior to 1845 increasing pressure of population obliged them to subdivide the land to provide a livelihood for their many sons, who in turn, given a scrap of land, married early. Thus was the birth-rate further increased and the pressure on occupiers of land to subdivide reinforced.

The only crop capable of supporting a large family which held mere scraps of land was the potato. Such a dependence on one crop became progressively more dangerous because the harvest failed from time to time in various parts of Ireland and sooner or later there was bound to be a nation-wide failure. This danger was exacerbated by the introduction of high-yielding varieties of potatoes which were less resistant to disease. The Famine is interpreted thus as an inevitable and classic Malthusian check upon a population which had outstripped its resources.

The popular story continues with a representation of how the Irish learned a bitter and unforgettable lesson from the Famine. They were determined that they would not leave themselves so vulnerable again and for the farmer this meant many unpalatable alterations to his traditional way of life. Abandoning the potato as the means of self-sufficiency signified a new kind of farming involving substantially larger units. Such a change-over obliged all but one of the farm children to leave the land and emigrate. The sons who remained postponed marriage, and if they did marry at all, they married prudently, with an eye to enlarging their holding. The long-term effect on Ireland of these enormous upheavals was a population decline which left the survivors with larger and more viable holdings.

Thus reads the popular story. It is an account of two very different Irelands, so different they might be separate nations. The destructive force of the Famine snapped all links between them so that economic and social developments are invariably given a pre-Famine or a post-Famine label. It is a story feelingly retold over the years by popular historians, novelists, playwrights, and journalists. It is much loved by schoolteachers and schoolchildren because it is easily expounded.

J. M. Goldstrom, "Irish agriculture and the Great Famine", in *Irish Population, Economy and Society*, J. M. Goldstrom & L. A. Clarkson (ed.), Oxford: Clarendon, 1981. By kind permission of Oxford University Press.

questions

1. What were seen as the economic causes of the Famine?
2. What were the main consequences?

The weaknesses in performance [...] basically amount to a failure to overcome the key problems which existed at independence. Although in the course of independence the structure of the economy has been changed substantially for the better, and dependence on the slowly growing UK reduced, many of the major problems still remain unresolved. Indigenous industry is still weak, the potential of the land has not been adequately exploited, the labour surplus problem is as daunting as ever, and living standards have fallen further behind all Western European countries except Britain. It may be asked then if independence made a fundamental difference to the development of the economy. Any answer to this question, of course, is highly speculative because it is impossible to know how the economy would have fared had the Republic remained part of the UK. In particular, since such an arrangement was politically unacceptable, it could only have been maintained by coercion involving an incalculable degree of violence.

Even in the improbable event that the Republic had remained peacefully within the UK, there would undoubtedly have been significant differences in some sub-periods and in some sectors as compared with the actual evolution of the economy. Irish agriculture, for example, would have enjoyed greater prosperity between the 1930s and the 1960s, but there would have been far less indigenous manufacturing activity in the 1930s and fewer multinational enterprises from the 1960s onwards. Over the period as a whole, the differences in many areas would probably be less marked, but with the likelihood that the overall growth of output and employment would have been somewhat lower had Ireland stayed in the UK. Population would probably have fallen even more, but on the other hand, living standards might very well have been higher given that Ireland would have benefited from the UK fiscal transfers and would not have incurred the burden of such a huge national debt. In other words, the pattern might have been very much a continuation of that established in the half century or so before independence. If so, then independence *did* make a difference. It raised the overall economic growth rate sufficient to at least arrest the decline in population, though not enough to absorb fully the perennial labour surplus or to secure a faster growth in average living standards. This achievement is of course much less than was expected at independence, but then, as we have said, such expectations were unrealistically high.

K. A. Kennedy, T. Giblin and D. McHugh,
The Economic Development of Ireland in the Twentieth Century,
London: Routledge, 1988. By kind permission.

2

Did independence matter?

While Irish nationalists had very high expectations at independence, its achievement did not solve every economic problem.

questions

1. What would the economic advantages have been if Ireland had remained part of the United Kingdom?
2. What economic progress was made?

3
A socio-economic profile of Ireland

The move from a closed to an open economy has profoundly changed socio-economic development in Ireland.

The underdevelopment of the Republic's economy prior to independence was a feature of British domination, the evolution of the capitalist word system and the subsequent divisive nature of the international division of labour within Europe. The contemporary form of uneven development has been shaped since the 1950s by the Republic's reintegration within the global economy, the evolution of neo-Fordist relations of production and the Republic's intermediate position within the New International Division of Labour. Reintegration, in this instance, was achieved through the abandonment of economic nationalism in favour of a pseudo-cosmopolitanism and almost total subservience to international capital (Smyth, 1991). The removal of the previous protectionist regime of economic development was based on a development path linked to industrialisation through invitation and outward-oriented growth (Munck, 1993). The main form of industrialisation during this period has been characterised by a disarticulated form of location based on fragmented production units and the decentralisation of manual execution (Perrons, 1981). The attraction of Foreign Direct Investment (FDI) has been a central strategy within the Neo-Fordist Regime (NFR). Although both economies have relied heavily upon foreign investment as a developmental structure, the Republic's continued and unfettered allegiance toward FDI has been more pronounced and ceaselessly illustrated by the growth in foreign capital ownership and the free importation of means of production and exportation of profits (Sklair, 1988). The demise of the indigenous sector and the promotion of export-led development during the NFR have meant that Transnational Corporations (TNCs) have come to play a decisive role within the Republic's economy. By 1989 over half (56 per cent) of the total gross output of manufacturing industries and 70 per cent of net output was controlled by TNCs (Department of Industry and Commerce, 1993).

It would appear that the main role of the Irish state within the NFR, as a facilitator of accumulatory activities of both the foreign and indigenous bourgeoisie, has been relatively successful. In relation to economic growth indicators the NFR has been characterised by improved terms of trade and significant growths in Gross National Product (GNP) and Gross Domestic Product (GDP), and a marked increase in labour productivity per employed person. For example, between 1981 and 1993 the value of GNP and exports grew by 61 per cent and £7152 billion respectively (Banc Ceannais Na hEireann, 1992; OECD, 1993).

Development Ireland, Contemporary Issues, Peter SHIRLOW (ed), Pluto Press, 1995.

questions

1. What role do multinationals play in Ireland's economy?
2. What are the implications of such a role for state sovereignty?

4

The manufacturing sector in Northern Ireland

The performance of the Northern Ireland economy between 1963 and 1989 has been profoundly influenced by the results of the manufacturing sector.

A

Although radical changes have taken place in Northern Ireland manufacturing during the past three decades, in some important ways the more recent developments can be seen as a continuation of an historical evolution that started after the First World War. Immediately after the foundation of Northern Ireland, the first Annual Census of Production in 1924 showed that three sub-sectors of manufacturing (textiles, food, drink and tobacco, and shipbuilding, engineering and metal) accounted for 89.8 per cent of gross output. At the start of the troubles in 1969, the share had declined only marginally to 85.8 per cent. The most recent ACOP for Northern Ireland that was available to us (for the year 1993) shows the continued dominance of these traditional sectors, with textile products, food, drink and tobacco, and transport equipment still accounting for over 55 per cent of total employment in manufacturing.

Prior to the UK entry into the then EEC in 1973, Northern Irelan, of course, always functioned within a regime of mainly free trade, with full access to the large British and Commonwealth markets. UK policy as applied in Northern Ireland included a regional employment premium scheme of wage subsidies, as well as other subsidy and grant-based policies to promote indigenous industry and attract external investment. However, Northern Ireland's main industrial sectors were in decline, and it failed to attract sufficient external investment to offset the inevitable job losses.

Since the Northern Ireland home market was so small, the local manufacturing sector simply could not efficiently supply all its different needs through local production of import substitutes. Rather, economic efficiency requirements dictated that it specialise in a narrow range of products, sell in highly competitive export markets, and import the goods not produced locally. However, analysis of the ACOP data since 1926 shows that local specialisation tended to continue in the same three areas that had characterised the Northern Ireland economy at its zenith; namely, food and allied products, textiles and a range of transport equipment (Bradley and McCartan, 1997).

Regional Economic and Policy Impacts of EMU: The Case of Northern Ireland.
Northern Ireland Economic Development Office, April 1998.

→

questions

1. Analyse the trend in manufacturing.
2. How does it compare with that of the Republic?

B

The Evolution of Manufacturing Employment: Northern Ireland, UK and the Republic of Ireland, 1963-1989

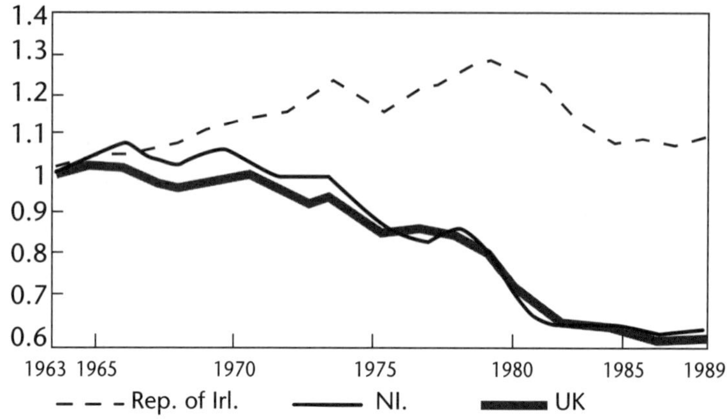

Northern Ireland and UK: *Business Monitor*, various issues; RoI; *Labour Force Survey*, various issues.

questions

1. Compare the differents trends.
2. Put forward some reasons which explain the differences in growth in the three cases given.

5
Public spending in the Republic

The economic development of the Republic of Ireland has depended heavily on both the state's financial support and foreign capital.

questions

1. How did public spending evolve?
2. What are the main implications of indebtedness?

Republic of Ireland public spending

	1983	1985	1987	1989	1990	1991	1992
Public spending as % of GNP	42.8	44	42.6	50	47.7	48.8	47.6
	Share of main categories of spending in total public spending						
Public investment	12.6	10.8	8.7	6.7	7.3	7.0	7.2
Productive infrastructure	5.2	4.5	3.3	3.1	3.5	3.4	3.5
Social infrastructure	4.1	3.8	3.3	1.4	1.5	1.3	1.3
Current spendings of central administration	53.3	54.9	52.8	43.1	43.5	44.2	45.4
Interest paid on national debt (of which proportion of interest on external debt)	9.9	11.5	10.5	9.3	9.3	8.8	8.2

Source: *Budget Statements*, CSO National Income and Expenditure.

6
Inside the Celtic Tiger

The Irish are very proud of their economic growth. However, the price to pay for new-found prosperity may be increasing economic dependence.

[…] Something has happened in Ireland in the 1990s. The popular view has been that the Southern Irish economy has become a 'tiger', the most dynamic economy in Europe and even in the OECD. While the figures show that Ireland is no tiger economy in the East Asian sense, one has to admit that its record of economic growth in the 1990s, especially since 1993, has been impressive. Most experts expect this dynamism to continue well into the next century. But few have looked closely at the structure of growth, and especially at the drastic levels of increasing dependence Ireland has had to encourage to achieve its rates of growth. Recent economic history raises the question about whether such dependent growth can be maintained in the long run, at least without the kinds of networked structures that have allowed domestic companies in the East Asian economies to emerge and upgrade. And even in East Asia there are limits to growth, including the 'glass ceilings" on technology upgrading that appear to keep the highest-tech product development in the US and Japan, or the chronic problems of maintaining levels of skill-formation that match the needs of an expanding economy. […]

It is the economic growth aspects of tigerhood that have drawn most admiration from observers of Ireland in the 1990s. I have tried to show that Irish growth may face structural limitations, especially if global downswings bite at the foreign-led sectors in which this growth is so concentrated. Surely, the recent Asian experience tells us that no country, even the fabled Asian tiger economies, can depend on rapid growth all the time. But it is not just growth, or even primarily growth, that raises questions about Ireland as a tiger economy. Even in its most successful phases – the years from 1993 onward – there have been nagging questions about whether Ireland, even with its high growth rates, can provide adequate work for its people or distribute the fruits of economic growth in an equitable way.

Denis O'Hearn, *Inside the Celtic Tiger, The Irish Economy and the Asian Model*, 1998, Pluto Press.

questions

1. Why the necessity for overseas industry?
2. How can the role of multinationals be assessed?

7
The industrialization of Ireland

See p. 100.

A multinational presence – Analog Devices, Limerick

question

Does this photo fit into your image of Ireland?

A feminist protest in Dublin (see p. 123)
Ph. © Betson / Inpho

CHAPTER NINE

Irish Women

In the 1990s, women emerged on the public scene to an extent previously useen in contemporary Ireland. The changes in Irish society, as has been seen in Chapter 7, have largely contributed to that situation. Prior to that, with some notable exceptions, they were, to a large extent, excluded from the life of the city. Inequality and discrimination are at the root of this exclusion. Added to this, one can find fault with the way historians have written women out of history. Women's real contribution to Ireland's past and present is only now being given its rightful place.

Women in Early Ireland

While little is known about women in Early Ireland, and what is known has been transmitted by monk-scribes, it would nevertheless seem that their status was higher than in other societies, notably that of Rome, during the same period. Equality between men and women, in the eyes of the law, was not however absolute. In early Irish law, often called Brehon law*, each person had a "price" which was calculated according to rank and worth within society. A crime against a man or woman was seen as an offence against his or her honour so an honour-price, and a further penalty, a form of atonement, had to be paid. The honour-price of a king, for instance, was the value of seven female slaves while that of his wife was only half as much. But articles of law tell us little about the way society actually worked. And the daily lives of Irish women for centuries still remain largely a closed book. It was not until the end of the 18th and in the 19th centuries that the mark that women left in a number of areas of public life became known. One thinks of the religious and educational fields, of the Land War,* of the suffragette* movement, and of the republican movement prior to independence.

WOMEN IN MODERN IRELAND

1 RELIGIOUS CONGREGATIONS

By the Penal Laws*, Catholics were forbidden from teaching school publicly or in private houses. Schools did exist, but their aim was to teach the children to speak and read English and to be instructed in the principles of the Protestant faith. With the relaxation of those laws at the end of the 18th century religious congregations of nuns and brothers were created to fight against the proselytism of the Protestant school system. Three congregations for nuns were created before Catholic Emancipation*: the Mercy Nuns, the Presentation Nuns and the Irish Sisters of Charity. To those must be added a number of French religious congregations which set up convents in Ireland. The areas where these congregations exercised their activities, in education or health, afforded an opportunity for Irish women, generally of comfortable rural stock or of the middle-class, who either were unable to marry for one reason or another, or who did not wish to do so, to participate in a social activity of immense value. In a period when women, all over the British isles, were excluded from public life, and confined more and more to the domestic sector, religious life offered an alternative existence. It is only recently that the work they accomplished is beginning to become the object of careful historical scrutiny.

2 THE LADIES' LAND LEAGUE

The Ladies' Land League* is a further example of the same phenomenon. Just like religion, the land problem was a fundamental issue in Irish politics and a major day-to-day preoccupation for the majority of the population of Ireland. The historic grievance resulting from confiscation, the unjust conditions imposed by many landlords, and the absence of legal protection meant that there was much to be done to right past wrongs.

In 1879 the Irish League* was founded in Dublin. Charles Stewart Parnell* was elected president and Michael Davitt* secretary. Because of the disastrous economic conditions of that year the immediate aim in 1879 was to gain rent reduction. According to the strategy adopted by the Land League, the tenants who were able to pay the rent were to refrain from doing so until the landlord reduced the rent of all the tenants.

In order to help finance its activity, Fanny Parnell*, a sister of Charles, founded the Ladies' Land League in New York (October 1880). In January 1881, a branch was set up in Dublin and Anne Parnell,* Fanny's sister, became its leader. Soon it had taken over most of the running of the Irish Land League: it processed the applications for relief and distributed help to the tenants who qualified. Anna Parnell travelled widely all over Ireland, and to areas in England and Scotland, where there were large Irish communities, explaining the aims of the Land League and encouraging the creation of new branches of the Ladies' Land League. In February 1881, when Michael Davitt, Charles Stewart Parnell and most of the other national leaders were imprisoned, the Ladies' Land League set about building up support for the no-rent campaign. Throughout the eighteen months of its existence friend and foe alike agreed that it had done remarkable work. Its activities constantly hit the headlines of the Irish, English and Irish-American press. Nevertheless, until recently, this work has received scant attention among Irish historians and Anna Parnell, who wrote an account of the Ladies' Land League, never found a publisher.

3 MILITANT WOMEN

While the end of the 19th century and the beginning of the 20th was a period of great cultural national awareness, it was also the period of the suffragette movement, of the revival of republicanism, and of the birth of a labour movement. In the general mobilisation of the period women were to play a large role and at the same time they set about creating women's groups in support of the nationalist cause. Women like Lady Gregory* were active in the Irish literary revival* and others, like Mary MacSwiney,* in the suffragette movement. Francis Sheehy-Skeffington* added his efforts to their action which soon extended to other areas.

Republicans

In 1909, Constance Markievicz,* an Irish woman, who having married a Polish count became Countess Markievicz, created a republican youth movement, Fianna Éireann.* Nine years earlier she had assisted Maude Gonne MacBride* in the creation of a separatist women's movement, Inghinidhe na hÉireann,* which was absorbed into a new women's movement, Cumann na mBan,* founded in Dublin at the same time as the Irish Volunteers,* of which it became the women's division. By 1916, it had 43 affiliated branches all over the country, all supporting the republican rising* of Easter week.

The national question vs women's rights

In the early 1900s, the role of women in Ireland was very circumscribed. Those women who had obtained qualifications were paid less than men with the same qualifications. Working-class women found themselves in a comparable situation to middle-class women with the important difference that their wages were abysmally low. After the 1910 elections, the Irish Party,* with 84 seats in the House of Commons of Westminster,* decided to support a government formed by the Liberal Party on condition that a bill for Home Rule* for Ireland would be introduced in Parliament. The Liberals, however, were opposed to the extension of the right to vote to women. Considering that the cause of a free Ireland was more important than the vote for women, Mary MacSwiney for instance, backed the Irish Party's decision.

Politicians

Refusing to limit themselves to purely auxiliary activities some of those women participated fully in the events of the period. During the rising Constance Markievicz was second-in-command to the forces in St Stephen's Green in Dublin.

Later she was sentenced to death but, just as with De Valera,* the sentence was commuted. This allowed her to stand as a Sinn Féin* candidate for the United Kingdom* general election in December 1918. She was returned and thus became the first woman to be elected to the House of Commons. It is to be remembered that in 1918 all men, aged 21 and over, and all women aged 30 and over, got the right to vote. However, like all the newly elected Sinn Féin members, Constance refused to take her seat in Westminster. With the creation of the Dáil* she was given the cabinet post of minister of Labour. It was thought that she was particularly suited for the post since during the famous 1913 Lock-Out* she had played a major role in organising the strike.

WOMEN IN CONTEMPORARY IRELAND

1 NORTHERN WOMEN

The contribution of women to the fight for independence and to the creation of a new State was such that it could be expected that they would play a prominent part in political life in the new Ireland. This was not to be the case for a long time. In Northern Ireland* women, until emergence of the Women's Coalition in 1996, have been noticeably absent from the political scene, having been clearly assigned a secondary role. Women are not allowed to join the Orange Order* and within the unionist party* they are organized separately. As elsewhere in the United Kingdom, women in Ulster* did not obtain the right to vote in the same conditions as men until 1928. Since the beginning of the conflict only one woman has represented the province in Westminster and that was the Catholic republican socialist, Bernadette Devlin,* who was elected in the early days of the conflict. The part played by women in the Republican movement and their intense activity in peace and reconciliation movements is of the greatest importance.

2 SOUTHERN WOMEN

In the South, the women who had been so active in the independence cause disappeared from the scene soon after 1922. One reason which explains this withdrawal was that all those who were elected to the Dáil opposed the Treaty and were absent therefore from the Dáil during the formative years of the new state. The growing influence of the Catholic Church, the increasing conservatism of the political elite and the economic difficulties of the period meant that, in spite of the fact that the 1922 Constitution allowed women to vote in the same conditions as men, the environment was in no way favourable to the expansion of women's rights. Unlike Northern Ireland, however, things began to change in the Republic in the 1970s. In 1973, a woman acceded to ministerial rank. In 1981, 6.6% of all deputies were women; in 1987, 8.4%

and in 1922, 12%. In a country where the majority of the electorate is female those figures indicate that there has been progress and nothing more. The election of Mary Robinson* as President of Ireland in 1990 did, however, constitute a significant event. Having been active for many years in the cause of women's rights, her accession to the highest post in the state could not but be interpreted as a victory for sexual equality. The fact that four of the five candidates for the 1997 presidential election were women, and that a woman, Mary McAleese, succeeded Mary Robinson, continued the progress made.

3 RIGHTS AND EQUALITY

Whether one considers rural women or urban women, much remains to be achieved in Ireland, both North and South in the field of specific women's rights and of equality. Women in rural Ireland have seen their status change considerably since the 19th century. With the modernisation of farm work the labour of rural women in the fields was required less and less. They did, however, retain power in and around the home. Indeed the efficient running of the farm depended heavily on women's labour. Developments within agriculture have forced more and more rural women out of such areas as milking, egg and poultry production, and calf and pig rearing. They have taken on a role more typical of the urban housewife and at the same time have lost their economic power.

With increasing urbanization and indeed with increasing numbers of women taking employment Irish women are faced with a number of problems inherited from the past and a number produced by the modernization of society. As seen in Chapter 7, until the late 1970s the sale of contraceptives was illegal. Abortion is still forbidden by law. Women's salaries are only 70% of those of men. Women suffer more from unemployement and poverty than men. It must be said though that thanks to the efforts of women's movements, to European intervention and to a certain amount of goodwill in governmental circles, efforts have been made to introduce reform. A first report by the Commission on the Status of Women* was published in 1972 and a second one twenty years later. Ignorance can therefore no longer be an excuse for not taking action. The principle of employment equality was adopted and new and fairer legislation has been introduced to protect the rights of the housewife.

FURTHER READING

CURTIN, C. et. al. (ed.), *Gender in Irish Society*, Galway: Galway University Press, 1987.
PYLE, J. L., *The State and Women in the Economy*, Albany: State University of New York Press, 1990.
SMITH, A., *The Abortion Papers*, Dublin: Attic Press, 1992.
WALSH, T. J., *Nano Nagle and the Presentation Sisters*, Dublin: Gill, 1959.

—1—
Irish women in the early 19th century

Landlord, radical, democrat, socialist and supporters of women's emancipation, William Thompson argues here in favour of their political rights. Such ideas were new at the beginning of the 19th century.

Political rights are necessary to women as a check on the almost inveterate habits of exclusion of men. It is in vain to sanction by law a civil right, or to remove an exclusion, if the law affords no means to those whom it designs to benefit of causing the right or permission to be enforced [...]. Though the present exclusions of women, particularly in marriage, from most of the rights of property, as well as from almost all other rights, were removed, it is very probable that, partly from want of inclination, partly from motives of convenience, numbers of women qualified would not offer themselves for offices, and would not exercice their political rights; yet would the consciousness in the minds of men of such powers of control existing amongst women cause them so to regulate their conduct, as to render for the most part unnecessary any party display of their power. In all cases where partiality was only suspected, women would of course exercice their rights. If but few women were themselves elected as representatives, their influence would cause such men to be elected as would enact equal laws between the two great portions of the race, or would cause such men as showed an inclination to revive the old reign of brutality and injustice to be replaced by other men or by women. Now it is possible to conceive that any set of legislators, male or female, particularly men, would not be more inclined to make and preserve laws of entire reciprocity and equal justice between women and men, when they knew that their constituents were equally balanced, and that injustice on their part would necessarily enlist a few of either party amongst the injured half, and thus create a majority of the whole constituents against them? Under the system of exlusive political rights, though nearly one half of men joined with the whole of women in reprobation of unequal laws, those laws, as long as there was a majority of one of the whole males in favor of injustice, could persevere in injustice, in contempt of the wishes of three fourths, wanting one, of the whole race. Under the system of non-exclusion, all men but one could not effect injustice against women. The one just man giving his casting vote for the equal votes of women, would wipe away from men the opprobrium of the meditated wrong. Who can doubt then of the necessity of the enjoyment of equal political rights by women as a preservative against the possibility of the monstrous evil of three fourths, wanting one, of every community being every day liable to be oppressed by one fourth, plus one? Nothing less than giving equal rights to all, men and women, can guard against such evils, can promote the equal happiness of all.

William Thompson, *An Appeal of one Half of the Human Race, Women, Against the Pretensions of the Other Half, Men...*, 1825.

questions

1. Why are political rights necessary to women?
2. What would happen, according to Thompson, if women had their political rights?

2
The Irish women's movement

The Ireland of the early 1900s was one of renewed awareness. The suffrage movement and the Gaelic Revival found many supporters all over the country. Mary MacSwiney came to nationalism through the women's movement.

A

The vote for women was a matter of justice to Mary. As contributing members of society, women should have the full rights of citizenship. To her, it was only logical that in a free society, women should share in the choice of governmental representatives. She rejected as illogical, and contrary to her own experience, the arguments of anti-suffragists that women were mentally inferior to men, that women's constitutions were too weak to withstand the rigours of politics, that God had put men at the top of the natural order, or that women were too emotional to be charged with choosing elected officials. She particularly resented the fact that denial of the vote placed all women on the "level of imbeciles and lunatics". Her association with the suffrage movement, through membership in the Munster Women's Franchise League, was the first gate through which Mary passed on her way to involvement in Irish politics. She did not go forward reluctantly as much as unsuspectingly.

B

The years 1912-14 were particularly vital ones for both the Irish Home Rulers and the suffrage movement. Following the second election of 1910, the Irish Nationalists controlled 84 seats in parliament, with Liberals having 272, Conservatives 272, and Labour 42. Because the Nationalists held the balance, it was a propitious time to seek action on Ireland. The Liberals, under Asquith's leadership, promised Home Rule if the Irish would support the government on other issues, one being the denial of the franchise to women. Although many of the Irish Nationalists supported the idea of female enfranchisement, they fell in line behind their leader, John Redmond, rejecting the extension of the franchise on the promise of Home Rule which had been presented as an "either-or" proposition. Many Irish parliamentarians echoed Mary MacSwiney's idea that "if Ireland were free, women would get the vote". This was a rather utopian belief, with little basis in reality, when the strong influence of the Church in Irish life is considered along with the poor support for the women's movement. Nonetheless it is illustrative of the rhetoric used in promotion of a free Ireland.

Charlotte H. Fallon, *Soul of Fire, A Biography of Mary McSwiney*, Cork and Dublin: The Mercier Press, 1986.
By kind permission.

questions

Text A

1. What was Mary MacSwiney's understanding of the suffrage movement?
2. Why does the author say that Mary went forward unsuspectingly?

Texte B

1. What sort of political blackmail damaged the women's cause in the years 1912-1914?
2. How did Mary MacSwiney compare women's rights to national rights?

3
Women and the 1937 Constitution

The 1937 Constitution gave a special position to women within the family in Ireland.

questions

1. What is the role of women within the Irish state?
2. How does the Constitution seek to protect women?

The Family ARTICLE 41

1. 1° The State recognises the Family as the natural primary and fundamental unit group of Society, and as a moral institution possessing inalienable and imprescriptible rights, antecedent and superior to all positive law.
   2° The State, therefore, guarantees to protect the Family in its constitution and authority, as the necessary basis of social order and as indispensable to the welfare of the Nation and the State.
2. 1° In particular, the State recognises that by her life within the home, woman gives to the State a support without which the common good cannot be achieved.
   2° The State shall, therefore, endeavour to ensure that mothers shall not be obliged by economic necessity to engage in labour to the neglect of their duties in the home.
3. 1° The State pledges itself to guard with special care the institution of Marriage, on which the Family is founded, and to protect it against attack.
   2° No law shall be enacted providing for the grant of a dissolution of marriage.
   3° No person whose marriage has been dissolved under the civil law of any other State but is a subsisting valid marriage under the law for the time being in force within the jurisdiction of the Government and Parliament established by this Constitution shall be capable of contracting a valid marriage within that juridiction during the lifetime of the other party to the marriage so dissolved.

Constitution of Ireland, 1937, Dublin: Stationery Office.

4
The role of women in Irish history

Margaret Ward, in her pamphlet on Irish history, voices her concern about the fact that women have no visible past, even now when Irish history is being rewritten.

There has been so much discussion over the political direction of the various new history texts that have emerged in recent years that now seems an appropriate time in which to raise another, possibly more uncomfortable question concerning those same histories: why are women not featured more prominently within their pages? Those engaged in the production of history have been mostly concerned with the implications of "revisionism". It is a political controversy, largely conducted by men, fuelled by those who want to distance the profession from any taint of nationalist sympathy, but what does all this mean for women? We seem to be invisible whatever the particular ideological view of the historian. Who are the people who make history? The argument rarely seems to touch upon the human content of the narrative. Conventional historiography has given us kings, with the odd queen thrown in, and rebellious chiefs and politicians, with the peasantry popping in and out of the picture. In the last couple of decades the working class has managed to shoulder its way onto the scene and the history of the Irish working class is now rapidly unfolding, thanks to the diligence of a new generation of historians. But it is all strangely women-free. Where are they? What have they been up to for the past few hundred years? Does anyone know or care, and can we get hold of the source material that will enable us to discover their hidden history? If we do, do we just "add women and stir" and let the stew of Irish history thicken with this female addition?

Men have written women out of history, that is an undeniable truth, and it has occured despite the fact that in many instances the history of women's struggles has been available for those who have had the inclination to look beyond their prejudices.

Margaret Ward, *The Missing Sex: Putting Women into Irish History*, Dublin: Attic Press, 1991.

questions

1. How have those who "make history" made it?
2. How have women been excluded from history?

5
Women in rural Ireland

Women in rural Ireland, until recent times, were valued above all else for their fertility

Once countryman of North Clare put that first year into words: "At first," he said, "the boy's people make much of the new woman. They would hardly let her work at all. This carries on for seven or eight months, and if then the old people don't see evidence of increase of young, they get angry and abuse her. But if they do, they don't let her do any work at all now and are so proud."

In such a situation barrenness is a curse and a disgrace. The husband has every right to express his disappointment and his displeasure. It is a source of shame to him as well. He fails in preserving the continuity of his line upon the land.

One childless woman of Inagh in Clare knew bitterly how much both family and community support these attitudes: "No matter how much money you have," she said, "no matter how good-looking you are, if you don't have children, you are no good. But if you are ugly as the worst and have children, you are all right." Then she went on, to perpetrate an Irish bull, perhaps, but to express the matter very forcibly: "The man wants children just as much as the woman. He is afraid others will tell him he is no good if he hasn't any. Children are the curse of this country, especially if you haven't any."

Accordingly, the chief duty of the "new woman" is to bear children. She succeeds or fails as a supplier of new persons to the family. Only →

with children can the new balance complete itself and the essential social continuity be assured.

The old couple appraise their daughter-in-law upon her success in this role. The first year of the girl's marriage is a time of apprenticeship. Her work is light. Highly ceremonialized custom grants her an occasional escape back to her own people. Her major duty is pregnancy, and the old couple watch her like a hawk for signs of fertility. All during her child-bearing years the old people will help her, praising her in terms of her increase, and showing as great an interest in the arriving children as she does herself.

Conrad M. Arensberg, *The Irish Countryman*, Gloucester, Mass: Peter Smith, 1959.

questions

1. What where the attitudes towards barrenness?
2. What was the chief duty of the new wife on an Irish farm?

6

The women's movement in the 1960s and 1970s

The 1960s and 1970s saw the birth and development of the Women's movement in Ireland. Its task was a difficult one.

Once contraception became available in the Western world on a wide scale the Women's Liberation Movement was almost inevitable. Women's control of their fertility altered their relationship to man, and to the world.

Other causes which brought the movement into being have been well documented: the suffocation of women and children in the nuclear family, the emphasis in modern society on doing rather than being, which stripped women of their traditional functions and conferred all power on men, the doers.

In Ireland the Women's Movement began with a small articulate group who launched straight into a campaign for contraception. From that grew reform groups, radical lesbian groups, groups who provided safety nets like the Hostel for Battered Wives. Women's liberation is no longer a joke, though it still arouses a great deal of antagonism. But slowly the bedrock is being chipped away with laws for equal pay, equal employment opportunity, equal division of family property.

Much remains to be done. Education is still sex based (cooking for girls, science for boys); illegitimacy is still seen as a girl's mistake, not the boy's, and she has to pay for it; the chaotic laws on separation, nullity and desertion usually militate most against the woman, who is least able to afford the legal costs of trying to sort them out; contraception is still a luxury and not a right; the Act still exists whereby a husband can sue a man who's estranged his wife for what the court believes to be the value in cash of her domestic and sexual services; women still only earn 65% of what men do, and only 3% of managers are female.

Most liberation movements fuel themselves on anger, a sense of injustice. The Women's Movement is no exception, though perhaps it is more dangerous, being as it were at the heart of the matter. Fear, the basis of all nastiness, will probably mean an increase in sexual violence before things settle down: rape increased by 100% in Dublin in 1977.

Rosita Sweetman, *On our Backs*, London: Pan Book Original, 1979.

questions

1. Why is women's liberation no longer a joke?
2. What remains to be done?

7

Women protest in Belfast

Ph. © G/M – Camera Press

Banging dustbin lids to warn of the arrival of British soldiers

questions

1. Why was this warning system necessary? 2. What did it achieve?

8

A feminist protest in Dublin

See p. 112.

Demonstrators protest outside government buildings in Dublin during the referendum campaign on abortion in 1992.

questions

1. What issues were involved in this referendum? 2. What solutions were found?

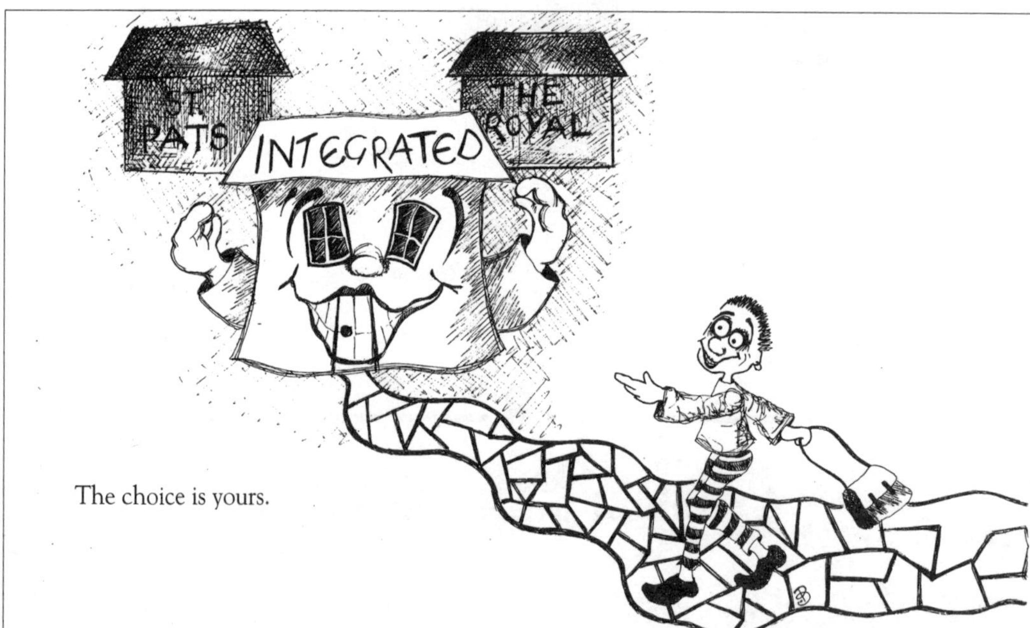

From separation to integration (see p. 134)
© Biddy Healy in *Integrated Schools, Information for Parents* by Dorothy Wilson and Seamus Dunn, Centre for the Study of Conflict, University of Ulster, Coleraine

CHAPTER TEN

Education

The Republic* and Northern Ireland* now have distinct educational systems. In both parts of the island, education is becoming the focus of increasing concern on the part of political and religious institutions, parents and teachers. New developments which will be interesting to follow are the creation of all Irish schools *(Gaelscoileanna)* both in Northern Ireland and in the Republic.

IRISH EDUCATION YESTERDAY

1 EDUCATION BEFORE 1831

Before 1831, there were few recognized schools in Ireland. During the Cromwellian Regime and later under the Penal Code* which operated until the end of the 18th century legitimate means of education for Catholics were suppressed. This was a cruel blow for a country which had attracted students to its monastic schools as early as the 6th century. The bardic schools* of the old Gaelic* Order had disappeared by the middle of the 17th century. The English had introduced schools in the 16th century. Their extension was however very limited since such schools taught only in English and were Protestant. Though it was illegal for Catholics to have their own schools, they did succeed in organizing lessons in hedge schools* from the 17th to the 19th centuries. It was in those makeshift schools that Irish Catholic children learned how to read and to write. Some would go on later to the Irish colleges in Europe for further education.There were two Irish colleges in Paris, one in Nantes, Douai, Bordeaux, Lille and Toulouse. There were also colleges in Italy, Belgium, Spain, Portugal and the Netherlands.

2 FROM 1831 TO PARTITION

The educational structure was to evolve differently at primary and secondary levels.

Primary education

The first Irish National School System* was set up in 1831 to anglicize Ireland and, it was hoped, to contribute to the reconciliation of the Protestant and Catholic communities. While being non-denominational, schools were to provide for religious education given by clergymen of the different churches. The state was to fund the building of schools. It also contributed to teachers' salaries and to the publishing and distribution of school books.

The churches, however, reacted against what they regarded as a reduction of their educational prerogatives. Consequently, the Powis Commission on Education (1870) recommended the official recognition of denominational schools, thereby reinforcing two features underlying Irish education ever since: denominational segregation and the hold of the churches on the school system.

Secondary education

Most secondary schools were under the responsibility of religious congregations which began to open Catholic schools at the end of the 18th century. Church or privately run schools catered for the needs of Protestant children. The Intermediate Education Act (1878) provided for the distribution to all schools of funds coming from the disestablishment of the Church of Ireland in 1870. But as the Act did not establish any official state education system at secondary level, the control of the churches and denominational segregation persisted.

Technical education

It was created by the Agriculture and Technical Instruction (Ireland) Act (1899). It was non-denominational and vocational.

Third-level

Elizabeth I founded Trinity College Dublin, in 1592 for Protestant Ireland. It was not until 1850 that Belfast, Cork and Galway got their Universities. The National University of Ireland (NUI)* was set up in 1908 incorporating the University Colleges of Galway, Cork and Dublin. Queen's University Belfast did not join the National University.

3 FROM PARTITION TO THE 1980S

Partition led to the complete separation and reorganization of the educational systems in the north and the south.

Northern Ireland

A New Structure

Successive measures and Education Reform Acts shaped the educational system of Northern Ireland.

- A Ministry of Education headed by Lord Londonderry was established in 1921.
- The Education Reform Act (1923) divided the system into state schools (fully state-funded and de facto Protestant as no Catholic pupils attended them) and independent schools, mainly attended by Catholic pupils.
- Religious education was left to each school's initiative.
- The question of funding, however, remained controversial – the fact that the state increased its financial contribution to independent schools angered part of the Protestant community which expected a "Protestant state" to support Protestant education exclusively.

The 1960s and the 1970s

The 1960s heralded in a long-term governmental policy the aim of which was to reduce conflict. Hence the Education Reform Act (1964) stipulated that most Catholic schools could be transformed into independent grant-maintained ones, with state funding up to 80% of capital expenditure, on condition that one third of their management committee be nominated by the government. As a result, by 1986, all independent schools had adopted the new status. As for Protestant schools, the 1964 Act stipulated that any new state school opening in Northern Ireland from 1968 onwards would be compelled to include members of the Protestant churches on their management committees. This was a way to reconcile all conflicting interests.

With the abolition of Stormont* in 1972, decisions regarding education in Northern Ireland came under the responsibility of the Secretary of State for Northern Ireland and particularly of the Junior Minister, responsible for Education. The

1972 Education Reform (N.I.) Act mainly restructured education authorities, replacing the former 8 county committees by 5 Education and Library Boards (ELBs), including representatives of both the Catholic and the Protestant Churches. This structure has since been maintained.

The Republic of Ireland

In the Republic, the evolution of the system was not guided by the political interests of opposed communities, as was the case in Northern Ireland, but rather by the predominance of the Catholic Church in the management of schools and the integration of Gaelic culture in school programmes. As of April 1st 1922, Irish was made a compulsory subject in all Irish national schools. It was used as the teaching language in many primary schools while its study and use were strongly recommended in secondary schools.

Primary schools

In 1922, the Irish education network was mainly composed of numerous small primary schools, most of which had only one or two teachers and were in bad condition. From 1927 onwards, school attendance became compulsory for children aged 6 to 14. From the 1960s onwards, the educational system was finally reorganized. A number of small scattered rural schools were closed or amalgamated. A national curriculum for primary schools became compulsory in 1971. The amount of the state budget devoted to schools increased from 3.05% to 6.29% of GNP between 1960 and 1973.

Secondary schools

The state started paying attention to post-primary education in the 1960s. In 1964, the first state capital grants were allocated to the expansion of secondary schools, while at the same time fully state-funded comprehensive schools were set up. In 1967, a "free education scheme" encouraged greater participation in post-primary schooling. In 1972, the compulsory school-leaving-age was raised to 15. Furthermore, the status of vocational schools was raised in order to bridge the gap between technical and academic education.

Higher education and teacher training

Attention also focused on higher education from the 1960s onwards. Many third-level institutions were created while existing ones were granted extra funding for capital and current expenditure. A new non-university sector was built. Regional colleges and national institutions were added to the colleges of technology. Research institutes also developed.

IRISH EDUCATION TODAY

1 NORTHERN IRELAND

Organization and funding

The Northern Ireland system is mostly composed of a rather scattered primary school network, whereas secondary education is more concentrated. While primary school attendance is obligatory, the nature of secondary education is determined by the results of the 11-plus exam,* which has been suppressed in England and Wales but maintained in Northern Ireland so far, and has to be taken by all children leaving primary school. The pupils with the best results are entitled to admittance to grammar schools.

In terms of funding, the educational system in Northern Ireland is composed of:

• controlled schools, owned and managed by Education and Library Boards (ELBs) and fully funded by the state;

• voluntary schools, mainly managed by the Catholic Church and largely maintained by public funds;

• voluntary Catholic or non-denominational grammar schools which receive grants from the Department of Education;

• and finally, independent schools, solely depending on private funding.

Just as in England, controlled or voluntary schools now have the possibility to "opt out": they may receive an annual grant directly from the Department of Education, and manage it according to their needs, the difficulty lying in the necessity to estimate expenses in advance. Such schools are called grant-maintained.

Segregation or integration?

The system is highly denominational and segregated. As voluntary and independent schools are mainly attended by Catholic pupils, controlled schools are de facto Protestant. The Catholic Church refuses to yield its hold on its schools in exchange for increased state funding.

However, the state, a large number of teachers and parents, and to a lesser extent the churches have become aware of the necessity to use education as a means to bridge the gap between the Protestant and the Catholic communities. Hence the birth of several projects meant to foster closer links between the pupils of both denominations. The most striking development in this field is integrated education,* which means schools with equal numbers of Catholic and Protestant pupils and teachers. The first integrated school, Lagan College, was opened in Belfast in 1981, thanks to private donations. A decade later, there were about eighteen integrated schools throughout Northern Ireland, including four secondary schools. Most integrated schools are now grant-maintained with the possibility to "opt out", and even controlled schools may turn into grant-maintained integrated schools (GMIS). Integrated schools were officially recognized in the Education (Northern Ireland) Reform Act (1989) promoted by Brian Mawhinney, the then Northern Ireland Minister of Education.

Another attempt at promoting cross-denominational school links consists in compulsory subjects included in the national curriculum for Northern Ireland: Education for Mutual Understanding (EMU), Cultural Heritage.* The Catholic Church, while refusing to support integrated education which would deprive Catholic children of a purely Catholic education, officially supports programmes such as EMU, and together with the main Protestant churches has even designed a common programme for religious education, to be implemented in all schools. Furthermore inter-school initiatives often foster opportunities for school exchanges or common activities.

Higher education however is not segregated. Except for 50% of student-teachers, Protestant and Catholic students attend the same universities and technological institutes. However, apparent integration may well hide forms of segregation and prejudice, still resulting from the long years spent in segregated primary and secondary schools. Furthermore, a large proportion of Protestant students choose to study in British universities, with the hope of being offered better job opportunities. This tends to unbalance the denominational distribution in Northern Ireland universities.

2 THE REPUBLIC OF IRELAND

In the Republic, the system is still marked by the Catholic Church's hold on education. In fact, each religion controls its own schools.

Structures

Like Great Britain and Northern Ireland, the Republic of Ireland has no pre-school system.

Children start primary school at 4 or 5 years old, proceeding to secondary education at the age of 12 or 13. The compulsory school age is from 6 to 16. At the end of the secondary junior cycle, around the age of 15, pupils take a Junior Certificate Examination, and around 80% of them enter the senior cycle to prepare their Senior Certificate which they take at the age of 18. If they pass, they may be candidates to attend universities or technological institutes.

Primary education: most primary schools are still denominational and have grant-aided status. There are more than 3,000 Catholic schools and about 100 Protestant ones. Secondary schools are also denominational, except for vocational schools and community schools.

The system suffers from the geographical distribution of schools, emphasized in some cases by the division into boys' and girls' schools. Consequently the state has to reconcile the financial necessity to amalgamate some schools, especially at secondary level, and the qualitative necessity to satisfy multi-faceted expectations and claims in terms of geographical position, religion and sex.

Secondary education: the main developments in the last twenty-five years have occurred in secondary and higher education. Enrolment has doubled at secondary level, and increased four-fold in higher education. Therefore the main difficulty is to find educational patterns for students unfit for academic studies. At secondary level, the curriculum is national, including Irish, English, mathematics, history, geography and one foreign language as compulsory subjects, with science increasingly becoming a core subject. But at third level, the system must be adapted both to the skills of the students and to the requirements of an unfavourable labour market. In the area of technical education, some people oppose the development of vocational education, arguing that Ireland is not sufficiently industrialized to provide work in that field.

Higher education: to meet the needs of industry many new regional colleges have been created and two new universities – Limerick and the City of Dublin were set up in the early 1990s.

Organization and control

The Irish system of education once again raises the question of school control. With the decrease of church attendance in the Republic of Ireland, an increasing number of parents see less and less point in enrolling their children in denominational church-controlled schools. They feel education should be handled and controlled by the state, both at national and local level, while the churches should have a consultative role.

Hence the Green Paper on Education* published in 1992 by the Irish government. This has so far given birth to a national debate on the issues of control, inequality, curriculum content and assessment. The Green Paper was to be followed by a White Paper and a parliamentary bill leading to the first legal national framework for education ever to have been elaborated in the Republic of Ireland.

Both in Northern Ireland and in the Republic of Ireland, political, economic, social, cultural, religious and demographic factors have recently combined to make change necessary. This has been accentuated by their common membership of the European Union. Consequently educational matters will probably remain priority issues in the years to come.

FURTHER READING

COOLAHAN, J., *Irish Education*, Dublin: Institute of Public Administration, 1991.

MULCAHY, D. G., & O'SULLIVAN, D., *Irish Educational Policy*, Dublin: Institute of Public Administration, 1989.

MURRAY, D., *Worlds Apart*, Belfast: Appletree Press, 1985.

1
The Churches and education

The school system in Ireland is here presented as a model of co-operation between Church and State. This was not always the case in the past, but now the school supplements the work of the parents.

In Ireland the schools and working conditions of the Presentation Sisters and other Catholic educators make the nearest approach of the actual to the ideal in the co-operation of the Church and State in education. The constitutional status of schools is not merely an acknowledgment of Irish tradition but also an acceptance of the principles formulated by Pius XI relating to the primary rights of the Church and family.

The basis of popular education is the modern adaptation of the system first introduced in 1831. The vindication of national independence in 1921 allowed the supersession of the former commissioners of education and a recasting of educational policy in harmony with religious and national aspirations. In the years that followed the national schools were proved instruments in the renaissance of Irish language and culture. Perhaps the most significant recognition of the national school system under the changed auspices is the fact that the Christian Brothers who had stood aloof since 1837 adopted the plan in 1926. Nowadays almost all primary schools, religious and lay, participate in the national system.

In the words of the Irish council of education, a consultative body established in 1950, the school exists to assist and supplement the work of parents in the rearing of their children. The function of the primary school is to provide an educational foundation; it supplies a basic education and prepares the child for further education. The council of education does not claim that the primary schools impart the full minimum education that is held to be necessary today; nevertheless, a foundation is laid that will serve the common needs of all.

In effect, therefore, the Irish national system is denominational. As far as possible the form and substance of the education visualized for the children of Ireland by Nano Nagle are integrated with the national plan in sixty-eight Presentation primary schools. And in the working of these institutions the subsidiary function of the State is exemplified. The training and qualification of the sisters is governed by statutory regulations. The State department of education determines the curriculum of secular subjects; a regular system of inspection and examination ensures satisfactory teaching methods and standards. The part cost of the erection of the schools, the payment of salaries to registered teachers are likewise the responsibility of the civil authority.

T. J. Walsh, *Nano Nagle and the Presentation Sisters*, Dublin: Gill & Son, 1959. By kind permission.

questions

1. To what extent can it be said that the Irish educational system is the ideal as regards Church-State cooperation?
2. Is it generally accepted that the function of the school is to assist the work of the parents?

2
Education and national consciousness

Successive governments have used the school system to impose their values.

In 19th century Ireland, the struggle to gain control of the national school system was explicitly a struggle to mould the consciousness of the Irish population. The British government pursued a policy of anglicization by operating constraints on the language and culture transmitted in the curriculum. The religious denominations sought and attained the development of a religiously segregated system. This ensured the perpetuation of their particular ideologies. Social control was the main concern of those who sought to shape the system; issues of moral socialization took precedence over issues of technical socialization, although the latter was catered for by the inclusion on the curriculum of such subjects as needlework, cookery and laundry, manual instruction and rural science.

The development of the national system in the Republic of Ireland since independence illustrates further the close links between education and values. The curriculum changes which were introduced after independence were inspired by the ideology of cultural nationalism. It was felt that schools ought to be the prime agents in the revival of the Irish language and Gaelic culture. The work of the infant school was to be entirely in Irish; no teaching of English as a school subject was to be permitted. For senior classes, Irish was to be the medium of instruction for history, geography, drill and singing, and all songs in the singing class were to be Irish language songs. The programme in history was to deal exclusively with the history of Ireland, the chief aim being to develop the best traits of the national character and to inculcate national pride and self-respect.

Patrick Clancy, *Ireland – A Sociological Profile*,
Dublin: Institute of Public Administration, 1987. By kind permission.

questions

1. What were the objectives of educational authorities in the 19th century?
2. Why and how was the trend reversed later?

3
Church-State conflict

Education in Ireland has been largely influenced by the Church-State relationship, sometimes to the detriment of educational progress.

Seen historically, the system of education in Ireland is the product of decrees that have come from outside rather than of any impulsion from within. It has been much less a history of educational ideas and principles than the history of a power struggle between Church and State. The unifying element had gone out of education with the entry of proselytism; it was never to return. The cohesive link was destroyed and with the expansion of education to all classes of the community, a vacuum was created. This the State sought to fill but, inevitably, it clashed with a Church then only beginning to turn from purely missionary aims to the serving of the social needs of her followers.

These were seen as being primarily educational, an extension of the apostolate in the serving of human needs, and the people, with the →

bitter memories of penal deprivation in their minds, welcomed the new schools which the religious orders began to establish. The mixed school as well as the lay school was doomed in a society which saw in the Church school a reassertion and reaffirmation of its faith. The Church placed its wealth and unpaid resources at the disposal of education and, in the nineteenth century, with the State doing nothing to build new schools or maintain existing ones, secondary education came to be almost a Church monopoly. Only the religious orders, with their unpaid resources of teachers drawn from their own members and their access to credit, could hope to build schools, equip them and pay for them. They did build schools, showing such evangelical fervour that no less than twenty-seven secondary schools were built in the post-Famine period before 1870. But, by doing so, they helped to make absolute the division between schools of different denominations so that, to the social barriers that separated Catholic and Protestant in nineteenth century Ireland, was added a formidable educational barrier. This barrier was not erected by accident; it owed its existence to the belief of the Catholic hierarchy that undenominational education would displace it from its dominant position of control.

T. J. McElligott, *Secondary Education in Ireland* (1870-1921), Dublin: Irish Academic Press, 1981. By kind permission.

questions

1. How did Church and State behave in the area of education?
2. How did the denominational division of schools come about?

4

Inequality in schooling

Socio-economic status is particularly relevant to the length of time spent at school.

% of students at various points in the system by socio-economic status

	Entering Post-Primary	Completing Junior-Cycle	Completing Senior-Cycle	Entering Third Level
Professional/ intermediate professional	98.1	90.9	66.9	24.0
Skilled	95.6	78.8	41.9	10.0
Partly skilled	92.1	73.0	38.2	7.9
Unskilled	78.0	50.5	19.8	4.4
Total	92.5	76.3	44.9	13.0

A Discussion Paper, issued by the Education Commission of the Conference of Major Religious Superiors, Dublin, September 1988.

questions

1. What picture can be drawn at the extremes of the social ladder?
2. Are there many variations at the centre?

Segregated education has an inbuilt tendency to be unequal education. Yet over half our primary school population are in single-sex schools and far more than half of our secondary pupils, a fact for which the Churches must be held largely to blame. Sinn Féin The Workers' Party is committed to the comprehensive integrated ideal and it is our conviction that such arbitrary separation is harmful to both boys and girls, creating as it does unnatural and unnecessary divisions between them.

[...] **Subject division** is even more acute in secondary schools where boys' schools frequently offer a level and range of subjects unavailable in most girls' schools. Higher mathematics and the "hard" sciences are generally not emphasised in girls' schools and girls are generally directed away from those subjects which would open up a broad range of the technical skills so vital for modern industry.

School textbooks pose another problem, almost invariably relying heavily on outdated and groundless assumptions about the role of women. Reading schemes for young children for instance show a cosy middle-class family whose mother cooks and cleans, father drives the car, son plays football/climbs trees and daughter plays with dolls or helps in the house. These concepts and roles are absorbed readily by children and reinforce the views they have already come across in other ways.

Teacher attitudes and expectations also reinforce this kind of stereotyping. [...] Teachers generally have different expectations of boys and girls, based on the old stereotypes, and children react accordingly.

Positions of authority in schools tend to be weighted heavily in favour of men, even though women predominate in the teaching profession. Such structures of authority also reinforce ideas about female inferiority.

It is scarcely surprising, therefore, that far fewer women than men go to university or other third-level colleges (with the exception of teacher training colleges), despite the absence of formal or legal barriers and despite the fact that more women than men sit – and pass – the Leaving Certificate. More disturbing again is the *pattern* of female participation in higher education. Over 70% of female university students are in the Arts or Social Science faculties for instance. In the Regional Technical Colleges there are fewer women again and most of these tend to opt for the Commercial/Secretarial courses. Predictably enough, there are more women than men in the Teacher Education sector – a traditional "caring" occupation, where the remuneration bears no relation to the heavy responsibility involved.

If education is genuinely to contribute towards equality, radical changes will have to take place in our schooling system.

Workers' Party Manifesto, 1987.

5
Sexual discrimination and education

The educational system prepares girls to play an inferior role in society. This is because of segregation, the contents of textbooks, and a generalized sexism.

questions

1. Are there any arguments in favour of segregated schooling?
2. How influential are other forms of sexism in education?

6
Integrated schools in Northern Ireland

Integrated education constitutes an attempt to defeat the prejudice generalized by the Northern Ireland segregated school system.

Even if the importance of differences is acknowledged, there are nonetheless a number of common understandings and levels of consensus within Northern Ireland about acceptable conventions with regard to some social and political structures. These conventions are both deep-rooted and conservative, and are common to the two groups, even if they are reflected in parallel but separate institutional forms. They can be thought of as metaphors, and there are at least two sets of metaphor operating. One reflects the Catholic-Protestant divide, and this results in two separate, vertical lines of schools, parallel but largely untouching. The second set of metaphors relates to a vision of society as pyramidal in which a smaller and smaller number of people are allowed to succeed and reach positions of influence and power. This is institutionalised in the separate grammar and secondary schools. [...]

The present situation is that integrated schools present challenges to both metaphors, and are therefore perceived as a danger to the status quo and to those whose power and influence, and even means of livelihood, depend on its continuance. The curricular difficulties may be perceived as a weakness, in that the integrated school metaphor is not yet strong enough to carry the weight of the challenge. Without an "integrated" curriculum, and with the emergence of Education for Mutual Understanding and Cultural Heritage for all schools, the integrated schools will be increasingly vulnerable to the criticism that they provide little extra over and above propinquity. However, if in time it turns out to be the case that mixed enrolment is the major achievement of the integrated schools, this may still be perceived as a challenge to the dominant metaphor.

C. Bowring-Carr, E. Cairns, S. Dunn, V. Morgan, *All the Things We Are*, Coleraine: Centre for the Study of the Conflict, University of Ulster, 1990.

questions

1. What social attitudes does integrated education challenge?
2. Why is the movement rather vulnerable?

7
From separation to integration

See p. 124.

Separated religions have until recently meant separated schooling in Northern Ireland. Integrated education is now beginning to modify the situation.

questions

1. What are the arguments of those who favour separate schools? **2.** Give the position of those in favour of integration.

8
Student flows in Northern Ireland

Instead of staying in Northern Ireland, Protestant students opt in ever increasing numbers for British universities. Many never come back and their places are taken by Catholic students and students from the Republic.

The flow of Protestant school-leavers from Northern Ireland to British universities continues to rise, new research shows. If previous patterns continue, only a third of them will return to the province after graduating.

Robert Cormack and Anthony Gallagher from Queen's University and Robert Osborne from the University of Ulster found that 44% of Protestants entering higher education in 1991 opted for Britain; the same was true for only 27% of Catholics.

The study is the fourth in a series dating back to 1973, when 37% of Protestants chose institutions across the Irish Sea. Due to rapid expansion since then, the number of Protestant "emigrants" has risen from around 640 to nearly 1,500 per year.

Recently there has been an attempt to focus on Protestant "alienation". Instead of a Protestant community previously thought of as ascendant, dominant and materially advantaged, there have been increasing portraits of the Protestant community as on the defensive and fearing the future.

A similar study in 1986 showed that two-thirds of the migrants had not returned some three or four years into their careers. They were joined by around 15% of those who studied in Northern Ireland but left after graduating.

This means Northern Ireland suffers a brain drain of well-qualified school-leavers and graduates. There is no compensating influx; this year, Queen's and the University of Ulster took in 5,781 students, but only 100 were from Britain. Northern Ireland does, however, have a substantial number of students from the Republic, rising from 130 in 1985 to more than 600 this year. About one student in 15 at Queen's University and one in seven at the University of Ulster is now from the South.

This influx from across the border has helped fill up courses at the University of Ulster and push up its entry grades, but it has been a mixed blessing. It has displaced local students with relatively poor qualifications who, in turn, have had to leave Northern Ireland for higher education.

Thus it appears that many high-flying Protestants go to British universities by choice, and are joined by both Catholics and more poorly qualified Protestants attending the former polytechnics. Well-qualified Catholics are more likely to remain in Northern Ireland and now constitute a clear majority of the student population at both universities.

The research shows the likely impact of Government policies, including the squeeze on expansion and the shift from student grants to loans. These changes could reverse the gains made during 20 years of expansion by Catholics, women, working-class families and mature students.

Guardian Education, February 22, 1994.

questions

1. Can it be said that Northern Ireland is undergoing a brain-drain?
2. What are the possible consequences of such a situation?

The west of Ireland-Connemara (see p. 143)
Ph. © Hires.

CHAPTER ELEVEN

Culture and the Media

In Ireland culture, though extraordinarily rich, has been fragmented and instead of contributing to the creation of a homogeneous society, it has contributed to its divisions. English culture has been the predominant one in Ireland for a long time, but the memory of a Gaelic* culture, expressed in the Irish language, is of particular importance. One can also talk of two other forms of culture, the Anglo-Irish* and Ulster* Protestant. The most important means for popular cultural expression is the media. Newspapers, radio and television are numerous and varied and have to confront severe competition from their British counterpart.

CULTURE

1 THE DEVELOPMENT OF ENGLISH CULTURE

Destruction of the Irish language

Following the Act of Union* (1801), Ireland's exposure to English culture became even more intense than it had previously been. The instrument of diffusion of this influence was, of course, the English language. The Great Famine* and the mass emigration* of the 19th century completed the destruction of the Irish language begun over two hundred years earlier. It is reckoned that on the eve of the Famine, 4 million people still spoke Irish as their mother tongue. Today it is the case with less than 2% of the population.

Anglicization

The forces operating in favour of the replacement of Irish by English were powerful. For the Irish people the path to economic advancement implied an exchange of the language of their ancestors for the language of the market. Who can blame them for having made such a choice? It must be said that they were encouraged to make it. The Catholic Church, for example, when it opened its seminary in Maynooth* in 1795 for the training of priests, adopted English. The great nationalist leader Daniel O'Connell* saw in English the language of progress and conducted his mass meetings in that language. The trend of anglicization* was to be further intensified by the setting up by the state of a primary school system. The teaching was carried out in English. It is not surprising, therefore, that English exercised a constant influence upon the habits of thought and the modes of life of the Irish. Today the English language is firmly entrenched in Ireland. The prose and poetry of such famous Irish writers as James Joyce,* Sean O'Casey,* Samuel Beckett,* Seamus Heaney,* Jennifer Johnston,* and John McGahern* are written in English.

2 GAELIC CULTURE

The basis of Gaelic culture is the centuries-old Irish civilization which, however, went into decline in the early 17th century. This meant that from then on its literature, language and customs were in retreat, and those who practiced it since decline set in were a rural and impoverished people.

First reactions against decline

As early as the 1740s some people, such as Charles O'Conor*and Sylvester O'Halloran,* reacting against the loss of a civilization, began studying the Gaelic past, and the image of a heroic and "natural" Celtic* world soon emerged from their work. Nevertheless the decline of the Irish language continued in the 19th century. This decline and the negative image of Gaelic culture were not, however, universally accepted. Imitating their predecessors of the 18th century, some scholars, like the romantic nature painter George Petrie,* turned to Gaelic Ireland and saw there not backwardness but a community which retained a continuity with the glories of its own religious and artistic past.

The birth of cultural nationalism

At the vanguard of this cultural nationalism in the 1840s came Thomas Davis* and the Young Ireland* group. A further attempt at giving new impetus to cultural nationalism, aspects of which are wonderfully described by Joyce in *The Dead*, was made towards the end of the 19th century with the creation of the Gaelic League* by Douglas Hyde* and Éoin MacNeill.* To preserve and to restore as a national medium the Irish language was the ambition of the new revivalists. A further dimension was the movement, embodied in the Gaelic Athletic Association,* in favour of developing nationalistic-inspired leisure activities, Gaelic games, Irish music and dancing being the best examples.

Attempts at gaelicization

With the creation of the Irish state the new government adopted a policy of gaelicization* which was founded on a double strategy of saving the Gaeltacht,* i.e. the Irish-speaking areas principally along the west coast, and promoting the use of Irish through the education system. While meeting some success, the Gaeltacht strategy never succeeded in halting the emigration from the west. The number of native speakers has continued to decline and with that decline a reservoir of folklore and of language in all its complexity and originality is dying out. It is difficult to say, too, that the second strategy has produced satisfactory results. All Irish school children have had full exposure to the Irish language but the market has, as yet, been more successful than the school room.

At the same time, in contemporary Ireland, there is a strong current of renewal at work in urban areas. Irish language classes are full in Belfast. All-Irish primary schools sprang up in the major towns in the 1980s. Publishing in Irish is making progress and such writers as the poet Nuala Ní Dhomhnaill* writing in that language are acquiring an international reputation.

3 ANGLO-IRISH CULTURE

The Anglo-Irish class

The Anglo-Irish are the descendants of the English settlers in Ireland who saw themselves as a privileged minority separated by ethnic origin and by religion from those whose land their ancestors had confiscated. Trinity College,* Dublin, was the bastion of their culture for hundreds of years. As a class the Anglo-Irish became more and more excluded as the 19th century developed. With the decline of their economic power and the growth of political democracy they were losing their very *raison d'être*. Some were to identify themselves with political and cultural nationalism, and even play a major role in the growth of both

Great Anglo-Irish names

In the first area, one thinks immediately of Charles Stewart Parnell,* and in the second, many names come to mind such as W. B. Yeats,* J.M. Synge,* and Lady Gregory* who launched an Irish literary movement in the English language, the Irish Literary Theatre.* The Abbey* Theatre was to become the symbol and the centre of their activity.

4 ULSTER PROTESTANT CULTURE

The fourth form of culture to be found in Ireland is that of Protestant Ulster. It is founded on conquest, on Calvinism and on industrialization. It also draws inspiration from the Scots tradition and its own patterns of resistance. Much of the material richness of that culture is to be found in the Ulster Museum of Belfast. Ulster poets and novelists are emerging as powerful voices in contemporary Ireland. One thinks of Michael Longley* and Derek Mahon.* A trait which could have united the Protestants of the North and the Catholics of the South in a common culture was their resentment of the Anglo-Irish ascendancy, but the force of Puritan* antagonism to Catholicism is such that it allows little room for common ground between those two communities.

THE MEDIA

The development of the media in Ireland has always been influenced by Britain. This can be explained by political dependence, geographical proximity, and greater relative poverty in the smaller island. The first newspapers defended the link with Britain and the first radio and television stations to broadcast in Ireland were English.

Those Irish people who tried to set up an indigenous system were confronted, from the beginning, with stiff competition. Although they are fighting an ongoing battle, they have been quite successful in the area of papers, radio and television.

1 NEWSPAPERS

The following tables give the Irish daily and Sunday newspapers today.

DAILY NEWSPAPERS	morning/evening	part of Ireland	year of creation
Belfast Telegraph	evening	Northern Ireland	1870
News Letter	morning	Northern Ireland	1758
Cork Examiner	morning	Republic	1841
Irish News	morning	Northern Ireland	1855
Irish Times	morning	Republic	1859
Irish Independent	morning	Republic	1891
Evening Herald	evening	Republic	1895

SUNDAY NEWSPAPERS	part of Ireland	year of creation
Sunday Independent	Republic	1905
Sunday News	Northern Ireland	1965
Sunday World	Republic	1973
Sunday Tribune	Republic	1980
Sunday Business Post	Republic	1989

The *Irish Times* and the *Belfast Telegraph* are the closest one comes to quality dailies in Ireland. The *Irish Press* was created by De Valera* and Fianna Fáil* in 1931. They later added an evening and a Sunday version. The heirs of the great Irish leader were unable in the 1990s to prevent the closure of the Irish Press Group. The *Sunday World* is a tabloid which models itself on the English Sunday gutter-press. The *Sunday Tribune* and the *Sunday Business Post* are both up-market papers. As regards English papers circulating in Ireland, both the qualities and the popular press from across the Irish sea have a large share in the Irish market.

2 RADIO

The Irish began first to familiarize themselves with the BBC before being able to tune in to their own radio and television. It is not surprising that wealthy Britain should have been in a position to occupy the wave lengths before its much poorer neighbour. A White Paper, published as early as 1923 by the Dublin government, provoked a major debate between those who favoured a radio controlled by the private sector on the American model and those who defended the British model of a public radio. The Wireless Telegraphy Act* (1926) created officially the new service which was placed under public control, but which was to be financed by licence fees, publicity and duties on imported radios and radio spare-parts. The function of the new service was to distract, to inform and to educate. On 1 January of the same year, at 7.45 p.m., the first voice over the wave length coming from the new Irish service was heard in Dublin. In 1960, with the creation of a television service, a new body was set up to administer the combined radio and television service.

3 TELEVISION

As early as 1949, people along the east coast of the island were able to capture images from television in Britain. In 1955, the British Broadcasting Corporation began to transmit images from Belfast. To benefit from the new service the number of television sets in the north east of the Republic* increased rapidly. This prompted the Dublin government to study the setting up of an Irish television station, so, in 1960, radio and television were combined in a new single body: Radio na hÉireann* became Radio Telefis Éireann* (RTE). It was a state-controlled service which guaranteed, notably, a significant place for the Irish language and Irish culture. The law which set up this new body stipulated that licence fees and publicity were to be its two principal revenue sources.

RTE and BBC Northern Ireland (television and radio) and Ulster Television compete successfully among themselves and with several overseas radio and television stations. The media, North and South, have had, since the 1970s, to deal with the controversial ban on interviewing spokes-persons of a number of organizations such as the IRA,* Sinn Féin* and the UDA.* It was only in 1994 that Dublin, followed later by London, put an end to that censorship.

The opening-up of Ireland to the world, the Northern Ireland conflict (see Chapter 6), and membership of the European Union* have had a profound ongoing effect on culture in Ireland. The distinctiveness that Irish writers, from North or South, continue to reveal corresponds much more today to a synthesis of those four cultures than it has done in the past. At the same time a certain cosmopolitanism is finding expression in different cultural forms in Ireland. The U2 rock group, and a flourishing film industry (see filmography, p. 4) producing such films as *The Snapper* or *My Left Foot*, as well as the creation of a new ministerial department of culture in 1992 indicate the increasing importance attached to culture. It suggests that some of the divisions of the past are undergoing a healing process. Culture in Ireland may now be beginning to move society in a single direction. The Irish media are doing much to contribute to that task.

FURTHER READING

BROWN, T., *Ireland, a Social and Cultural History*, London: Fontana, 1986.
CROZIER, M., (ed.), *Cultural Traditions in Northern Ireland*, Belfast: Institute of Irish Studies, 1989
MCLOONE, M., & MACMAHON, J., *Television and Irish Society*, Dublin: RTE/IFI, 1984.

1
A new perception of the Irish past

Since the 1970s the Irish have begun to look at themselves and at their past in a more open and a more critical way.

[...] In a more hopeful reading of recent Irish cultural and intellectual history in its social context, such discussions about Irish identity conducted in literary and artistic terms could be seen as merely particular expressions of a more general intellectual current that has only begun to flow with any real vigour in Ireland in the last twenty years. This I take to be a steadily increasing urge towards an informed Irish self-understanding, a critical concern for origins and for contemporary fact and a desire to comprehend and accept modern Ireland in its fullness. It is in the last twenty years, as we noted, that the historiographical revolution, begun in the 1930s, has borne its first real harvest. Economic and social history have begun to be added to constitutional and political history as foci of historical concern. In social anthropology and social geography the pioneering work of Arensberg and Kimball has been followed by further studies of Irish social patterns. The artistic and literary traditions have attracted increasing numbers of Irish historians and critics. The study of religion has admitted sociology as a tool, and the literary imagination as a guide. At a popular level books and pamphlets about Irish craftwork, folklore, music, design, architecture, shop-fronts, town planning and natural history have raised Irish self-awareness to an informed level it did not possess in the early decades of independence. In a country that remains small and intimate in scale, there is a new openness to the inheritance of the past that has rejected much of the prejudice and many of the entrenched attitudes so characteristic of earlier decades. A healthy eclecticism is characteristic of the contemporary cultural scene, and a youthful enthusiasm remains a principle feature of the social atmosphere in a country that still reckons itself one of the ex-colonial nations at the beginning of its life. With a confidence bred of twenty years of economic improvement large numbers of young people are expectant of a worthwhile future and dismissive of the ideological constraints that in more hesitant years inhibited cultural and social experiment.

The change in consciousness of Irish identity [...] might, one hopes, have some effect over time in contributing to an ideological shift in Irish society as a whole as the humanistic values that currently govern intellectual activity in the country achieve a wider currency. At present of course such a nascent humanism is a fragile dyke against the cultural and social depredations of a rampant commercialism in an Ireland which could lose, before long, any distinctive identity it may once have possessed. But without it one could have little hope that the tides of commercialism could be resisted or that in future a new humanely comprehensive ideological imperative be defined for Irish society – one which would take account of the material and social gains of modernization but which would also allow a sustaining and challenging role for the products of the imagination and of the mind.

questions

1. What new tools are being used to reassess the past?
2. What may be the consequences on definitions of Irish identity?

Terence Brown, *Ireland: A Social and Cultural History* (1922-1979), Glasgow: Harper Collins Publishers Ltd, 1981.

2

The west of Ireland

See p. 136.

Against a background of natural beauty this Connemara road beside the sea is shown in the official language of the country and in English.

questions

1. Can the revival of the Irish language come from the west? **2.** How successful is the Irish tourist effort?

3

The Gaelic revival

The Centenary of the Gaelic revival has led to much questioning. However, hope still remains that the aims of the revivalists can be achieved.

Perhaps the greatest tribute to Conradh na Gaeilge is that it has survived at all, if not in particularly great shape. Centenary celebrations for the organization which led indirectly to the birth of the independent Irish State have, for the most part, gone unnoticed. Many would argue that shows the lack of interest in Irish today, and is a comment on the approach of Conradh na Gaeilge itself.

When the Gaelic League was established in 1893 there were 500,000 native Irish-speakers. In 1990, the writer and broadcaster Breandán Ó hEithir (since deceased), in a report for Bord na Gaeilge which was never formally published, estimated the number of native speakers at 10,000 "nó mar sin". He added that this would equal the attendance at a county football final, and was just ahead of the then membership of the British Communist Party.

But there are also positive signs for the survival of the language, including the phenomenal growth in the number of all-Irish schools. Twenty years ago there were 11, and now there are 73, including five in the North. Adult-education classes in Irish are mushrooming and the "What use is Irish?" attitude is dying out. Hostility to Irish has faded, though few still use it in their daily activities. And interest in other aspects of Irish culture, such as heritage, music and dancing, has flourished.

The Irish language movement in general and Conradh na Gaeilge as the main language body have been repeatedly criticized for not harnessing that enthusiasm, for being "middle-aged" and unrepresentative of that revived interest. But the organization can point to the high numbers attending Irish classes.

As the debate goes on about the current role of Irish, *The Irish Times* sought the views of some prominent people on the state of the language, its prospects for the future and their own interest in it. A view commonly held was the need for reform in the way the Gaeltacht areas →

questions

1. How is the hundred-year-old revival seen by contemporaries?
2. What is being done to improve the situation of the language and the Gaeltacht?

are treated and the necessity to recognize the efforts of people in urban areas such as Ballymun, Tallaght and Clondalkin in Dublin, who have tried to create a living Irish-speaking area in their communities.

As the poet Nuala Ní Dhomhnaill put it, the Gaeltacht is not so much a geographical as a mental contour, and wherever people speak Irish they have created a Gaeltacht.

Those canvassed hold a variety of views about where responsibility lies for the demise of Irish, but there were no doubts that the way the language has been treated in the school system is, at the very least, "unfortunate".

The Irish Times, July 31, 1993.

4
The roots of Protestant support for partition

questions

1. What cultural elements explain the support for partition in Northern Ireland?
2. What were the historical and contemporary circumstances which made the South abhorrent?

As any of the communities at grips with each other in that small province could have testified, support for partition was formidable, not because it was the last remnant of an outmoded colonialism, but because it was rooted in a variety of historical and contemporary circumstances which made the south abhorrent and an object of dark suspicion to the northern Protestant. The power of the Roman Catholic church in education, welfare, and society in general; the lingering influence of the civil war in the public life of the twenty-six counties and the ambiguous attitude of responsible politicians towards the IRA; the restrictions on family life and on the freedom of the individual implied in the denial of divorce, the ban on contraception, and the operation of the *Ne Temere* decree which in effect dictated that the children of mixed marriages should be brought up as Catholics; the censorship of books (and, to a lesser extent, of films); the emphasis upon compulsory Irish – all this conveyed to the northern Protestant mind an overpowering impression of Catholicism, Gaelicism, and authoritarianism triumphant and triumphalist.

F. S. L. Lyons, *Culture and Anarchy in Ireland (1890-1939)*, Oxford: Clarendon Press, 1979. By kind permission of Oxford University Press.

5
Censorship

The Censorship of Publications Act of 1929 allowed the young Irish State to prohibit the sale and

A selection from the 1,700 (approx.) books prohibited (1930-1946)

[...] BECKETT, Samuel	*More Pricks than Kicks* (23 October 1934)
[...] CALDWELL, Erskine	5 titles, inc. *God's Little Acre* and *Tobacco Road* (20 March 1934) (15 December 1933)
[...] COLETTE	5 titles, inc. *Chéri*, (7 April 1931)

[...] DURRELL, Lawrence	*Pied Piper of Lovers* (17 December 1935)
[...] FAULKNER, William	7 titles, inc. *Sanctuary* and *As I Lay Dying* (27 October 1931) (17 December 1935)
FRANCE, Anatole	*A Mummer's Tale* (27 November 1936)
FREUD, Sigmund	*Collected Papers* (vol. II) (11 August 1944)
[...] GREENE, Graham	*Brighton Rock* (14 February 1939) *It's a Battlefield* (11 February 1938) *Stamboul Train* (18 October 1938)
[...] HEMINGWAY, Ernest	*A Farewell to Arms* (31 March 1936) *Fiesta* (12 September 1941) *For Whom the Bell Tolls* (10 June 1941) *To Have and Have Not* (11 February 1938)
[...] HUXLEY, Aldous	*After Many a Summer* (9 February 1940) *Antic Hay* (12 August 1930) *Brave New World* (8 March 1932) *Eyeless in Gaza* (1 September 1936) *Point Counter Point* (13 May 1930)
[...] JOYCE, James	*Stephen Hero* (10 November 1944)
[...] LAWRENCE, D. H.	*Lady Chatterley's Lover* (22 March 1932)
LEWIS, Sinclair	2 titles, inc. *Elmer Gantry* (27 January 1931)
LLEWELLYN, Richard	*How Green was My Valley* (12 July 1940)
[...] MALRAUX, André	*The Royal Way* (14 February 1936) *Storm in Shangai* (La Condition humaine) (10 March 1936)
MANN, Thomas	*The Transposed Heads* (13 February 1942)
[...] MAUGHAM, S.	6 titles, inc. *Cakes and Ale* (7 November 1930)
MEAD, Margaret	*Coming of Age in Samoa* (15 August 1944) *Growing Up in New Guinea* (15 August 1944)
[...] MONTHERLANT, H. de	*The Lepers* (12 July 1940)
[...] MORAVIA, Alberto	*Wheel of Fortune* (11 March 1938)
[...] O'CASEY, Séan	*I Knock at the Door* (16 May 1939) *Pictures in the Hallway* (8 May 1942) *Windfalls* (4 December 1934)
O'CONNOR, Frank	*Dutch Interior* (12 July 1940)
O'FAOLAIN, Sean	*Bird Alone* (1 September 1936) *Midsummer Night Madness* (22 April 1932)
O'FLAHERTY, Liam	5 titles
PROUST, Marcel	*Remembrance of Things Past:* Vol. 9 – Vol. 12 (9 April 1943)
[...] SHAW, Bernard	*Adventures of the Black Girl in her Search for God* (5 May 1933)
[...] STEINBECK, John	*The Grapes of Wrath* (9 February 1940) *To a God Unknown* (16 August 1935)
[...] TOYNBEE, Philip	*A School in Private* (27 March 1942)

Register of Prohibited Publications, 31 December 1943.

distribution of books and publications which the Censorship Board found to be "indecent or obscene". Here are some examples.

questions

1. What have these authors in common?
2. Comment on some of the books on the list.

6
Newspapers in Ireland

The Irish are a newspaper-reading people. This is reflected here.

National Newspapers of Ireland: Circulation Figures

Mornings	1990	1998
Irish Independent	151,927	162,715
The Irish Times	94,058	111,486
The Examiner	57,061	58,536
The Star	53,533	90,262
Irish Press	60,461	
Total Mornings	**417,040**	**422,999**
Evenings		
Evening Herald	98,529	106,989
Evening Echo	30,525	26,973
Evening Press	95,857	
Total Evenings	**224,911**	**133,962**
Total Dailies	**641,951**	**556,961**
Sundays		
Sunday Independent	230,344	309,912
The Sunday Tribune	101,680	86,621
Sunday World	328,702	308,753
The Sunday Business Post	25,853	47,934
Sunday Press	207,507	
Total Sundays	**894,086**	**753,220**
Irish Farmers' Journal	70,979	74,407

questions

1. Identify the different papers
2. What changes can be detected in newspaper sales?

7
English Newspapers

English newspapers have also a wide circulation in Ireland and some of them have even Irish editions.

Circulation Figures for UK Titles in the Republic of Ireland

Dailies	1990	1998
Daily Mirror	59,812	47,418
Sun	29,627	86,818
The Express	4,506	3,587
Daily Mail	3,812	6,670
Daily Telegraph	3,526	3,804
Guardian	1,537	3,102
Independent	1,345	2,749
Times	2,100	5,615
Financial Times	2,862	4,640
Daily Record	—	1,159
Totals	**109,127**	**165,562**

Sundays		
News of the World	169,240	162,012
Sunday Mirror	64,985	43,120
The People	71,830	64,422
Mail on Sunday	0	10,616
Express on Sunday	21,645	8,134
Independent on Sunday	0	6,074
Observer	12,212	8,284
Sunday Telegraph	5,046	3,805
Sunday Times	31,188	80,412
Totals	**376,146**	**386,879**

ABC (Audit Bureau of Circulation), 1998.

questions

1. What trends can be identified?
2. What does a comparison of Irish and English circulation figures in Ireland suggest?

8

A newspaper stand

The "Yes" to Europe in the Maastricht referendum hits the first pages of the papers in Dublin.

questions

1. Describe the Irish newspaper scene.
2. How important is the penetration of English newspapers in the Irish market?

St Patrick's Pilgrimage, Co. Mayo
(see p. 157)
Ph. © G. Peress/Magnum

CHAPTER TWELVE

Religion

It is sometimes said that the Republic* of Ireland has the highest religious practice rate in the world and that Northern Ireland* has the second highest. What can certainly be said is that religion was of great importance in the past. In more recent times it has been an instrument of control and service in both private and public matters. Nevertheless today there are signs indicating that its influence is on the decline.

Religion in the Past

1 The Celtic Church

Christianity did not come to Ireland until the 5th century. It was brought by Saint Patrick* and his followers who succeeded in reconciling pre-Christian Celtic* religious practices and their new ritual. The influence of the Celtic religion and more generally of Irish culture of the time, and the difficulty in maintaining strong links with Rome throughout what were particularly troubled centuries all over the continent, meant that the Christian religion in Ireland, during the period after its introduction, took on a different hue from its counterpart elsewhere in Europe. A specific form of Irish Christianity was therefore to evolve, embodied in a monastic system rather than in a diocesan one. The Irish monastery corresponded, on the religious level, to that of the tuath* on the political level. The personalities of many monastic founders, if one is to judge by their names, marked Irish religious history. One thinks of St Eude of Aran, St Finnian of Clonard, Colum Cille of Derry, Ciarán of Clonmacnoise, Brendan of Clonfert, Fionnbar of Cork, etc. From the 6th century onwards the Irish monastic system was to produce missionaries who contributed to the reintroduction of Christianity to parts of Europe after the barbarian invasions (see Chapter 13).

2 CONTINUITIES

Over a thousand years later, in the 19th and early 20th centuries, Irish Catholic missionaries, inspired by the example of their ancestors, were this time to follow in the footsteps of the British and try to convert the conquered peoples of the Empire to the Catholic faith. Those two periods were ones when the Church in Ireland was powerful and wealthy. In early Ireland the numerous monasteries, the manuscripts, and the gold ornaments reflected that wealth, as in more recent times did the hundreds of churches built in the 19th century, the schools, the hospitals, the land and the money. The Irish monastic system also produced a set of penitential practices based on the mortification of the body which were also, in the 19th century, to contribute to a type of Catholicism which placed a heavy emphasis on celibacy and virginity, accorded a superior status to the religious life over married life, and through the use of the confessional increased the power of the priest over the body and soul of the Catholic Irish. Between the period of the early middle-ages and the 19th century, religion in Ireland underwent, however, major changes.

3 CHANGE

The decline of the early Irish church led to its reform being decided upon by Rome in the 12th century. The introduction of the continental mediaeval religious orders like the Cistercians and later the Dominicans and the Franciscans as well as the reorganization of the Church along diocesan lines bore witness to the end of the old Celtic Church and to the extension of the influence of Rome on religious matters in Ireland.

A further major upheaval occurred as a result of the religious Reformation of the 16th century. Henry VIII,* who was the first English King to have himself crowned king of Ireland, also became head of the new Anglican Church* which he set up after his break with the Pope. As elsewhere in Europe, the people had no option but to follow the religious choice of their masters. In Ireland, the Gaelic* chieftains, ignoring Henry's claim to temporal and spiritual sovereignty, decided to retain the old religion, whereas many colonizers of English stock and all those whose function it was to defend the English interest in Ireland adopted the new reformed religion, embodied in the Anglican Church of Ireland.

With the plantation* of Ulster* in the early 17th century a third religion was introduced from Scotland: Presbyterianism,* an offspring of Calvinism* and Puritanism.*

Since then those three religions have dominated the religious life of the country, Catholicism being the most important since it was and still is confessed by the majority of the population. Other religions have come since then and have found adepts, particularly in the north east of the island. One thinks of the Methodists,* the Baptists,* the Quakers,* dissident Presbyterians and other forms of Protestantism. One also thinks of the Jews who constitute a small community and among more recent arrivals the Moslems, the Hindus and the Buddhists.

4 PERSECUTION

The Catholic religion in the 18th century was the object of very severe repression on the part of the Anglican government as was, to a lesser extent, Presbyterianism. It was not until the late 18th century and more especially the 19th that an end was put to religious discrimination, and public positions began to be opened up to Catholics and Presbyterians. The notion of an official religion disappeared with the disestablishment of the Church of Ireland in 1870 and since then, from a legal point of view, all religions are equally tolerated.

RELIGION IN MODERN IRELAND

Control

In the 19th century the churches opted to have a decisive influence in the civilizing process by elaborating a system of religious control over the bodies and the minds of the Irish, and later over the state. The aim was to modify social customs, to obtain control over marriage and sexual behaviour, and to influence public life.

To create a new order the Catholic Church, more particularly, counted on the presence of the priest in every parish all over the country. The priest was to be a model himself of civility and virtue and he was the instrument to bring morality into the lives of the parishioners. To increase his chances of fulfilling with the utmost efficiency his moralizing role the priest had to add to his traditional religious functions of presiding over the principal rites of passage (birth, marriage and death) a further function: that of moral censor. Through formal pastoral visitation and confession the local priest was placed in the position of exercising a permanent role in the daily lives of the people. His chief instrument was the catechism, in other words a detailed code of behaviour or body of rules to be followed by all good Catholics. According to this code the faithful were obliged to attend church, by going to mass weekly and to confession at least once a year.

The church thus became the principal place where control could be exercised over a population which, it must be added, accepted the extension of Church power over their lives. Attendance at Catholic masses and Protestant services increased throughout the 19th century and became a permanent feature of the religious life of the people for most of the 20th. Penitential practices increased among Catholics, places of pilgrimage became very popular, the Virgin Mary appeared in a small village, Knock, in the west of Ireland and new forms of piety emerged. An ever-increasing number of young men and women espoused religion, thus choosing a life of celibacy.

Service

The churches did not limit their activity to meeting the religious needs of the population. Different types of institutions were created to render essential services.

First of all came the schools. New congregations of nuns and brothers were created to meet the huge educational needs of the Irish masses and to ensure that those needs would be satisfied in accordance with Catholic teaching. They built numerous primary and secondary schools with the result that by the mid-20th century the vast majority of secondary schools were in the hands of religious bodies. In spite of the efforts by the British state to create a secular primary school system in the 1830s catering for the educational needs of both Catholic and Protestant children, Catholic schools for Catholic children and Protestant school for Protestant children later became the rule in both parts of the country.

The Catholic Church also moved into other areas of public life where it could also serve. Hospitals, old people's homes, orphanages, reformatory schools, and homes for the handicapped were opened by the religious congregations, and thanks to state aid still largely remain under their management.

It would be wrong to generalize of course about all religions in Ireland. The forms of piety which developed within the Catholic religion in the 19th century remained foreign to Protestantism. This is understandable, given the latter's opposition to representations and icons and also its essentially private nature, since most Protestant Churches in Ireland would see their role as that of helping the individual create a relationship with God.

1 RELIGION AND THE STATE

After independence, in Southern Ireland, the Catholic religion gained more and more influence in every walk of life. When Éamon De Valera* was preparing a new constitution he consulted widely in order to find the correct terms to define the status of the different religions in the state. Finally the text of the 1937 Constitution* gave a "special position" to the Catholic Church while, at the same time, according recognition to the other churches as well as to the Jewish religion. This article of the constitution was removed in 1972 in a referendum in an effort to facilitate North-South relations. In Northern Ireland, when the province was created in 1921, the unionist* leaders set out to create what was later called a Protestant state for a Protestant people. The result was that between the 1920s and the 1970s, though neither part of Ireland possessed an official religion, a de facto Catholic state in the South stood face to face with a de facto Protestant state in the North.

The influence of the Protestant Churches on the new regime in Northern Ireland was to remain less evident than that of the Catholic Church in the South. In that part of the island the creation of what was in fact a Catholic state was not the work of the Catholic hierarchy but rather that of the politicians of the new state, the majority of whom held strong religious beliefs and acted politically in accordance with their Catholic convictions. The forbidding of divorce and contraception, and the introduction of a particularly severe censorship system in the 1920s and 1930s, illustrate both the force of Catholic influence and the obedience to the Catholic Church of the majority of Dublin's political leaders. However, change, when it did come, was to affect both the state and society all over the island.

2 SECULARIZATION

Today religion is clearly on the wane in Ireland. The following table gives the frequency of global church attendance in % in 1981 and 1990. The figures in parentheses relate to Mass attendance for Catholics.

Church attendance	Republic of Ireland		Northern Ireland		European average
	1981	1990	1981	1990	1990
More than once a week	28 (30)	22 (24)	18	12 (14)	7 (10)
Once a week	55 (57)	59 (61)	34	38 (71)	23 (32)
Once a month	6 (5)	7 (7)	15	19 (4)	11 (12)
Christmas or Easter	3 (2)	5 (5)	4	3 (2)	8 (9)
Less often	9 (6)	7 (4)	29	28 (9)	51 (37)

The troubles in Northern Ireland, which translated into religious terms what was fundamentally an ethnic conflict in a post-colonial society, served to underline the extraordinarily divisive nature of religion in Irish society. Most Irish people have certainly the negative effects of such divisions in mind since the beginning of the Ulster crisis. At the same time, with the modernization of society, new forms of behaviour and new value systems are contributing to the marginalization of the Churches. The Bible, the ten commandments, the commandments of the Church, the catechism and more generally the teachings of both Protestant and Catholic Churches on such fundamental questions for them as sexuality and procreation are becoming more irrelevant to the everyday lives of ordinary people. Contraception is now common, and homosexuality has been depenalized both North and South. The Churches therefore are no longer being obeyed. The church buildings, however, are still full on a Sunday morning though, there too, decline in religious practice has set in. It cannot be said that the Irish are undergoing a process of rejecting religion and adopting the principle of a secular society. Rather they are turning away from the Churches on those issues which for them are now a question of private conscience.

Secularisation underwent a process of acceleration in the latter half of the 1990s and, indeed, is very likely to spill over into the years 2000, when many acts of child-abuse, committed by priests, brothers and nuns, were largely publicized in the media. Those revelations came after the discovery that one of the most charismatic bishops of the hierarchy of the country was the father of a boy of 15, living with his mother in the United States. When some very sordid affairs of pedophilia were subsequently made public many Irish Catholics were profoundly shocked and felt deeply betrayed in the faith and confidence they had placed in the Catholic church and in the trust which they had expressed for two hundred years by confiding their children to the religious for their education.

FURTHER READING

BRENNAN P., *La Sécularisation en Irlande*, Caen: Presses Universitaires, 1998
INGLIS, T., *Moral Monopoly*, Dublin: Gill & Macmillan, 1987.
HUG, Ch. *The Politics of sexual morality in Ireland*, London: Macmillan, 1999
WHYTE, J. H., *Church and State in Modern Ireland*, Dublin: Gill & Macmillan, 1980.

—1—
The Popery code

After the battle of the Boyne in 1690 which witnessed the defeat of the Catholic King James by the Protestant King William, the Irish Parliament enacted a series of anti-Catholic laws, the Penal Laws.

"Whereas it is notoriously known that the late rebellions in this kingdom have been contrived, promoted and carried on by Popish archbishops, bishops, Jesuits and other ecclesiastical persons of the Romish clergy. And forasmuch as the peace and public safety of the kingdom is in danger, by the great number of the said archbishops which, not only endeavour to withdraw His Majesty's subjects from their obedience, but do daily stir up and move sedition and rebellion...

No Catholic may sit in the Irish Parliament.

No Catholic may be a solicitor, game-keeper or constable.

No Catholic may possess a horse of greater value than £5. Any Protestant offering that sum can take possession of the hunter or carriage horse of his Roman Catholic neighbour.

No Catholic may attend a university, keep a school, or send his children to be educated abroad. £10 reward is offered for the discovery of a Roman Catholic schoolmaster.

No Catholic may buy land or receive it as a gift from a Protestant.

No Catholic may bequeath his estate as a whole, but must divide it among all his sons, unless one of those sons become Protestant, where he will inherit the whole estate.

No Catholic may be the guardian of a child. The orphan children of Catholics must be brought up as Protestants."

And this is a summary of only some of the Penal Laws. No Catholic could hold a commission in the armed forces, or sit on the Bench, or hold any government office at all. Catholics were debarred from standing for Parliament; they didn't even have a vote. The Catholic Church itself was proscribed, as were Catholic pilgrimages. The whole point and purpose of this penal legislation was to keep the Catholics in permanent subjection to a Protestant minority. For instance, the clause about not owning a horse worth more than £5 was designed to prevent the possibility of Catholics ever again building up a cavalry force. The clause on divided inheritance was designed to make it virtually impossible for a Catholic ever to become a major landowner. The total burden of the Popery Code was aimed at preventing the emergence of an educated, or professional, or landed, Catholic leadership. In the face of this relentless pressure, many notable Catholic landlords and lawyers abandoned their old religion and went over to the established church, the episcopalian Church of Ireland. By the end of the eighteenth century, scarcely 5% of Irish land was owned by Catholics.

Magnus Magnusson, *Landlord or Tenant?* London: The Bodley Head, 1978.

questions

1. What were the economic dimensions of the Penal Laws?
2. What did the Penal Laws set out to achieve?

2
Women and religion

While the majority of Catholic women in Ireland practise their religion, contradictions exist today between belief and behaviour. The changing role of nuns in Irish society is a further illustration of these contradictions.

The question of the relationship of women to organized religion is an important one in Ireland because the overwhelming majority of the population practises religion, normally Catholicism. While the figures for some of the signs of religious observance have been falling over the past two decades, both successive surveys and measures of observance show a continued attachment to Catholicism. The women's movement in Ireland will not be able to advance without taking account of this.

Many aspects of Catholic traditional teaching, however, especially those relating to the role and rights of women, are challenged or rejected. Contraception is widely practised, the birth-rate outside marriage is now one of the highest in Europe and still rising, while family size has halved in the past twenty years, the Church itself champions the equal rights of women at work, men and women who leave religious life to marry are accepted and welcomed in their communities.

A little-noticed aspect of this has been the changing role of nuns, both in the Church itself and in the wider community. While the religious life offered women in the nineteenth century a socially-useful and relatively powerful role outside the confines of restricted domesticity, for a long time they accepted their subordinate role within the Church. More recently nuns have come to challenge this role within the Church, and in the broader society theirs have often been the most radical voices, criticising the patriarchal traditions of the Church and also urging it to be more involved in the concerns of the poor. Nuns have also been deeply involved in the development of locally-based women's groups, both in inner city communities and in country areas, groups which confronted issues like inequality of educational opportunity for working-class women, violence against women and reproductive rights. They have been to the fore there in urging women to assert their rights, against the "sanctity of the family" if necessary.

Carol Coulter, *Women and the State in Ireland: The Hidden Tradition*, Cork: Cork University Press, 1993. By kind permission.

questions

1. What aspects of traditional Catholic teaching are challenged by women?
2. What new roles are nuns assuming?

3
Losing an Empire and finding a role

The religious congregations, female and male, which

In recent years the most audible sound in Irish education has been that of an empire collapsing. For almost two centuries religious congregations have dominated the education of Roman Catholics. They managed most schools and provided a substantial number of the teachers. In 1969-70 there were 2,300 religious receiving teachers' salaries representing approximately a third of the teachers in voluntary secondary schools. By 1995-6 this had declined to 753 (5,9% of the total). In addition of the religious working in secondary schools, it is calculated that about 40% are within ten years of compulsory →

contributed so much to the extension of education in Ireland in the past are now quickly disappearing from the educational field.

retirement whereas less than 5% are aged under 35. Severe decline in vocations and the assignation of some religious to alternative ministries help account for this free-fall.

So religious are disappearing from our schools as quickly as snow under the mid-morning sun. Their fall is proving as rapid as their rise in the nineteenth century. In 1800 there were only 120 nuns in the country, a number that had risen to 8,000 by the end of the century. Caitriona Clar in her "Nuns in Nineteenth Century Ireland" shows that the major expansion took place in the second half of the century. Nuns multiplied eight-fold between 1841 and 1901 even though the Roman Catholic population halved during this period. In 1861 there were 68% more nuns than there had been a decade earlier. From then until 1901 the rate of increase every ten years never fell below 20 per cent. Religious institutions were founded with such frequency in those years that the novelist, George Moore, caustically commented that "Nothing thrives in Ireland like a convent, a public house and a race meeting."

It is time to write the obituary on this once-powerful entity in Irish education that like all human endeavours had its success and failures?

Kevin Hegarty, *Ceíde*, March-April 1998.

questions

1. How can 19th century growth of religious vocations be explained?
2. Why the relatively rapid contemporary decline?

4 Mixed marriages

Married couples from different religious backgrounds in Northern Ireland have often to face major difficulties, not only in their neighbourhood but in their respective Churches, notably in the Catholic Church.

"They shoot mixed marriages, don't they," Martha said nervously. The Protestant wife of a Craigavon Catholic had just heard the early morning news that loyalist gunmen had murdered Margaret Caulfield, also a Protestant, and seriously wounded her Catholic husband Gerald as the couple lay sleeping in their North Belfast home.

Martha's reaction is indicative of the many people who have married outside their religion and who run the gauntlet of disapproval from one side or the other [...].

The inter-weaving of politics and religion is more evident among mixed marriages in working class areas where unemployment is high and wages low. Couples take a house where ever they can get one, the main concern being whether or not the area is safe from gunmen. Whichever partner is the more ardent in their religious or political beliefs usually determines where the couple live. Middle class couples who have enough money to choose where they live tend to settle in mixed areas. [...]

In South Belfast for example, in the Holy land area – a collection of terraced streets with middle Eastern names – and around Queen's University, "mixed" couples live in relative harmony with neighbours of different religions and political viewpoints. According to Queen's Methodist chaplin Rev. David Turtle, who is also a member of the Northern Ireland Mixed Marriage Association, a new concept of "double belonging" has evolved in recent years which gives equal recognition to the religion and the tradition of both partners in a marriage. In the past some couples have ceased to be practising Christians and instead have adopted an attitude of "a plague on both your houses". Recognizing both religions and backgrounds, he claims, has given hope for the future.

In contrast, the Catholic Church, which perceives itself as the only true church, has always taken a "hard line" on mixed marriage – seeing it as a dilution of the faith. The Church insists that any children must be raised as Catholics and that the Protestant partner must promise not to interfere. [...]

The Catholic Church's dogmatic position is met with a certain amount of resentment among the the Protestant Churches. [...] Many Protestants regard such conditions as an invasion of any couples' liberty which tend to emphasize differences rather than similarities. [...]

The Irish Catholic Bishops have rejected concelebrated baptisms in which both a priest and a minister are in attendance and they have stated they are not in favour of having the child registered in both churches.

Many mixed couples send their children to integrated and independent schools such as Lagan and Forge. The Catholic Church has steadfastly refused to appoint a chaplain to these schools unlike its Protestant counterpart.

Fortnight, June 2, 1986. By kind permission.

questions

1. How does class affect mixed marriages?
2. Is the Catholic position on mixed marriages understandable?

5

A pious people

See p. 148.

Following in the footsteps of Saint Patrick, here we see pilgrims participating in the march up the mountain, Croagh Patrick, in Co. Mayo.

questions

1. How can Irish Catholicism be characterized? **2.** Do Irish Protestants manifest similar signs of piety?

—6—
Religion and the conflict

Religion has also played a part in North-South relations. For a majority of Protestant unionists, the 1912 anti-Home Rule slogan – "Home Rule is Rome Rule" – became a reality in the South.

On social and religious issues the policies pursued since the 1920s progressively converted what might have been a pluralist state into a confessional state. Censorship of all literature that was offensive to the Catholic Church was imposed. The possibility of obtaining a divorce was eliminated. An explicitly Catholic Constitution was adopted in 1937. And many other laws and practices were adopted to give effect to the views of the Catholic majority regardless of those of the Protestant minority. In the cultural and educational sphere an exclusively Catholic and Gaelic, and often an anti-British, ethos was promoted. The numbers in the minority Protestant community declined very rapidly, both through emigration and through the rigid application of the Catholic Church's rules respecting the religion of children of mixed marriages. The 343,000 Protestants in the twenty-six counties of the Republic in 1901 had by 1961 declined to a mere 144,000.

It is sometimes argued that these developments were an inevitable consequence of partition, which had created an overwhelming Roman Catholic majority in the South. But that is altogether too charitable a verdict on a state that ignored or overrode the values of the Protestant minority both within the twenty-six counties and within the thirty-two counties over which the Republic aspired to rule. While it was natural for a newly formed state to assert its independence from Britain and essential for it to create a distinctive cultural identity, the manner in which these aims were pursued reinforced the prejudices of the northern unionists and made their policies more difficult to criticize from within Northern Ireland and from without. When to the indisputable evidence that "home rule" had in fact become "Rome rule" is added the ambition expressed in Articles 2 and 3 of the Irish Constitution to incorporate Northern Ireland into the Republic, the substance of the criticism that the Republic carries its own responsibility both for the hostile nature of North-South relations and for the state of majority-minority relations within Northern Ireland is amply demonstrated.

Kevin Boyle and Tom Hadden, *Northern Ireland: A Positive Proposal*, Harmondsworth: Penguin Books, 1985.

questions

1. How was a pluralist state transformed into a confessional one?
2. Did this correspond to a deliberate choice?

—7—
Attitudes towards religion

Traditional religious values, by age group (% believing), see page opposite.

question

How significant is age as a factor in understanding changing religious values?

	God			Life after death			A soul			Heaven			Hell			The Devil			Sin		
	Ireland		Europe	Ireland		Europe	Ireland		Europe	Ireland		Europe	Ireland		Europe	Ireland		Europe	Ireland		Europe
	1981	1990	1990	1981	1990	1990	1981	1990	1990	1981	1990	1990	1981	1990	1990	1981	1990	1990	1981	1990	1990
18-26	92	92	62	67	69	39	74	75	56	72	78	36	41	39	18	45	41	20	80	79	47
27-35	93	96	67	69	76	39	74	79	55	79	82	34	46	40	18	51	43	21	81	84	49
36-44	97	93	73	75	68	41	86	81	59	86	80	41	57	48	22	60	49	24	86	83	55
45-53	98	97	78	87	84	45	90	90	66	93	87	45	66	53	25	68	58	27	90	88	62
54-62	98	97	81	83	88	50	90	91	68	92	92	52	65	60	30	67	63	32	91	87	66
63 +	96	100	85	84	85	52	91	94	71	92	95	58	66	62	33	67	64	35	91	87	69
TOTAL	95	96	73	76	78	44	83	85	62	84	85	44	55	50	24	58	53	26	86	84	57

Christopher T. Wheelan, *Values and Social Change in Ireland*, Dublin: Gill & Macmillan, 1994.

8
A Catholic country

A statue of the Sacred Heart in O'Connell Street, Dublin's main thoroughfare.

question

How representative is the statue of contemporary Irish Catholicism?

The Irish presidence of the European Council of Ministers –
John Burton in 1996, between Jacques Chirac
and Helmuth Kohl (see p. 171)
Ph. © Chesnot / Sipa Press

CHAPTER THIRTEEN

Ireland and the World

For hundreds of years Ireland sustained close links with continental Europe. Later those links were, to a large extent, to be mediated by Great Britain* though direct contact in certain areas continued to be maintained. In the 19th century, for a period of roughly one hundred years, new links, to the detriment of the old bonds with Europe, were forged with the United States of America and with different countries making up the British Empire. Finally, in the 20th century, after an initial period of elaboration of its foreign policy, the new Irish state was to turn back to Europe, thus reestablishing the centuries-old relationship.

1 IRELAND AND CONTINENTAL EUROPE

Early Christian Ireland

Though the evidence is fairly scant, it can be said that strong ties bound Ireland and Europe together for hundreds of years after the introduction of Christianity. Trade existed with the west coast of France, bringing with it the exchange of scholars and of manuscripts. Apart from the Bible, which was the basic text of Irish Christianity, the Latin poets Virgil and Horace were known in Ireland, as were the Lives of such saints as Martin of Tours and Germanius.

The Irish monastic system spread beyond the shores of the island and in the 6th and 7th centuries Saint Columbanus* and his disciples built monasteries in such places as Jumiège, Péronne, Auxerre, Luxeuil, Laon, Liège, St. Gall and Bobbio. Travelling to Europe the Irish monks took manuscripts with them. A mid-8th century Epistle of Saint Paul, glossed in Old Irish and in Latin, is now in Würzburg and another manuscript, glossed in the same manner, can be seen in the Ambrosian Library in Milan.

Other evidence of the Irish presence in Europe is the records of the dispute over the dating of Easter which in the 7th century opposed the Celtic* party and the Roman party. There was also an Irish scholarly presence in the court of Charlemagne, for instance, and in that of Charles the Bald. A fusion of Irish and Latin culture appears in 7th and 8th century Irish art. Indeed it can be said that early Irish Christian culture is a welding together of the continental European and Irish heritages.

Troubled times

Throughout the 9th and 10th centuries contact was diminished due, undoubtedly, to the Viking* presence in and around Ireland, and to Norse, Magyar and Moslem plundering of monasteries on the continent. The bilateral links were again strengthened in the 11th and 12th centuries with the creation of Irish monasteries in the Empire, in such places as Ratisbon, Vienna, Eichstätt, Memmingen, Würzburg, Constance and Nuremberg. Pilgrimages to Rome became common at the same period. In the opposite direction, moving from the continent to Ireland, came the church reform movement, the aim of which was to restructure the Irish Church, and have it abandon its monastic system in favour of the Roman one of dioceses and provinces. New monastic orders, the Cistercians and the Augustinians, were introduced into Ireland.

The Irish in Europe

Literary and linguistic French influence was strong on Irish throughout the 13th and 14th centuries. In the 15th century, translations from Latin of medical texts and works of piety also bear witness to direct contact between Ireland and the continent. From the 16th to the 19th century contacts were more conditioned by the political and religious situation in Ireland. The destruction of the Gaelic* order led to the flight of fighting men, the Wild Geese, to the armies of France, Spain and other continental powers. The penal* legislation against the Catholic religion led to the organization of Irish Catholicism in Europe. Irish colleges were created to educate young Irish scholars and to form some of them for the priesthood. The largest of those colleges were in France, in Paris and Nantes. Others were opened in cities such as Toulouse, Louvain, Santiago and Seville. With the disbanding of the Jesuits and the French revolution most of those colleges had closed down by the end of the 18th century.

European allies

Political protest in Ireland and the search for political allies abroad led to the establishing of further patterns of relationships with Europe. Revolutionary France helped republican Ireland. On three occasions in the 1790s it tried to be of military assistance to the United Irishmen* movement. Napoleon in 1803 and Lamartine in 1848 refused, however, to do the same.

During the First World War, republican elements sought military help from the Germans, and during the Second World War, the IRA* did the same. Unlike revolutionary France at the time of the United Irishmen, Germany never seriously studied the possibility of using the Irish approach in its projects to attack England. More than anything else, however, Irish neutrality during the Second World War, however powerful the internal reasons for declaring it may be, symbolized the profound gulf that then existed between the European continent and Ireland which, since the middle of the 19th century had turned for aid to its emigrant sons and daughters in the English-speaking world.

2 IRELAND AND THE ENGLISH-SPEAKING WORLD

The relation between Ireland and the English-speaking world is a product of Irish emigration.* Prior to Catholic emigration a steady flow of Protestants had been emigrating to America since the 17th century.

By the end of the 19h century, Irish Catholics had arrived in the United States in their millions. Paradoxically, coming from a rural background as they did, they opted massively for urban America. From there they proceeded to organize themselves politically in some of the major cities, and in the Democratic party. The arrival of the Kennedys to power in Washington was to crown all their efforts and to symbolize their integration.

Canada, Australia and New Zealand also received hundreds of thousands of Irish emigrants. The appointment of Mr Mulroney as Prime Minister of Canada in 1987 and that of Mr Keating as Prime Minister of Australia in 1991 bear witness to the successes of Irish emigration to those countries.

3 IRISH FOREIGN POLICY

Anglo-Irish relations

When the new Irish state was created (1922) and when it set about elaborating its foreign policy, it soon became evident that Anglo-Irish relations would be dominant. To a large extent that has been the case ever since, though the relations are now mediated to a large extent through the European Union* and the international arrangement set up under the Good Friday Agreement (1998). The fact that the 1922 Treaty* accorded dominion* status to Southern Ireland explains the importance of those relations. Indeed the 1920s and early 1930s were dominated by Dublin's efforts, which were on the whole successful, to achieve greater independence for each member country, i.e. for each dominion, and to reduce Britain's role to one of equality within the Commonwealth.*

When De Valera* came to power (1932), the efforts of the new Fianna Fáil* government were clearly oriented towards achieving sovereignty. This meant in fact dismantling the 1922 Treaty. Between 1932 and 1937, when he published the new constitution and had it adopted by referendum, De Valera through a step by step process broke all remaining ties with Britain.

The proclamation of the Republic* (1949) was the logical consequence of De Valera's efforts during those years. The achievement of formal sovereignty did not, however, reduce the importance of Anglo-Irish relations in foreign affairs. Britain remained by far Ireland's most important market, taking as it did about 90% of all Irish exports.

And just as Ireland was about to diversify its trade, the Northern Ireland* conflict (see Chapter 6) broke out bringing London and Dublin together in a number of attempts to find a solution. This coming together assumed new proportions with the signing of the Anglo-Irish international agreement (1985) – sometimes called the Hillsborough Agreement* – according to which the Irish Government obtained the right to put forward views and proposals on matters relating to Northern Ireland in an Anglo-Irish institutional framework. Collaboration was further strengthened in 1993, 1994 and 1998 on the Northern Ireland problem. The relationship had, however, been also reinforced by Ireland and the United Kingdom* joining the European Community* together in 1973.

First steps towards international recognition

Anglo-Irish relations did not obscure the necessity to develop ties with other countries and to obtain a place within international bodies. In order to underline its independence in the eyes of the world Dublin designated a plenipotentiary to Washington in 1925. It was the first Commonwealth country to take such a step, and was soon followed by Canada. In 1929 an envoy was appointed to Paris, to Berlin and to the Vatican. Seven years only after the Treaty, the new state was officially present in the most important capitals of the world. With time the list was lengthened, the development of Ireland's trade being on some occasions an important motivation in opening a new embassy abroad.

International bodies

In 1924 Ireland joined the League of Nations, and in 1929 the International Court of Justice. A certain continuity in this area of foreign policy was maintained when De Valera came to power since, in the same year, he also became president of the Council of the League (1932). In 1948 Ireland joined the Organization for European Economic

Cooperation – which became the OECD* in 1960 – and in 1949, it joined the Council of Europe, i.e. the same year as it proclaimed the Republic and decided not to apply for membership of NATO.* In 1950, it signed the Convention on Human Rights and Fundamental Freedoms. Five years later it became a member of the United Nations, and in 1957 joined the International Monetary Fund.

4 IRELAND AND EUROPE

The decision taken to apply for membership of the European Economic Community, announced in 1961, was a logical consequence of the political and economic opening-up process begun in the 1950s. After De Gaulle's veto on Britain's entry in 1963, Ireland withdrew its candidacy. New negotiations began in 1969, and finally in 1972 membership was approved in a referendum by 83% – in a turnout of over 70%. Though such enthusiasm was not repeated, Ireland's commitment to European Union was reaffirmed in the Single European Act (1987) referendum and again in the Maastricht Treaty (1992) referendum. Northern Ireland as part of the United Kingdom became a member on 1st January 1973.

Since 1973 the state's involvement in international affairs has increased considerably and the action of the European community has penetrated large sections of Irish public and even private life. Financial support, coming through the Common Agricultural Policy and the Structural Funds, has largely contributed to economic growth in Ireland. By joining the Euro on 1st January 1999 Ireland confirmed its previous choices. The interaction between the international and the national means that European affairs are no longer purely a question of foreign relations and in the same way many questions, which were traditionally of a domestic nature, now assume a European dimension.

European institutions

Ireland, like all other member states, participates fully in the work of the four principal institutions of the European Union:

- the Commission,
- the Council of Ministers,
- the European Parliament, and
- the Court of Justice.

Being one of the smaller states, Ireland nominates 1 commissioner to the Commission. As for the Council of Ministers, it has a President, held on a rotating basis for a period of six months. This system has the advantage of allowing small states to play a central role, a role that Ireland fulfilled on five occasions between 1973 and 2000. The European Parliament is composed of 518 members, 15 of those come from the Republic of Ireland and a further 3 from Northern Ireland. Nevertheless, in spite of the continuing europeanization of general policy, foreign policy as such has, to a considerable extent, remained in the hands of the national governments. Ireland has, for example, retained its neutrality.

The world has greatly influenced political development in Ireland and, in a small way, as becomes a small state, Ireland has also influenced the world. It has contributed, for example, to United Nations peace-keeping operations in different parts of the globe. It no longer lives in the shadow of Great Britain, playing as it does its full role within the European Union.

FURTHER READING

KEATING, P., *A Place among the Nations*, Dublin: Institute of Public Administration, 1978.
FISK, R., *In Time of War*, London: André Deutsch, 1983.

1

Ireland and the French Revolution

Revolutionary France tried to help Republican Ireland. Its efforts, however, were thwarted.

France had sent little over four and a half thousand men to the Irish coasts in 1798. Even that had been scraping the bottom of the barrel, for French forces that summer were peculiarly overstretched. They were all badly equipped and poorly financed. Shortages of ships and sailors meant severe overcrowding and certain capture if challenged by the British. With the knowledge of hindsight it is almost inconceivable that the French government or the United Irish exiles there should have expected success with such forces. They did so because of a serious misconception about popular rebelliousness in Ireland. Tone had convinced the first Directory that the Irish would rise only after the French had landed in sufficient strength and won some notable victories against the defending forces. But Ireland was not very high on the second Directory's list of priorities. It suited them to believe that the Irish people as a whole were poised for rebellion and no longer needed substantial help. In this belief they were encouraged by the exaggerations of one set of United Irish exiles, and the understatements of others who feared a French military takeover. The timing for a successful fusion of forces had long gone by the summer of 1798 and the United Irishmen themselves were no longer relevant to the internal Irish crisis. They continued negotiations for several more years to secure another invasion by the French. It was a difficult and ultimately fruitless task under the Consulate and Empire. Bonaparte was no Hoche, and the growing recognition by the exiled leaders that their struggle might simply replace English with French domination was part of the motivation of Emmet's rebellion in 1803. It foundered because the United Irish Society could not simultaneously reject its popular base and the French military assistance which substituted for it. The remnants of the organisation disintegrated rapidly thereafter.

Hugh Gough and David Dickson (eds.), *Ireland and the French Revolution*, Dublin: Irish Academic Press, 1990. By kind permission.

questions

1. How ready were the Irish to rise in the 1790s?
2. Was Ireland important for France?

—2—
The American support to Ireland

A joint resolution was introduction to the United States' House of Representatives on May 14, 1917, on the Irish question.

65th CONGRESS
1st Session.

H. J. RES. 88.

IN THE HOUSE OF REPRESENTATIVES

May 14, 1917

Mr Mason introduced the following joint resolution; which was referred to the Committee on Foreign Affairs and ordered to be printed.

JOINT RESOLUTION

To declare the liberation of Ireland one of the purposes of the present war.

Resolved by the Senate and House of Representatives of the United States of America in Congress assembled, That Ireland, a distinct and historic nation, anciently possessed of freedom, in the opinion of Congress and of the American people, of right ought to be free and independent; and be it further

Resolved, That as the Irish nation has contributed a very numerous and valuable element to the American Nation, and as the United States is committed by American traditions and by recent utterances of the President to the principle of freedom for small nations, the liberation of Ireland from all foreign domination is hereby declared one of the objects for which the United States fights in this present war; and all money hereafter voted by Congress for the prosecution of this war, and all loans hereafter authorized to be made to any nation now at war shall be voted and authorized with the condition that the liberation of Ireland is one of the purposes of the war; and be it further

Resolved, That the liberation of Ireland means the complete separation of the island of that name, together with such small islands as are now administered as part of it, from all involuntary and subordinate political connection with any other nation and the complete freedom of the adult inhabitants to decide by full and fair vote upon their form of government, and the complete freedom of such government as they may erect to determine its relations with other nations and to exercise all the functions of an independent nation, and the recognition of Ireland as a free nation, in accordance with this definition, shall be a part of the peace terms secured by the representatives of the United States in negotiations with any and all of the belligerent nations; and be it further

Resolved, That if the people of Ireland shall request the assistance and advice of the United States in the establishment of their future government the President, the Vice President, and the Speaker of the House of Representatives shall appoint a commission of five American citizens to proceed to Ireland and render such assistance and advice up to, but not beyond, the time when the people of Ireland shall adopt a constitution; but the United States shall not attempt to mold the course of the Irish nation and shall assume no responsibility for the new government to be erected in Ireland; and be it further

Resolved, That upon the adoption of a constitution by the people of Ireland, if said constitution shall erect a republican government, the Secretary of the Treasury is hereby authorized to purchase bonds of the Irish government so established, provided said bonds bear interest at not less than three per centum, to the amount of $100,000,000, and to reimburse the Treasury by the sale of United States bonds to an equal amount and bearing an even interest.

Library of Congress Public Affairs Office.

questions

1. How supportive was the House of Representatives for the liberation of Ireland?
2. How was Irish liberation defined by the House?

3
The Irish in America

The Irish in America have been particularly successful in gaining positions of authority in the public arena.

The range of occupations in which the Irish have achieved their successes in the United States is suggestive about the group as a whole. The Irish have evinced an unusual interest in gaining positions of authority in the most conservative institutions in our society – not only in the Catholic Church, which is readily understandable, but also in government and political parties, banking, the judiciary, the police, and the public schools. If there is a single concept that distinguishes the Irish in America, it is their dual preoccupation with security and power. The fact that the Irish in many large cities control City Hall, the police, the courts, and sometimes the public school system gives them a distinctive attitude toward issues affecting public order, the security of the streets, and civil liberties. They are for law and order in part because it is they who enforce and administer the laws and maintain order.

Fundamentally, the Irish have been a people outside of the business system and never fully have been reconciled to its values. At the lower levels, they have been obsessed with the security of civil-service jobs because they have been more impressed by the failures and vicissitudes of capitalism than by its opportunities and rewards. At the higher levels, this same alienation reappears as an aristocratic disdain for mere money-making. Repeatedly, there recurs an aspiration for the honors of high public office and a belief that government service is really the highest calling. The Kennedys are archetypes. Joseph Kennedy accumulated a huge fortune, but what he really coveted was the Ambassadorship to Great Britain, and his ambition was to found a family dynasty to rival the Adamses or the Roosevelts. His son John epitomized this attitude when he remarked of politics: "It beats chasing a dollar." In the same spirit, Thomas E. Murray, successful inventor and industrialist, devoted the last two decades of his life to public affairs, including a term on the Atomic Energy Commission and an unsuccessful bid for a US Senate nomination in New York in 1958. James Forrestal left Wall Street for service in the Navy and Defense Department. A *protégé* of his, John Connor, resigned the presidency of Merck & Co., the drug manufacturing firm, to become Secretary of Commerce in the Johnson Cabinet in 1965. The Irish are not unique in their esteem for public life, but it remains their most distinctive common concern and tradition.

William V. Shannon, *The American Irish: A Political and Social portrait*, London: Macmillan, 1986. By kind permission.

questions

1. Examine Irish success in the public sector.
2. Discuss the Irish-American attitude towards business.

4
St Patrick's Day Parade

Saint Patrick's Day, 17 March, is celebrated in style in New York along Fifth Avenue.

Ph. © Levy-Halebian/Gamma

questions

1. Why such a celebration in New York?

5
De Valera and Churchill

De Valera answers Churchill's condemnation of Irish neutrality during World War II.

Unfortunately, that outstanding matter, the matter of Partition, which affects so deeply every man and every woman of Irish blood throughout the world, was left unsettled, and it remained unsettled at the outset of this war. But we had settled the points of difference so far as the immediate territory under the jurisdiction of this Government was concerned, and we had hoped that these matters were settled for ever and that never again was there going to be any question of the right of the people of this part of Ireland to exercise complete sovereignty over this territory and to be able to choose the policy which would best seem to serve the interests of the community that lived in the territory.

No doubt, giving us back what was our own may appear to many to have put a burden upon those who gave it back. To restore that which has been taken does, I suppose, always imply a sacrifice for those who restore it. But, if justice is to be done, that sacrifice has to be faced and we fully expected that, not merely on the part of the British Government, but on the part of the British people, that was completely and fully understood. I want to say before I say much more that, up to the present certainly, it has been understood and that there has not been since the beginning of this war a single suggestion that this community of ours was not entitled to act as we have acted and to remain out of this war.

It is because I am anxious that that should continue that I am choosing this opportunity to address the House and to speak to our people and to the people of the adjoining island. We have chosen the policy of neutrality in this war because we believed that it was the right policy for our people. It is the policy which has been accepted, not merely by this House, but by our people as a whole, and nobody who realizes what modern war means, and what it means particularly for those who have not sufficient air defences, will have the slightest doubt that that policy was the right one, apart altogether from any questions of sympathy on one side or the other.

We want friendly relations with the people of Britain, as we want friendly relations with all other peoples, but we naturally want them with Britain because Britain is the nearest country to us on the globe. We have many relations of various kinds which make it desirable that the two peoples should live in friendship. It was partly for that reason, and partly because I knew perfectly that it was a condition of neutrality, that, years before we came into office and several times since we came into office, I announced that it would be our policy to use our strength to the utmost to see that this island was not going to be used as a basis of attack upon Britain. We have never swerved in the slightest from that declaration. Everything that we could do has been done to make sure that that policy would be made as effective as it was within our power to make it.

De Valera's reply to Churchill, *Dáil Éireann Debates*, vol. 81, 582-586, 6 November 1940, Dublin: Stationery Office.

questions

1. On what conditions can there be good relations between Ireland and Britain?
2. How convincing are De Valera's arguments in favour of neutrality?

6
Agenda 2000

Be it under CAP or the Structural and Cohesion fund, the European Union has been good for Ireland.

Ireland and the European Union

Ireland's membership of the European Union has been a very positive experience. There has been much comment on the monetary benefit of the transfers to Ireland over the period and indeed these have been extremely significant. Since 1973, Ireland has received a cumulative net transfer of some £23.5 billion in receipts from the EU. The Common Agriculture Policy has enabled Irish Agriculture to develop and helped to preserve our rural communities. The Structural and Cohesion Funds have facilitated significant infrastructural investment whilst also assisting the development of a range of programmes encompassing sectoral economic development, human resources and the fight against social exclusion.

The indirect benefits of our EU membership have been equally important. Ireland as a trading oriented economy has greatly benefited from access to a single market of over 370 million people. Access to the single market has played a key role in generating significant levels of foreign direct investment. The single market has been further underpinned by the completion of Economic and Monetary Union from the 1st January of this year. The advent of the Euro should enhance the prospects of continuing stable and sustained economic growth.

→

Ireland in turn has made a positive and constructive contribution to the European Union. Ireland has always adopted a positive approach in negotiations on the ongoing evolution of the Union's policies and institutional architecture. It is generally agreed that the Irish Presidencies of the EU have been successful and helped to ensure the advancement of the Union's agenda. We have not been afraid of change, but have always sought to participate actively in shaping change, in the best interests of Ireland and Europe. This general philosophy also governs our approach to the Agenda 2000 negotiations.

Background to Agenda 2000 Negotiations
It is important, in the context of the Agenda 2000 negotiations, to put Ireland's recent economic performance in a proper perspective and to consider its impact on our development needs. Ireland's recent economic performance has indeed been most impressive. Growth has well outstripped the European average and our unemployment rate is now below the EU average.

These developments have enabled living standards in Ireland to converge towards the European average. This improvement is, however, a relatively new development. When we joined the EEC in 1973 Irish Gross Domestic Product (GDP) per head approximated to 60 per cent of the EU average. Whilst the gap had been halved by 1993, it will be clear that most of the convergence of the Irish figure towards that for the EU has taken place in the very short period since 1993. The nature of this rapid convergence needs to be kept in mind in judging the extent to which we have "caught-up" with our Partners.

Statement by The *Taoiseach* Mr Bertie Ahern,T.D., in advance of the opening of negociations on Agenda 2000.

questions

1. Given Ireland's new found prosperity should it continue to benefit from European funding?
2. How solid are the arguments put forward by the Taoiseach to justify the Irish case?

7
The European Community and Irish foreign policy

One would have thought that European unity would have done away, to a large extent,

National foreign policies have [...] resisted the logic of integration to a considerable extent. Decisions on Irish foreign policy still rest with the government in Dublin [...]. When taking its turn for six months every six years in the rotating EC presidency, the Irish government is actually responsible for the management of EPC, giving both Foreign Ministers and Taoisigh opportunities to play the "statesman's" role in public. [...] Moreover, in so far as EPC positions on major international issues are consistent with Ireland's interests and values, if they are advanced on behalf of 325 million people they are likely to bear more weight than statements on behalf of a society of 3.5 million.

At this level of generalization it may seem that, so far, an acceptable balance has been found between the way in which Irish governments see their national foreign policies and the rather loosely framed obligations of EPC. This may not remain the case, though. Irish governments arrive at many foreign policy decisions with the minimum input from political parties, and enjoy relatively large domestic freedom of manœuvre given that the Oireachtas is the only western European parliament without a standing foreign affairs committee. But the Treaty of Maastricht, by introducing the possibility of a European defence policy, may clash with a long standing element of Irish foreign policy – the stance of neutrality.

Nevertheless, Ireland's participation in EPC over the last 20 years does on the whole support the proposition that opportunities to pursue foreign policy objectives were enhanced by EC membership. Some examples may illustrate the point. So far as East-West relations were concerned, the EC states jointly were an important positive influence in the Conference on Security and Cooperation in Europe (the "Helsinki process"), which maintained a modicum of diplomatic engagement with the USSR during the tension of the "new cold war" of the early 1980s. In the Middle East, the Irish government's position on the Arab-Israeli conflict was mirrored in the EC's gradual receptiveness to the Palestinian case. For most of this period Ireland remained, as it had been before joining the EC, a consistent and credible contributor to United Nations peace-keeping operations.

Patrick Keatinge and Brigid Laffan, "Ireland in International Affairs", in J. Coakley and M. Gallagher, *Politics in the Republic of Ireland*, Galway: PSAI Press, 1992.

with national foreign policies. Such is not the case, because of the rather loose European process of foreign policy coordination known as European Political Cooperation (EPC).

questions

1. Is it valid to say that Ireland's foreign policy has resisted the logic of integration?
2. What is Ireland's contribution to European foreign policy?

8

The Irish presidence of the European Council of Ministers

See p. 160.

John Bruton, Taoiseach *in 1996, takes a photo-call with other European leaders, after presiding over a meeting of the European Council of Ministers.*

question

What benefits have small countries drawn from their membership of the European Union?

Award Ceremony Nobel Peace Prize: David Trimble and John Hume, December 10, 1998
Ph. © Knut Fjeldstad, NTB Pluss, Sipa Press

CHAPTER FOURTEEN

Ireland on the Move

From being among the most backward countries of the European Community,* Ireland* has since 1973 been catching up the other member states. The Irish modernization process has not conformed to any clear set of rules. Rather it would seem that elements taken from more developed societies have been here accepted and there rejected. Irish Catholicism has changed, new attitudes towards sexuality, marriage and the family are emerging and politics in Ireland are being redefined. The Irish in the new century will be seeking, more than ever before, a lasting solution to the Northern Ireland* problem.

1 Catholicism

The influences of secularization in Ireland, though weak, are being increasingly felt. Religious practice, from being a universal phenomenon, is now more varied and more influenced by age, education and residence. Frequency of church attendance is lower among the young than the old, among urban dwellers than rural dwellers, among the manual than the non-manual. Religious values, however, remain strong. This can be understood if one remembers that Catholicism is not the object of a general disenchantment. Irish Catholics today have, nevertheless, adopted a much more questioning attitude towards their Church, and their confidence in its ability to provide satisfactory answers to moral and social questions is clearly on the decline. They are increasingly asserting their right to think for themselves, notably on matters of private sexual morality.

2 Sexual Morality, Marriage and the Family

Contradictions abound in this whole area. Traditional values were, for example, vindicated in referendums on abortion and divorce in the 1980s. At the same time the Status of Children Act* (1987), abolished the former legal disabilities suffered by children born outside marriage, and the Judicial Seperation and Family Law Reform Act* (1989), introduced a liberal, no-fault regime as regards judicial separations. The fact that the Irish elected a feminist, Mary Robinson,* as head of state in 1990, and another feminist, Mary McAleese in 1997, the high percentage of births outside marriage, and the depenalization of homosexuality today tilt the balance in favour of the European liberal tradition. This was to be confirmed in the 1995 divorce referendum which finally allowed for divorce.

3 POLITICS

A sense of the need for change would seem to be very influential in contemporary politics in the Republic.* This has undermined the traditionally solid basis of each political party's support among the electorate and has led to the reshaping of strategies by the parties. This search for change has produced some surprises, such as the election of Mary Robinson to the presidency, and the election in 1997 of a Northerner to the same function, in other words to a post traditionally held by elderly male politicians at the end of a long and prestigious political career. A further surprise was the heavy swing to the left in the 1992 General Election, followed by Fianna Fáil* and Labour forming a coalition government. This lasted to December 1994 when a new Fine Gael* Labour-led coalition was voted into office. Hence the voter volatility of the early 1990s, confirmed in 1997, if it persists, could reveal further surprises in the coming years.

4 A SOLUTION FOR THE CONFLICT

Dublin and London, hand in hand (early 1990s)

The interest of the Irish and British governments was to see the end of the conflict. It brought much suffering to the people of Northern Ireland and it cost a considerable amount of money. It was indicative of the incapacity of the two governments to impose a compromise political solution. Their interest was therefore to work closely together on the Northern Ireland question. Brussels and Washington also brought pressure to bear on them to do so. Internal political pressure, too, was exercised in a similar way. In the Republic, by the early 1990s all the political parties were convinced that a compromise was necessary to try to solve the central problems which the conflict posed. The vast majority of the electorate supported them in their position. The British, while less concerned with the conflict than the Irish, have never opposed any initiative by their government in that direction.

The Joint Declaration (1993)

It was hoped that the Downing Street Declaration* of 15 December 1993 would bring an immediate end to the political violence. It constituted a high point in the development of the collaboration between Dublin and London on Northern Ireland. The text of the Declaration was itself the product of several months of contacts, talks and negotiations involving all the bodies engaged directly in the conflict. Its immediate origin dates back to February 1992 when Albert Reynolds,* the newly elected Taoiseach,* and John Major, the British Prime Minister, pledged themselves to achieving peace in Northern Ireland during their respective terms of office. Later, in April of the same year, Albert Reynolds met John Hume,* the Northern Ireland nationalist leader, who began talks some time after with Gerry Adams,* the leader of Sinn Féin.* What emerged from those talks was a draft document which was submitted to Dublin. In June 1993 the Dublin government presented to London a document which the Taoiseach believed contained propositions which could produce peace. This draft had the approval of John Hume and Gerry Adams. It therefore constituted a unanimous expression of Irish nationalist and republican positions. For the first sime, since 1921, Irish nationalists and republicans shared a common position on the future of the island. The Dublin document was amended by London and became the Joint Dublin-London Declaration* (December 1993).

Reactions (1994)

The initial reactions were largely very favourable. The Declaration was warmly welcomed in Europe and in the United States. All the Irish and British political parties praised its balanced contents. In Northern Ireland the Ulster* unionist party* gave it a guarded approval and even the Protestant paramilitaries were in favour of it. The sole exception among unionist was Ian Paisley's* DUP* which opposed it. Several months were to elapse, however, before the IRA* and Sinn Féin gave their official reaction. Sinn Féin's came in July 1994 and it was negative. The principal reason for the refusal was what Sinn Féin called the unionist veto over change. By that they meant that with their in-built majority in Northern Ireland the unionists would automatically dictate the outcome of any vote on the question of unification with the South. However, some weeks later, on 31 August, the IRA decided to lay down its arms and thenceforth to give its backing to the political campaign for peace being waged by Sinn Féin. The Protestant paramilitaries followed their example in October 1994. The hope generated by the Declaration soon turned sour on account of the Unionist demand that the IRA surrender its arms before any negotiations and the failure of the British government to convince the Unionists to adopt a less intransigent position. The publication of the joint Framework Document by London and Dublin on 22 February 1995 and President Clinton's visit to Belfast in December of the same year hardly influenced a deteriorating climate. There was little surprise therefore when the IRA abandoned its cease-fire in February 1996. Its strategy seemed to have a solid backing since during the Assembly elections of 30 May 1996, with 16% of the votes, Sinn Féin became the third most important party in Northern Ireland. The violence surrounding the Orange marches of that summer seemed to indicate that a settlement was as far if not further away than ever. However the May 1st general election victory of Labour in the United Kingdom, Sinn Féin's success during the same election, Gerry Adams and Martin McGuinness being elected in Northern Ireland, and the Fianna Fail victory in the general election in the Republic on 6 June profoundly modified the global situation. Having, obviously, obtained the necessary assurances from London and Dublin, the IRA declared a new cease-fire on 20 July 1997. And in September Sinn Féin had joined the negotiations which were to lead to the Good Friday Agreement on 10 April 1998. In spite of the firm intention expressed to set up new political institutions before the first anniversary of the Agreement, this ambition was not achieved. So while the theory of reconciliation is written down since Good Friday 1998, the practice is still running into formidable difficulties.

Compromise in Dublin and London

The people of the Republic of Ireland and their government have shown in the past that they are willing to go to great lengths to arrive at an accommodation.

As for the British government, it is now committed to withdrawing from Northern Ireland if a majority in the province so decides.

Face-saving in Belfast

The unionist position had varied very little over a period of thirty years. It rejected categorically any form of unification or institutionalized link with the South. It also rejected for years power-sharing with the representatives of the minority. The Good Friday Agreement was to profoundly modify unionist political thinking. The principle of a coalition government composed of members of all the principal political parties in the province was accepted as was that of the setting up of a North-South political institution. In the eyes of the SDLP such movement on the unionist side could not but be warmly welcomed since the unionist compromise corresponds to the position advocated by John Hume for many years. At the same time, the unionists were successful in obtaining what some people called a council of the

Isles, that is a council in which representatives of the two sovereign Parliaments of Dublin and London would sit with members of the Parliament of Scotland, the Assembly of Wales and the Assembly of Northern Ireland. In unionist eyes such a council would help to strenghten the unity of the United Kingdom. One may wonder whether such a scheme does not correspond to the thinking of Tony Blair's Labour government.

But then any strengthening of the United Kingdom could not but be totally opposed by Sinn Féin and, one would think, by the Fianna Fail party in power in Dublin in 1999. The latter, however, surprised many observers when, in 1998, its leader, Bertie Ahern, spoke about the possibility of Ireland reintegrating the Commonwealth. One may wonder whether Sinn Féin is now alone in defending the Republic as first imagined by Wolfe Tone in the 1790s. By signing the Good Friday Agreement, Sinn Féin clearly manifested its willingness to compromise, but to what extent?

Historically compromise has been impossible for either side since for both the term is synonymous with betrayal. Yet there can be no solution without compromise unless, of course, there is an important decrease in the influence of one or the other, or of both. It is true that unionism is declining. The Catholic proportion of the total population is slowly increasing. Catholics are moving into more and more positions of power in civil society. The Protestants, on the other hand, have few friends and their cause few allies. Is the only solution therefore a creeping long-term victory for the Catholics which will leave the distrust and the hatred undiminished? As long as there is no compromise, such is the most likely direction of future events. Or is the intransigence only on the surface? Is there some face-saving formula which can reconcile the conflicting political aspirations? The Good Friday Agreement is that formula since it allows for compromises without betrayal.

The Celtic Tiger

The economic upturn since 1995 has taken on such proportions that now one hears of the Irish economic miracle or the Celtic Tiger. With the highest growth rate among all the OECD countries and sharply declining unemployment, Ireland, for the first time in its history is becoming an economic model. The image of economic success today is founded on the facts that output and employment growth are three times the EU average. The low corporation tax on business profits, which explains the massive multinational presence in Ireland, is surely the key to this success story. So where does all the newly earned money go? Much of the profit is immediately expatriated by the multinational parent companies. If one is to judge by the numbers of new cars and holidays abroad, the professional middle class are also benefiting from it. However there are those who are left behind: the poor. Most of them are made up of the long-term unemployed. The fact that the problem of poverty has not been fully faced up to means that the inequality gap is widening in the new Ireland.

FURTHER READING

BOWYER Bell, J., *The Irish Troubles*, Dublin: Gill & Macmillan, 1993.
O'TOOLE, F., *Black Hole, Green Card*, Dublin: New Island Books, 1994.

1
Ireland's Foreign Policy

For the first time in the history of the state a public debate on Irish foreign policy was opened up in 1994. The result was a White Paper, published in 1996. The following test is a brief extract from that document.

Our membership of the European Union and of the United Nations and other international organisations affords us the opportunity, despite our size, to speak on equal terms with many larger countries. Our voice in world affairs is strengthened by the fact that we are a democracy. The particular nature of our democratic institutions allows our people an influence on policy that, while not unique, is greater than that enjoyed by the citizens of most of the world's states. The extent of our influence also reflects the reality that, by world standards, we are relatively wealthy and can devote more of our time and resources to promoting our interests and concerns than can those whose daily life is dominated by the struggle to exist.

Ireland's foreign policy is about much more than self-interest. For many of us it is a statement of the kind of people we are. Irish people are committed to the principles set out in the Constitution for the conduct of international relations –

• the ideal of peace and friendly cooperation amongst nations founded on international justice and morality;

• the principle of the pacific settlement of international disputes by international arbitration or judicial determination; and

• the principles of international law as our rule of conduct in our relations with other states.

Challenges and Opportunities abroad. White Paper on foreign Policy, 1996.
Department of Foreign Affairs.

questions

1. How influential has Irish foreign policy been ?
2. Can it be said that the country in its foreign policy has lived up to its constitutional principles?

2
A new moral order

Here is a short extract from the conclusions of Crystel Hug's study of change in contemporary Ireland

Politics and sexual morality

Irish Catholics have reclaimed the right to think for themselves as far as sexual morality is concerned, thus overriding disciplinary norms and rejecting the Church's moral authority.

If the true value of a society, as is said, can be measured by how well it deals with its minorities, Ireland has found a balance between the traditional notion of an Irish identity imbued with Catholicism and that of a pluralist and therefore liberal democracy, which does not undermine the social order. In this process, the 'moral majority' (the militants in the pro-life and divorce campaigns, the ultra-Catholic lay groups, the conservative vote) has become a minority like the others,

questions

1. What do you understand by natural law?
2. To what extent has morality been secularized in Ireland?

– the homosexuals, the women who choose to terminate their pregnancy, the couples with marital difficulties, the couples cohabiting, the single-child families, the single-parent families. They bear witness to the 'widening of the ethical dissensus', in the phrase of Lipovetsky, which could very well be the supreme expression of democracy, a more convincing one than majority rule.

Chrystel Hug, *The Politics of Sexual Morality in Ireland*, Macmillan Press Ltd, 1999.

3
Pardon

In March 1998 the Christian Brothers took out advertisements in the principal national newspapers to express their regret to those who had been abused by members of the Congregation.

Message from
the Irish Christian Brothers

Over the past number of years we have received from former pupils serious complaints of ill-treatment and abuse by some Christian Brothers in schools and residential centres.

We, the Christian Brothers in Ireland, wish to express our deep regret to anyone who suffered ill-treatment while in our care.

And we say to you who have experienced physical or sexual abuse by a Christian Brother, and to you who complained of abuse and were not listened to, we are deeply sorry.

We want to do more than say that we are sorry. As an initial step, we have already put in place a range of services to offer a practical response. Further services will be provided as needs become clearer.

For independent and confidential help and advice phone:

Freephone Faoiseamh Helpline
1 800 33 1234 Republic
1 800 97 3272 Northern Ireland
(Monday to Saturday 10.00 a.m. to 10.00 p.m.)

or contact us directly:

The Irish Christian Brothers
P.O. Box 6245
Freepost
Dublin 7

The Irish Christian Brothers
Freepost
Dept. IE 8018
P.O. Box 788
Belfast
BT1 1XX

questions

1. What are your reactions to the wording of the advertisement?
2. What gave rise to this message?

4
An outraged victim

One victim reacts to the advertisement which came years after revelations of abuse had first become known.

One victim outraged by 'sorry' advert

One of those who were abused by a number of Christian Brothers during the '70s has reacted furiously to the Brothers' apology.

"An apology for something you are denying is a sham. What are they doing to weed out these abusers?

"Why don't they call on the guilty to admit their crimes and spare their victims the long drawn out ordeals they are going through? What are they doing to ensure it doesn't happen again?

"What I want to say to them is, if you did it, who did it and what are you doing about it?

"The people of Ireland are being made a mockery of.

"I hope those who suffered at their hands bring the advertisement to court with them when they go looking for damages.

"This apology is because of damage done to the Christian Brothers image and their huge financial interests. They are just covering their asses, which is more than the boys in their care could do."

Sunday Tribune, 29 March 1998.

questions

1. What do damages mean?
2. Ought the victim forgive and forget?

5
The socio-economic gap in Northern Ireland

False perceptions continue to be of great importance in Northern Ireland. Catholic poverty and unemployment are, nevertheless, still part of a harsh reality.

An outspoken loyalist woman from the Shankill Road summed up a firm perception among many Protestants: "We've seen the nationalist community crying out for years for things and now they're getting them. They've better housing than us now. They get all the jobs they want now and it's all turning full circle. We're ending up with nothing."

A number of Protestant politicians and clergy are now making similar points. As a rising Catholic middle class makes advances and becomes more visible, the impression is widespread that the Catholic community as a whole is now winning out.

There is certainly Protestant poverty and unemployment in the province, yet almost every objective measurement of disadvantage indicates that, after more than two decades of direct rule from London, the Catholic community remains far behind.

The scale of Catholic disadvantage was starkly laid out in a confidential →

government document which stated: "On all the major social and economic indicators Catholics are worse off than Protestants. They are more likely to be unemployed, more likely to experience long-term unemployment and significantly less likely to hold professional, managerial or other non-manual positions.

"More Catholics than Protestants leave school lacking any formal educational qualifications. There is a greater provision of grammar school places for Protestant than Catholic children. Significantly more Catholics than Protestants live in public sector housing and experience overcrowding. Catholic households have a lower income than Protestant households. Almost double the proportion of Catholic households are dependent on social security. Catholics suffer from higher levels of ill-health."

Nearly 70% of the long-term unemployed are Catholic, and their community has a higher rate of premature live births and a lower vaccination uptake.

The worst Catholic ghettos are marked by low skill levels, a weak private sector, depressing physical environment, low morale and job expectations, high levels of criminal and paramilitary activity, inter-community conflict and friction with the security forces.

In one survey, 31% of Catholics and 19% of Protestants cited unemployment as Ulster's biggest problem. Asked which single change was most needed to end the troubles, one-third of Catholics said "equal opportunities for Protestants and Catholics" compared to 13% who said "a united Ireland".

David McKittrick, *The Independent*, July 5, 1993.

questions

1. Why do the Protestants think they are losing out?
2. How great is Catholic disadvantage?

6 Birth rates in Northern Ireland

Birth Rates by Religious Denomination

Catholic fertility has been above the level achieved by Protestants since at least the 1920s and is the most enduring fertility differential in Northern Ireland. Yet it has always been difficult to measure because births are not registered by the religious denomination of the parents and it is therefore necessary to resort to indirect procedures of estimation. The census of population has constituted one such source; in 1961 and 1971 actual fertility questions were posed and the birth rate differential can therefore be determined reasonably accurately for these two years. Otherwise census-based estimations come from the respective age structures of the two denominations. A second source is the baptismal records of the Catholic Church published in the Annuario Pontificio which can be converted into annual birth rate estimates. [...]

The background to the emergence of the differential by religion is to be found in the history of demographic transition in Ireland – that is the passage from high to low fertility which has affected all advanced countries at some time during their demographic history. Protestants in the north east of Ireland underwent this process at roughly the same time as the GB population, while it occurred somewhat later for Catholics.

Catholic and Protestant Live Birth Rates, Northern Ireland, 1971-1992

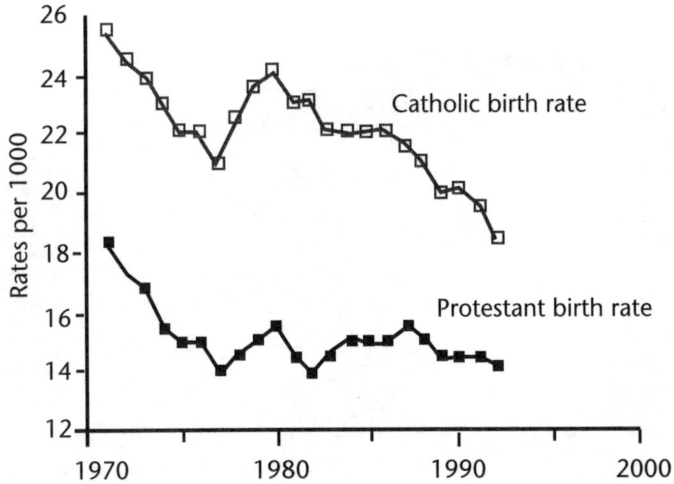

Paul Compton, *Demographic Review*, Northern Ireland 1995. Northern Ireland Economic Development Office.

Since the creation of Northern Ireland the fertility differential between Catholics and Protestants has been a source of hope for the former and a source of fear for the latter.

questions

1. Analyse the differential between the two rates.
2. What could some of the consequences of such a differential be?

7
How permanent?

John Hume of the SDLP and Gerry Adams of Sinn Féin are seen here tattooing «peace» on the body of the IRA. The unionist in the background remains sceptical (cartoon A) since the IRA ceasefire provoked an initial rejection among some unionists (photo B).

A

Ph. © Steve Ben, 1994, *The Guardian*

B

Ph. © P. Stumpf / Sipa Press

questions

Cartoon A

1. Why the joint effort by Hume and Adams?
2. What has the unionist reaction been?

Photo B

1. Trace the history of the unionist's «no surrender» stance.
2. Will the unionists be able to continue saying no?

8

We've grown up

Obviously impressed by the fact that a British Prime Minister should address the Dail this article suggests that Ireland ought to join the Commonwealth and evokes the ghostly approval of De Valera.

Although I am no admirer of the more ardent advocacies of bilingualism, the moment which for me best symbolised the high emotion of Mr Blair's address, to the joint Houses of the Oireachtas was a simple, almost clichéd salutation in fractured Irish: "Go raibh míle maith agaibh."

What Mr Blair said in Irish, or how well or how badly he said it mattered nothing. What mattered was that the first British PM ever to address the Oireachtas spoke Irish at all. It symbolised that spirit of inclusiveness characteristic of every aspect of the Blair visit, that same inclusiveness which inspired the flying of the Union Jack side by side with the Tricolour over the entrance to Mr Ahern's old Christian Brothers' school in Whitehall.

Those few words of Irish also sent an unmistakable signal to Sinn Féin. It distinguished the magnanimity of Mr Blair's inclusive world from the petty hatreds of the tribal cocoon still inhabited by those political pygmies in the Northern Assembly who invariably respond to all utterances in Irish with venomous derision.

Mr Blair sent a similar signal on the issue of decommissioning in the shape of his bald assurance: "I am not asking anyone to surrender. I am asking everyone to declare the victory of peace."

What also made it so appropriate is that the unprecedented invitation to speak in Leinster House was our way of saying 'Go raibh mile maith agat' to Mr Blair. It is a thank-you he richly deserves because no British PM since Gladstone, not even Lloyd George, has ever devoted so much time, energy and sympathy to Ireland.

Mr Blair's feeling of a profound sense of history is something we all should share. The Ceann Comhairle, Mr Seamus Pattison, went part of the way to explaining why when he described Mr Blair's presence as symbolising "the ever-maturating nature and indeed the coming of age of the relationship between our two countries."

I would put it more bluntly. November 26, 1998, was the day when independent Ireland finally grew up.

Look at some of those who have been accorded the honour of addressing the Oireachtas; three US Presidents; a German Chancellor; heads of government from India, Australia and South Africa. All worthy recipients, but none of them – not even Clinton and certainly not the Anglophile Kennedy – as potentially significant for this State as the British PM, if only because of his or her role as the ultimate arbiter of governmental authority in Northern Ireland.

Ronan Fanning, *The Sunday Independent*, November 29, 1998.

questions

1. Identify politically the author.
2. Is this text a good example of what certain specialists describe as the alienation of colonialism?

IRELAND: A TO Z

The purpose of this A to Z is to give further information on names, terms and acronyms used in the Chapters.

Abbey Theatre Founded (1904) in Dublin, the home of the Irish literary revival. Yeats, Lady Gregory, Synge and O'Casey are playwrights closely associated with it. Still at the centre of Irish theatrical creations.

Act of Union Passed (1800), came into force (1801), creating the UK by suppressing the Irish Parliament and placing Ireland under the control of Westminster.

Adams, Gerry (1949-): interned (1971). When liberated (1976), favoured republican engagement in politics. Elected (1983) MP to Westminster and President of Sinn Féin. His contribution to the peace process is primordial.

Anglican Church Church of England. Founded by Henry VIII in opposition to Rome.

anglicization the process whereby the Irish adopted the English language and culture.

Anglo-Irish the descendants of former English settlers in Ireland

Anglo-Irish Free Trade Agreement Signed (1965), came into effect (1966), gradually removing tariff barriers on imports and exports between the two countries.

Anglo-Irish Treaty see **Treaty**

Anglo-Normans The descendants of the Norman barons who accompanied William the Conqueror to England.

Baptist a Protestant body objecting to infant baptism

bardic schools Secular schools dating back to early Ireland where the Irish language, literature, history and Brehon law were studied. Disappeared with the old order (17th cent.).

Beckett, Samuel (1906-89) Born in Dublin, settled in Paris (1937), novelist and playwright. Wrote in English and French translating his own works (*Molloy*, *Waiting for Godot*).

Birmingham Six Bombs exploded in two pubs in Birmingham (England) killing twenty-one people (1974). Six Irishmen were arrested and received life sentences. They had to wait until 1991 for their innocence to be recognized.

Black and Tan War an auxiliary force dressed in black and tan uniforms sent by London to fight against the IRA

Boyne A river between Dublin and Belfast. The famous battle which witnessed the defeat of the Catholic King James II by William of Orange (1690) was fought on its banks.

Brehon Law the old Irish legal code (abolished, early 17th cent.)

Brighton, Grand Hotel An IRA bomb destroyed this hotel during the annual conference of the Conservative party (1984) nearly costing the life of the then British Prime Minister Margaret Thatcher.

Britain Term used to designate the UK. Great Britain includes England, Scotland and Wales.

B-Specials One of the categories of the Ulster Special Constabulary (the A and C were not used after the 1920s) established to supplement the official police force, the Royal Ulster Constabulary (RUC). An entirely Protestant force, with many of its members in the Orange Order.

Calvinism A particularly austere form of Protestantism based on the teaching of Jean Calvin (1509-64). The Presbyterians of Ulster situate themselves in that tradition.

Carson, Edward (1854-1935): Irish unionist politician opposed to Home Rule, leader of the Irish Unionist Party (1910), later a member of the British war cabinet

Catholic emancipation According to a law voted in Westminster (1829) Catholics could henceforth sit in Parliament and fill a number of functions from which they had been excluded by law till then.

Celts, celtic Of Indo-European origin, the Celts settled in Gaul and Spain c.800 BC and some hundreds of years later in Ireland.

Centre Party, or **National Centre Party** Founded (1932-33), favoured monetary reform, integrated the new Fine Gael party (1933).

Civil War Began (Apr. 1922), ending (Apr. 1923) with the defeat of the republicans who had opposed the Anglo-Irish Treaty accepted by the Dáil (Jan. 1922). It left profound and bitter divisions among the Irish for decades.

Clann na Poblachta [klɒn nə 'pɒbləktə] = the republican family. Founded (1946) by Seán MacBride and three other politicians, it got support from some members of the IRA and aimed at being the modern voice of republicanism.

Columbanus, Saint A 6th century Irish monk. Founder of monasteries in Europe.

Commission on the Status of Women Set up by the Dublin government (1970) to promote equal participation in public life for women, published two reports (1972, 1992). The Equal Opportunities Commission in N.I. defends equality for women there.

Commonwealth the association of countries previously part of the British Empire

Constitution The newly independent Irish Free State adopted a liberal democratic constitution (1922). Prior to that, the Dáil had adopted a Constitution (1919). Many changes occurred and a new constitution, heavily influenced by the teachings of the Catholic Church, came into force (1937).

Control of Manufacturers Act This 1932 legislation aimed at prevening foreigners from being able to control Irish industrial organizations. Repealed (1958).

Craig, James (1871-1940): Ulster Unionist politician, played an important role in the mobilization of Northern Protestants against Home Rule and became N.I.'s first Prime Minister.

Cromwell, Oliver (1599-1658): head of the government in England (1653-58). His military efforts in Ireland to put an end to royalist resistance were particularly violent. Remembered for the massacres of Drogheda and Wexford.

Cultural Heritage It reflects the necessity to cherish both the Catholic and the Protestant cultural traditions in Ireland.

Cumann na mBan ['kɒmn̩ nə ˌmɒːn] = the Association of Women. Founded in Dublin (1913) at the same time as the Irish Volunteers of which it became the women's branch, it supported the 1916 rising and later the republican movement.

Cumann na nGaedheal ['kɒmn̩ nə ˌgeɪl] = the Association of the Irish. The pro-Treaty party created as a result of a split within Sinn Féin over the acceptance of the 1921 Treaty, held power (1922-1932) and transformed its name to Fine Gael (1933). See **Fine Gael.**

Dáil ['dɔɪl] = assembly. The lower house of the Irish Parliament. The first Dáil (1919) was composed of those candidates elected under the Sinn Féin banner (1918 General Election) and who refused to take their seats in Westminster.

Davis, Thomas (1818-45): one of the leaders of the Young Ireland movement, also a poet and a journalist who contributed to the development of Irish nationalism

Davitt, Michael (1846-1906): a member of the IRB. To a large extent instrumental in organizing the agitation around the land question (1870s, 1880s) and creating the Land League.

Democratic Left a political party in favour of democratic socialism, and the product of a split within the Workers' party (1992). See **Workers' Party.**

Democratic Socialist Party (DSP) It emerged in Limerick (early 1980s). Its leader Jim Kemmy, being unsuccessful in creating a nation-wide party reintegrated the Labour party.

Democratic Unionist Party (DUP) A loyalist party founded by Ian Paisley and Desmond Boal (1971). Defends the union with Britain, opposes a united Ireland and is in favour of Protestant supremacy. Electoral support: about 12%.

De Valera, Éamon (1882-1975): born in New York, reared in Ireland, he participated in the 1916 rising. President of the 1919 Republic, he opposed the Anglo-Irish Treaty (1921). On winning the 1932 General Elections he set about undoing that Treaty. Head of the executive (1932-48, 51-54 and 54-59), he was elected President of Ireland (1959-66, 66-73). He defended the territorial unity of the island and was an enthusiastic Irish speaker.

Derry N.I.'s second city, previously called Londonderry

Devlin, Bernadette (1947-): elected with republican support to Westminster (1969) and active in politics since then

dominion a member country of the British Commonwealth, e.g. Canada, Australia.

Downing Street Declaration joint Anglo-Irish Declaration (15 Dec. 1993) reaffirming the necessity of consent in solving the N.I. conflict and opening the way to a ceasefire

DSP see **Democratic Socialist Party**

Dublin Castle Built 1260. The forbidding symbol of English power in Ireland.

Dublin-London Declaration see Downing Street Declaration

DUP see **Democratic Unionist Party**

Economic War Started (1932) with Dublin's refusal to continue paying London the land annuities owed by the Irish farmers in the framework of the settlement of the land question, it became a tariff war between the two countries but ended with a number of new Anglo-Irish Agreements (1938).

EEC European Economic Community. See **European Union.**

Éire the official Irish name for Ireland

ELB Northern Ireland Education and Library Board

emigration While beginning before the Famine, emigration became a mass phenomenon after 1845. Throughout the union (1801-1921), around 8 million people emigrated. Since 1921 it has remained a factor of major importance in Irish society both North and South.

EMU Education for Mutual Understanding

European Union (EU) After a referendum (1972) when over 80% of the voters in the Republic opted in favour of joining, Ireland became a member (1 Jan. 1973). N.I., with the rest of the UK, also became a member on the same day. The Single Act Referendum (1987) and the Maastricht referendum (1992) confirmed the initial choice in the republic.

Famine Often called the Great Famine (1845-49) to distinguish it from the numerous famines which struck Ireland (18th, 19th cent.). The worst catastrophe the country has witnessed, it was caused by the potato blight. One million people died, another million fled the country.

Fianna Éireann ['fiːnə 'eərən] = Scouts of Ireland. Republican youth movement founded (1909)

Fianna Fáil ['fiːnə ,fɔɪl] **(FF)** = Soldiers of Destiny. A political party created by de Valera in 1926. Since first coming to power (1932) it has remained the biggest political party in the Republic.

Fine Gael ['fiːnə ,geɪl] **(FG)** = the Irish Party. A political party which was the direct successor to the Cumann na nGaedhal Party. Set up (1933), it was a government party (1948-51, 54-57, 73-77, 81-87, 94).

Free Presbyterian Church founded (1951) by Rev. Ian Paisley

Free State see **Irish Free State**

Free Trade see **Anglo-Irish Free Trade Agreement**

Gaels Irish word for the Irish; adj. **Gaelic.** Sometimes used to distinguish the Irish of Celtic origin from the English of British origin. See **Celts; Anglo-Irish.**

Gaelic Athletic Association (GAA) Created (1884) for the promotion of national pastimes, e.g. Gaelic football, hurling and handball. Unionists do not participate in its activities.

Gaelic League Founded (1893) by Douglas Hyde, Éoin MacNeill and Fr. Eugene O'Growney, aimed at the "de-Anglicization of Ireland" through the revival of Irish as a spoken language.

gaelicization the return to the use of the Irish language and of a Gaelic way of life. See **Gaelic League.**

Gaeltacht ['geɪltɒkt] = an officially designated Irish-speaking area mainly along the west coast

gerrymandering the drawing of electoral boundaries to one's own advantage

Gonne MacBride, Maude (1866-1953): particularly active in republican and cultural activities, also a defender of women's rights. Autobiography, *A Servant of the Queen* (1939).

Government of Ireland Act Passed in Westminster (1920), it partitioned Ireland in two, thus creating N.I. out of the 6 north-eastern counties of the island (see map, p. 21).

Grattan, Henry (1746-1820): a prominent MP (end of the 18th cent.), advocated the independence of the Irish Parliament and Catholic emancipation

Green Paper on Education a Dublin government published discussion paper (1992), the first ever on education

Gregory, Lady (1852-1932): a dramatist and a folklorist, involved in the Irish Literary Theatre (with Yeats and Martyn) and the setting up of the Abbey Theatre which she directed until 1928.

Guilford Four Bombs planted in a pub frequented by soldiers in Guilford (England) killed five people (1974). Four innocent Irish people were condemned and remained in prison before being finally released (1989).

Hanna, Rev. Hugh (1824-92): a Presbyterian clergyman and pamphleteer, often inciting violence against Catholics in his sermons

Heaney, Seamus (1939-): the best known of contemporary Irish poets, born into a Northern Irish Catholic farming family

hedge schools They owe their origin to the suppression of all legal means for Catholics to educate their children, initially during the Cromwellian period, later under the Penal laws. The teacher was obliged to teach out of doors behind a hedge to avoid detection and to be able to flee if necessary.

Henry VIII (1491-1547): a Tudor king, first English king to proclaim himself King of Ireland. See **Anglican Church.**

Hillsborough Hugh Hanna made a famous speech there (1834). It later became the official residence of the Governor of N.I. The 1985 Anglo-Irish (Hillsborough) Agreement was signed in that former residence.

Home Rule Political autonomy for Ireland. Three Home Rule bills (1886, 1893, 1912) were presented to the House of Commons.

Hume, John (1937-): born in Derry, founder of the SDLP.

Westminster and European Parliament MP, one of Ireland's greatest politicians

hunger strike Inspired by a traditional form of republican resistance, Bobby Sands of the IRA went on hunger strike (1 March 1981) and died after 66 days. His example was followed by other republican prisoners, 9 of whom died that summer. They demanded, in vain, political status.

Hyde, Douglas (1863-1947): first President of Ireland (1938-45), a Gaelic scholar. Founder of the Gaelic League he spent much of his life in promoting the Irish language. He also tried to convince his fellow Protestants of the importance of his cause and tried to keep politics and the language revival movement separate.

Independence see **War of Independence**

Inghinidhe na hÉireann ['ɪnjiː'niː nə 'heərən] = Daughters of Ireland. A women's movement, founded (1900) by Maude Gonne and Countess Markievicz, in favour of the Irish cultural revival and Irish separatism.

IRA see **Irish Republican Army**

Ireland The official English name for the Republic of Ireland. Very often used for the whole island.

Irish Free State The official name of the new state created (1922) and composed of 26 of the 32 counties of the island. It was a dominion within the British Commonwealth.

Irish Literary Revival The literary movement (late19th-early 20th cent.). It concerns writing in English. See **Yeats, Lady Gregory** and **Synge.**

Irish Literary Theatre see **the Abbey Theatre**

Irish Party name generally given to the Irish Nationalist Party sitting in the House of Commons in Westminster during the period of the Union

Irish Republican Army (IRA) Initially, the army of the Republic (1919). After 1922, an illegal body banned in the North and the South.

Irish Republican Brotherhood (IRB) Founded (1858) and popularly known as the Fenian movement. Implanted in North America and Britain. Attempted a republican rising (1867).

Irish Volunteers Founded (1913), inspired in fact by the Ulster Volunteer Force (UVF) founded the same year but which split (1914) into the National Volunteers favouring involvement in the war (while the Irish Volunteers opposed it and were to become the IRA at a later date).

James, King James II (1633-1701) see **Boyne**

Johnston, Jennifer (1930-): a novelist (*Fool's Sanctuary* and *The Old Jest)*

Joint Dublin-London Declaration see **Downing Street Declaration**

Joyce, James (1882-1941): born in Dublin, the most famous of all Irish writers (*Ulysses*, *Dubliners*, *A Portrait of the Artist as a Young Man*, etc.)

Judicial Separation and Family Law Reform Act legislation on marital separation introduced (1989) in the Republic

land annuities see **Land War; Economic War**

Land League Founded (1879) in Dublin at a meeting attended by Michael Davitt and Charles Stewart Parnell, it aimed at protecting the tenant and abolishing landlordism by using different methods, including boycotting which it invented.

Land War Fought by the Land League (1879-1903), initially a violent struggle aiming at putting an end to the old landlord system set up during the English conquest of Ireland. The transfer of the land to the tenants became law (1903), the latter being expected to pay land annuities for a fixed number of years to the government.

Larne gun-running the landing in Larne (April 1914) of 35,000 rifles and 5 million rounds of ammunition bought in Germany for the UVF

Law, A. Bonar (1858-1923): a British Conservative politician, leader of that party (1911) and totally opposed to Home Rule. Prime Minister (1922).

Lock-Out (1913) The arm used by the Dublin employers against Jim Larkin and those union members trying to organize Dublin workers in a trade union. The conflict lasted six months.

Longley, Michael (1939-): one of N.I.'s best known poets

MacNeill, Éoin (1867-1945): Contributed to the founding of the Gaelic League. A historian and politician, became Chief-of-Staff of the Irish Volunteers, then Professor of Early Irish History in UCD (1908) and later Minister of Education in the Free State government.

MacSwiney, Mary (1872-1942): came to republican politics through the Gaelic revival and the women's movements. Elected to the Dáil, she opposed the Treaty and until her death refused to recognize the legitimacy of the new Irish state.

Maguire Seven Mrs Maguire, her husband, their two sons, their lodger and her brother were condemned (1975) to prison on the false accusation that the Maguires' home was used for making bombs. Mrs Maguire was not released until 1985. Meanwhile her brother, father of one of the Guilford Four who had simply come to Britain on hearing of his son's arrest, had already died in prison.

Mahon, Derek (1941-) one of the trio (with S. Heaney, M. Longley) of great poets from N.I.

Markievicz, Constance (1868-1927): Of the Sligo Gore-Booth family, particularly active in women's movements, she took part as a soldier in the 1916 rising and later opposed the Treaty.

Maynooth St Patrick's College. Founded (1795) as a seminary by the Irish Parliament with the encouragement of the London government which preferred to see Catholics trained in Ireland rather than in revolutionary France. Today a seminary, a pontifical university and a lay constituent college of the National University of Ireland (NUI).

McGahern, John (1934-): born in Dublin, his literary roots are in rural Ireland *(The Barracks, The Dark, Among Women)*.

Methodist a Protestant body drawing inspiration from the teachings of John Wesley (1703-1791)

Molyneux, William (1656-98): born in Dublin, participated at different periods in the government of Ireland. His inquiries into the effect of English legislation on Irish industry led him to write *The Case of Ireland's Being Bound by Acts of Parliament in England Stated* (1698).

National League a political party founded (1926) and modeled on the old Irish Party, proposing co-operation with Britain

National Progressive Democrats (NPD) a left-wing political party founded (1957) by Dr Noel Browne

National School system the primary school system set up in the 1830s

National University of Ireland (NUI) Established under the Irish Universities Act (1908), it consisted of the University Colleges of Dublin, Cork and Galway. Maynooth was a recognized college of the NUI until 1967 when it became a full constituent college. Trinity College (Dublin) was not incorporated and Queen's University (Belfast) became a full university.

NATO North Atlantic Treaty Organization

N.I. see **Northern Ireland**

NICRA see **Northern Ireland Civil Rights Association**

Ní Dhomhnaill, Nuala (1952-): one of the major poets writing in Irish today

Northern Ireland (N.I.) Established under the Government of Ireland Act (1920), it is part of the UK and made up of 6 of the 32 counties of Ireland (see map, p. 21). The 1920 Act was later modified by the Northern Ireland Constitution Act (1973) and the Northern Ireland Act (1979).

Northern Ireland Civil Rights Association (NICRA) founded in Belfast (1967) to end discrimination in the province and notably to obtain "one man one vote" in local elections and a fair system of allocation of houses

Northern Ireland Emergency Provisions Act Enacted (1973), it replaced the Special Powers Act. It was hoped that it would be acceptable and would deal efficiently with terrorism. Like its predecessor it constituted a suspension of the rule of law.

NUI see **National University of Ireland**

O'Casey, Seán (1880-1964): A dramatist. Born in Dublin, he moved to England (1926). His three major plays were produced at the Abbey: *The Shadow of the Gunman*, *Juno* and *the Paycock* and *The Plough and the Stars*.

O'Connell, Daniel (1775-1847): a lawyer by profession and the first great Catholic leader. His contribution to the politicization of the Catholic masses is particularly important. He succeeded in obtaining Catholic emancipation and numerous other reforms from Westminster but failed to have the Act of Union repealed.

O'Conor, Charles (1710-90): founded the first Catholic Association; a member of the Royal Irish Academy, wrote *Dissertations on the Ancient History of Ireland* (1753).

OECD Organization for Economic Cooperation and Development

O'Halloran, Sylvester (1728-1807): remembered for his plea for the preservation of Irish manuscripts and for his *General History of Ireland*

Oireachtas [əʊ'rɒktəs] = legislature. It consists of the President and the two Houses of Parliament: the Dáil and the Seánad.

Orange Order Protestant organization founded (1795) to protect Protestants against Catholics, support the Protestant religion and maintain the Protestant monarchy and constitution

Paisley, Rev. Ian (1926-): a clergyman and a politician, he has always defended the union with Britain; proclaimed his hostility to Dublin and denounced the Catholic Church. An MP and a N.I. representative in the European Parliament since 1979.

Parliament Dublin Parliament (1297-1800). See also **Dáil, Stormont, Westminster**

Parnell, Anna (1852-1911): organized a famine relief fund (1870s), visited the USA to raise funds, founded the Ladies' Land League. Among the first Irish women in modern history to take an active and public part in politics.

Parnell, Charles Stewart (1846-91): a Protestant landlord, the leader of nationalist Ireland. He fought to win Home Rule for Ireland in Westminster but failed, though successful in obtaining measures of land reform. His implication in a divorce suit led to his destitution as leader of the Irish party. He died soon afterwards.

Parnell, Fanny (1849-82): a poet, and a sister of Anna and Charles, she sympathized with the Fenian movement. Set up the Ladies' Land League in America.

Patrick, Saint Coming either from France or Britain, he arrived in Ireland (432). The spread of Christianity in the country is due to his efforts which explains his status as patron saint of the island.

Penal Laws Sometimes called the Popery Code. The first anti-Catholic law was voted by the Irish Parliament (1695) and followed by others, notably by the 1704 Act creating an anti-Catholic code of an extraordinary repressive nature.

Petrie, George (1789-1866): As an antiquarian, he made an immense contribution to the preservation of Irish music.

plantation the system used by London to confiscate land in Ireland and donate it or sell it to English Protestants

Popery Code see **Penal Laws**

Presbyterian a form of Protestantism originating in Scotland and of calvinist inspiration

Prevention of Terrorism Act emergency legislation introduced (1974) for the whole of the UK, extending the powers of arrest and detention

Programme of Economic Expansion The three programmes for economic expansion (1958-1972). An attempt to modernize the Irish economy particularly through a strategy of industrialization.

Progressive Democrats (PD) Created (1985) by dissidents from Fianna Fáil, it initially situated itself on the right.

Puritan, Puritanism see **Calvinism**

Quakers The Society of Friends. Its members in Ireland, Britain and America were very active in relief operations during the Famine.

Radio na hÉireann = Irish radio. The Irish national radio network.

Radio Telefis Éireann (RTE) the Irish national radio and television network

Republic of Ireland It formally came into existence on Easter Monday, 1949, and is made up of 26 of the 32 counties of the island. See map, p. 21.

Reynolds, Albert (1932-): several times minister in Fianna Fáil-led governments, Taoiseach (1992-Nov 94)

rising Usually refers to the republican Easter rising of 1916 though there were other republican risings (1798, 1848, 1867).

Robinson, Mary (1944-): University professor of law, senator, president of the association of single parents, founder of the European Centre for European Law, President of Ireland (1990)

Royal Ulster Constabulary (RUC) the police force of N.I. replacing the RIC (Royal Irish Constabulary) after 1921

Sands, Bobby (1954-81) Died in the Maze prison in N.I. See hunger strike.

SDLP see **Social Democratic and Labour Party**

SF-WP see **Workers' Party**

Sheehy-Skeffington, Francis (1878-1916): a socialist, journalist and pacifist, he was active in favour of equality for women. Though he did not participate in the rising he was shot by the British (1916).

Sinn Féin ['ʃɪn ˌfeɪn] = We ourselves. Developed from 1905 on, it finally became the republican political party which it still is today.

SLP see **Socialist Labour Party**

Social Democratic and Labour Party (SDLP) principal N.I. Catholic party, founded (1970)

Socialist Labour Party (SLP) founded in Dublin (1977), largely controlled by Troskyites

Special Powers Act emergency legislation in force in N.I. since its creation, amounting to a permanent suspension of the rule of law

Status of Children Act It put an end to the legal status of illegitimacy (1987).

Stormont Village near Belfast. Seat of the N.I. Parliament (1932-72) and government.

Stuarts Coming from Scotland they succeeded the Tudors on the English throne. The Stuart monarchs were James I, Charles I, Charles II, James II and later, Queen Ann.

STV single transferable vote

suffragette a woman who campaigned (end of the 19th, early 20th cent.) for the right to vote for women

Sunningdale A town in England which has given its name to the Agreement signed (Dec. 1973)

by Dublin, London and the Executive-Designate of the first Protestant-Catholic coalition in Belfast.

Supreme Court the Court of Final Appeal in matters of law or fact, civil or criminal and in constitutional matters

Swift, Jonathan (1667-1745): born in Dublin, author of *A Modest Proposal* (1729) and *Gulliver's Travels* (1726), Dean of St Patrick's, Dublin (1713)

Synge, John Millington (1871-1909): born in Dublin, this dramatist played an active role in the founding of the Abbey Theatre. Most famous play: *The Playboy of the Western World.*

Taoiseach (pl. Taoisigh) ['ti:ʃək] = Prime Minister

Taxi, taxi-driver The black taxis in Belfast were well-known in Catholic areas where they replaced buses which for long periods did not service those areas.

Treaty Usually designates the 1922 Anglo-Irish Treaty leading to the creation of the Irish Free State in Southern Ireland. Since then there have been other Anglo-Irish treaties (1938, 1965).

Trinity College Dublin University

tuath ['tu:hə] the basic territorial unit in early Ireland, headed by a king, in Irish a rí ['ri:].

Tudors The Tudor royal family included Henry VII, Henry VIII, Edward VI, Mary and Elizabeth I.

UDA see **Ulster Defence Association**

UK see **United Kingdom**

Ulster the most northerly of the 4 provinces of Ireland (Leinster, Munster, Connaught and Ulster). 6 of its 9 counties make up N.I. See map, p. 21.

Ulster Defence Association (UDA) Protestant paramilitary organization

Ulster Volunteer Force (UVF) Founded (1913) to resist Home Rule. As an illegal Protestant paramilitary body it resurfaced (1966) and still existed in the mid-1990s.

UN United Nations

Union see **Act of Union**

Unionism political ideology founded on maintenance of link between Ireland and Britain

Unionist Party (UP) Created (1905) to maintain N.I. as an integral part of the UK. It controlled the government of the province (1921-72).

United Irishmen Society Founded in Belfast (1791), it initially sought parliamentary reform but later became a secret society with the aim of creating a republic. It staged an armed uprising in 1798 which failed.

United Kingdom (UK) England, Scotland, Wales and Northern Ireland

Viking initially raiders from the northern countries (8th-10th cent.)

vocationalism sometimes called corporatism, i.e. a manner of organizing society in socio-economic groups

voluntary bodies Very numerous in Ireland, they play an important role notably in the social area, e.g. the National Council for Travelling People.

War of Independence Usually refers to the guerrilla waged by the Irish republicans against the British police and army (1919-1921).

Westminster seat of the UK Parliament (House of Lords and House of Commons)

Whitehall seat of the British government

William of Orange (William III) (1650-1702) see **Boyne**

Wireless Telegraphy Act set up the national radio station (1926)

Wolfe Tone, Theobald (1763-98): founder of Irish republicanism, inspired by the French revolution, helped to create the United Irishmen movement. Aided by the French, he attempted to set up an Irish republic. Captured in Ireland (1798) and being refused a soldier's death, he committed suicide.

Workers' Party (WP) The Sinn Féin movement split (1971) between Provisional Sinn Féin and Official Sinn Féin, reflecting the division between the provisional IRA and the official IRA. Soon the latter was officially abolished and the Official Sinn Féin became Sinn Féin-the Workers' Party (SF-WP), later simply the Workers' Party. It favoured Leninist type socialist politics.

Yeats, William Butler (1865-1939): Nobel Prize for Literature (1923), this great Irish poet contributed to the creation of the Irish Literary Society and to the founding of the Abbey Theatre.

Young Ireland A nationalist and later republican movement whose leaders, Thomas Davis, Charles Gavan Duffy, John Blake Dillon and John Mitchel contributed greatly through their newspaper *The Nation* to the development of Irish nationalism. The movement disintegrated after the failure of the rising it organized (1848).

zinc Discovered with other minerals in Tynah, Co. Galway.

Collections d'anglais HACHETTE *Supérieur*

HU anglais Littérature

An Introduction to English Literature: From Philip Sidney to Graham Swift, F. GRELLET, M.-H. VALENTIN

An Introduction to American Literature: "Time Present and Time Past", F. GRELLET

**Les Grands Classiques de la littérature anglaise et américaine*, P. CASTEX, A. JUMEAU

**Anthologie de la poésie britannique*, M. PORÉE, P. McDONALD

**Figures libres, figures imposées : l'explication de texte en anglais (fiction)*, H. AUFFRET-BOUCÉ, A. BLEIKASTEN, Y. CARLET, M.-D. GARNIER, P. LAGAYETTE, F. MacPHAIL, S. MARRET, M.-Ch. PAUWELS, S. PIGNOT, C. RIHOIT

A Handbook of Literary Terms: introduction au vocabulaire littéraire anglais, F. GRELLET

**L'Explication de texte : méthode et pratique* É. TAANE

**La Nouvelle anglo-saxonne Initiation à une lecture psychanalytique*, P. BADONNEL, C. MAISONNAT

HU anglais Civilisation

**Civilisation britannique*, P. JOHN, P. LURBE éd. actualisée

**Civilisation des États-Unis*, M.-Ch. PAUWELS éd. actualisée

**Grande-Bretagne et Irlande du Nord : géographie économique*, C. MOINDROT

**États-Unis : géographie économique*, C. MOINDROT

Contemporary British Institutions and Culture A Glossary, F. GRELLET

HU anglais Phonétique

**Initiation raisonnée à la phonétique de l'anglais*, R. LILLY, M. VIEL, éd. révisée avec CD audio

**La Prononciation de l'anglais : règles phonologiques et exercices de transcription*, R. LILLY, M. VIEL, éd. révisée et augmentée, avec CD audio

HU anglais Linguistique

Grammaire exploratoire de l'anglais : exercices de syntaxe commentés, M. YAGUELLO

**Les Théories de la grammaire anglaise en France*, P. COTTE, A. JOLY, D. O'KELLY, C. DELMAS, G. GIRARD, É. GILBERT, J. GUÉRON

HU anglais Grammaire

Grammaire anglaise : thèmes construits, P. CHANTEFORT, M.-L. et G. GROUSSIER

Pratique de la traduction

Traduire en anglais... les mots grammaticaux, D. SOULIÉ

Initiation à la version anglaise : "The word against the word", F. GRELLET

Initiation au thème anglais : The Mirrored Image, F. GRELLET

**La Presse économique : versions et thèmes anglais*, F. GALLIX, M. WALSH

**Recueil de thèmes anglais*, K. JULIÉ, C. GRIMAL

**Recueil de versions anglaises*, F. GUSDORF, F. OGÉE

**La Traduction littéraire, textes anglais et français : XXe siècle*, F. GALLIX, M. WALSH

Les Fondamentaux

**Histoire de la littérature anglaise*, É. ANGEL-PEREZ

**Civilisation américaine*, M.-Ch. PAUWELS

**Histoire du cinéma américain*, B. GAUTHIER

**Civilisation du Royaume-Uni*, P. LURBE

**L'anglais : comment traduire*, I. PERRIN

**Le Théâtre anglais*, É. ANGEL-PEREZ

**La Grande-Bretagne au XIXe siècle*, J. CARRÉ

**Histoire de la littérature américaine*, P. LAGAYETTE

**Le Rêve américain*, M.-Ch. PAUWELS

**Les Villes américaines*, S. BODY-GENDROT

**Shakespeare*, M. VIGNAUX

---

*Série transversale dirigée par Michel VIEL, Professeur à l'Université de Paris-Sorbonne (Paris-IV)

Imprimé en France par I.M.E. 25110 Baume-les-Dames

Dépôt légal n° 5569 - 09 / 1999 - Collection n° 37 - Édition n° 01

14/5334/9